D1557395

The Politics of Utopia

The Politics of Utopia

A Study in Theory and Practice

Barbara Goodwin
and
Keith Taylor

St. Martin's Press   New York

© Barbara Goodwin and Keith Taylor 1982

ISBN 0-312-62933-8

Library of Congress Cataloging in Publication Data
Goodwin, Barbara.
  The Politics of Utopia.

  Bibliography: p.
  Includes index.
  1. Utopias – History. I. Taylor, Keith. II. Title.
HX806.G648 1983   321′.07   82-21556
ISBN 0-312-62933-8

Contents

Acknowledgements

I would like to thank the Social Science Research Council and the Centre National de Recherche Scientifique for an exchange grant which helped me to pursue research into French views of utopianism, and Brunel University for granting me special leave to do so. I am grateful to the Fondation Nationale des Sciences Politiques for its hospitality. My thanks are also due to Miguel Abensour, Louis Marin and Lyman Sargent for some valuable cross-cultural conversations about utopianism.

B.G.

The Central Research Fund of Coventry (Lanchester) Polytechnic assisted me greatly by providing finance for some of my research. A large number of individual friends and colleagues, too numerous to mention, have contributed to my work on utopianism through their willingness to discuss problems and issues with me. I have also been saved from making many errors of judgement by my wife and by several students, past and present, whose own utopianism has been a constant source of inspiration. I trust that my future students will draw my attention to other, yet undiscovered, mistakes.

K.T.

Preface

To some people the idea of utopia signifies, first and foremost, a special kind of political fantasy. In this book, however, we try to show that utopianism as a tendency is a key ingredient of the whole process of modern politics, from theoretical conception to fruition in political practice. The utopian impulse makes the link between political theory and practice quite explicit and public, unlike some forms of political thought and activity which operate by camouflage and intrigue. Utopianism is thus a phenomenon which is particularly suitable for systematic study and analysis, since it attempts to free itself from many of the compromises often associated with political power and its exercise.

The book is intended to provide both an introduction to utopianism, and a general perspective on modern politics for the interested reader, hopefully with sufficient detail and critical analysis to satisfy someone who already has some knowledge of utopianism and who wants to go deeper into the subject. We do not offer a survey of the extensive secondary literature on utopia, although certain fundamental texts figure prominently in our discussions because they offer important insights. Nor do we offer a historical anthology of utopia, a task performed more than adequately by the Manuels in their monumental *Utopian Thought in the Western World*. Rather, we seek to develop an approach which relates social causes to political theory and practice, and which examines the material determinants of political thought as well as its inner logic.

Part One of the book (by Barbara Goodwin) treats utopianism as a form of political theory with unique characteristics, one whose special advantage is its ability to transcend the ubiquitous, seemingly unassailable present. In Chapter 1 there is particular emphasis on the critical and constructive force of the utopian model by contrast with other devices of political theory. In Chapter 2 a brief account of some of the more salient works of utopianism leads to an assessment of utopia in terms of the familiar political polarities, for example, the egalitarian/

elitist distinction. Chapter 3 deals with some key interpretations of the functions and flaws of utopianism, including that of Marx, and makes a plea for a polyvalent reading of utopian texts, while Chapter 4 considers those critics who identify utopians as would-be totalitarians.

Part Two (by Keith Taylor) considers utopianism as an expression of fundamental social impulses and as an ingredient of modern political movements. Detailed attention is given in Chapter 5 to the relationship between the emergence of capitalist industrialism and the origins of socialism as the most distinctive utopian tradition of modern times. Liberal and socialist conceptions of history as progress towards perfectibility are contrasted in Chapter 6, and the role of such practical factors as leadership, organization and propaganda in stimulating commitment to the socialist cause is examined. In Chapter 7 Marxism, anarchism and Russian Bolshevism are studied as movements which grew out of early socialist utopianism, and which faced similar problems of mobilizing support and maintaining high levels of commitment. The fortunes of liberalism and conservatism in an age dominated by the rise of socialism are considered, and the emergence of a unique positivist–technocratic utopian school in the nineteenth century is highlighted. In Chapter 8 the focus of attention shifts to the development of small-scale utopian communities with particular reference to the experience of America and Israel. The contribution of architects and planners in the advocacy of design utopias is also noted.

Part Three offers a defence of utopianism as both political theory and practice. Chapter 9 (by Barbara Goodwin) justifies the utopian approach to political thought and method in the light of various recent theoretical trends, and, furthermore, argues for the necessity of utopianism if political ideas are not to decline into a narrow pragmatism and sterility. In Chapter 10 (by Keith Taylor) the impact of utopianism on the practice of politics in the twentieth century is surveyed through a discussion of what has happened to socialism, liberalism and conservatism, and of how movements such as Fascism, technocracy, communitarianism, ecology and feminism have contributed to the ongoing effort to find solutions to the many practical problems which confront modern industrial societies.

While working on this book we were struck by the lack of investigations by English scholars into the relationship between utopianism and politics. There are considerable national variations of interest in utopianism, and the Americans and the French are by far the most prolific writers on the subject. American commentators frequently take a theme such as the machine, the family or education and analyse how it is treated in utopian texts. In France there has always been a lively interest in utopianism, but especially so since 1968, with utopianism being regarded as a speculative form of political thought and practice which could supersede the tired orthodoxy of Marxism. French academics from many disciplines make forays into the territory of utopia to plunder its wisdom for their own subjects. In France, one feels, everyone lives near a utopian frontier. By contrast the English have hived off utopianism as a small, fringe section of political theory, or have confined it to the realm of literary studies. The feeling that utopianism could be an active force in British social and political life is rarely encountered. It would be interesting to unearth the cultural reasons for this isolation of a mode of thought which many others consider central. The intellectual predominance of empiricism may be one reason, as Chapter 4 suggests. But is the notorious pragmatism of British politics a cause or a result of the absence of utopianism? Undoubtedly there are social explanations, too, of British non- and anti-utopianism, probably linked, as Part Two tries to show, to the development of class structure under a form of capitalist industrialism which, in the case of Britain, has hitherto seemed to satisfy most of our immediate material needs, and which has given the British the taste of an impressive, although temporary, industrial and commercial success.

To the best of our knowledge no previous book on utopian political theory and practice has emerged from English scholarship. If our work encourages others to take utopianism more seriously, and perhaps to undertake further research, it will have served its chief purpose.

Part One

Utopia and political theory

1 Taking utopianism seriously

When a word as contentious as 'utopia' appears in a book's title the first chapter is usually bristling with definitions and refutations of counter-definitions. To start with a stipulative definition of the term here would be self-defeating because, in dealing with the place of utopianism in political thought, we must consider theories which have been called utopian by their critics, perhaps erroneously, as well as works conforming to the traditional utopian form – a voyage to a lost island or into the future. Hence, the utopian aspects of works by such writers as Marx and Rousseau will not be neglected, although some definitions of the term would exclude them from consideration. The readers of this book doubtless already have definitions of utopia in their minds which range from the pejorative to the laudatory, and long debates at cross purposes still take place between those who use 'utopian' to mean 'unrealizable because hopelessly idealistic' and those for whom it connotes an ideal society, a real alternative. This book endeavours to show which of these judgements is more appropriate.

The essentially contested nature of the concept of utopia and the chequered history of utopian thought can be traced back to the paradox at the heart of the pun which More coined: is the good place (eutopia) by definition *no* place (utopia)? Differently put, is utopia necessarily unrealizable because of its ideal nature? According to the answer given, utopianism signifies either the birth or the death of political optimism. The nature of utopian thinking has changed historically, depending on whether or not utopia was regarded as realizable. Enlightenment utopians, such as Mably and Morelly, created utopias which were little more than ideal codes of law, imbued with a spirit of unreality and abstract idealism, and primarily intended to be didactic, like most such enterprises since More's *Utopia*. But the French Revolution suggested to some that the course of history *could* be diverted, and utopia (of a sort) *could* be implemented – in other words, that abstract ideals could be incarnated in society by deliberate human action. This discovery helps to account for the increased optimism and activism of nineteenth-century utopias. Although the utopian socialists repudiated the label 'utopian' because the unflattering connotations of fantasy and unreality lingered on, they expected their ideas to be realized in their own lifetimes. Despite Marx's .disapproval of their approach to socialism,[1]* the various successes which they and their followers had helped to revive the positive sense of the concept of utopia. In the twentieth century it has become more fashionable to talk of 'utopianism' than utopia, a term that embraces forms of thought incorporating utopian elements while not purveying complete utopian blueprints.

The question then arises whether there is a common core in all these attempts to create utopia and in differing uses of the term that will enable us to understand the concept of utopia. Above all, 'utopia' denotes an elaborate vision of 'the good life' in a perfect society which is viewed as an integrated totality: such a vision transcends normal idealism, and is inevitably at variance with the imperfections of existing society and so, *per se*, constitutes a critique of social institutions. Of course, it is not the case that utopians have a monopoly of ideas about the good life; rather, the ability of utopianism to establish itself as a powerful form of thought in the West rested on the prior existence of the Christian notion of the virtuous life, on the political notion of public good implicit in Locke's dictum that 'salus populi suprema es lex'[2] and, latterly, on the utilitarian 'proof' that the greatest good of the greatest number was the only sound basis for morality. Such established doctrines facilitated the development and acceptance of utopian ideas. Similarly, the intellectual roots of modern utopianism were nourished by the central ideas of the Enlightenment – historical progress, perfectibility and optimism[3] – while the theory of evolution, especially Spencer's version, whose possible consequences for man and society he elaborated in *Principles of Ethics* (1879), offered a more scientific grounding for optimism and the utopian idea of progress. Twentieth-century utopianism, equally, has sought to make itself intellectually respectable by drawing on quasi-scientific theories such as behaviourism and post-industrialism: as in the past, utopia emerges from established currents of thought, positing its own credibility on their acceptance, and reforming and modernizing the vision of the good life and the perfect society, from which derives the perception of our own imperfections. This constant updating of utopian ideas, and their reliance on the social and intellectual context, evidently make it hard to define the concept generally, except in an anodyne and empty phrase such as 'an account of an ideal society'. However, this will serve as a

* Superior figures refer to the Notes and references on pages 255–74.

preliminary filter, and will allow us to explore the nature of utopia in the next few chapters. The basis of utopia's claim to be taken seriously as political theory is its critical analysis of socio-political reality, as much as its ideal vision. Social criticism is not the particular prerogative of utopians, but they conduct it in an idiosyncratic, forceful fashion, by demonstration rather than by reasoned argument. One cause of the widespread hostility to admitting utopian 'fantasy' to the corpus of political thought is the extent to which it subverts, or renders unnecessary, reasoned argument and replaces it by symbols, inversions and the all-powerful *reductio ad absurdum*. Yet such techniques are effective: although we are no longer Renaissance men imbued with the myth of El Dorado, the force of More's description of the use of gold for shackles and chamberpots still strikes us like an expletive. Hence the risk that academic writing about the significance of utopias will seem both long-winded and blunt beside the originals. The prolonged exclusion of utopianism from 'serious' disciplines recalls the hostile reception of surrealism, the artistic movement dedicated to subverting received, 'bourgeois' logic, and to destroying normal, self-congratulatory perceptions of the world, and many similarities might be detected between utopianism and surrealism as forms of thought. Clearly, the more orthodox advocates of logical exposition and reasoning will not readily agree to be outclassed by what they consider to be tricks of literary rhetoric, and one mode of self-defence has been to devalue utopianism by making it a synonym for fantasy and illogicality. This book is intended to show the injustice of such dismissals and to argue the importance of this unorthodox approach in political theory.

Identifying utopia

The constructive or 'eutopic' aspect of utopianism is perhaps what most fixes the concept in the popular mind. Utopianism depicts an ideal form of social life which, by definition, does not currently exist. In this respect it appears to differ from the kind of political theory which in principle accepts the framework of existing society while idealizing some elements within these parameters, such as the maximization of liberty. The intimate relationship of utopia to ideals which are themselves debatable poses problems from the start for the application of the term. One man's Paradise is another's Inferno. Should not a book purporting to deal with utopia include in its scope *Mein Kampf* as well as the *Republic*? But then, could it truly maintain that utopia explores the nature of the good life? There is a strong temptation immediately to stipulate further criteria to distinguish acceptable or 'real' utopias from dystopias and perverse fantasies, such as most people would consider Hitler's vision to be. But this must be resisted on methodological grounds since such criteria would have to invoke and impose other ideals and personal preferences, also debatable, and the final result would be to render 'utopia' an entirely empty class, since some people would consider Plato's Republic dystopian, some More's Utopia, while others would pass the same judgement on the higher stages of communism.

But perhaps a criterion can be devised which passes no judgement on the content of a utopia, yet rules out theories which exalt one section of the population and degrade another by redefining humanity, as did Hitler. On such grounds, Servier distinguishes utopias from millenarian doctrines, pointing to the hubris implicit in the notion of a Promised Land for the Elect.[4] From the Elect's standpoint, the Promised Land *is* utopia - but what about the non-elect, including those formerly inhabiting it? On similar lines, Mucchielli argues that the 'community of humanity' must be universal since, if it excludes some by invoking special laws, it will destroy those outside the boundaries and, ultimately, those who enforce the boundaries. A closed utopia is thus immoral, and only utopias which reinforce the solidarity of mankind merit the name.[5] From an ethical viewpoint, then, it can properly be stipulated as a minimal requirement that anything purporting to be a utopia should have universal scope and offer benefits to all those within this frame of reference. A separate question is whether such benefits must be distributed equally. Readers often condemn the *Republic* on the basis of Plato's vindication of slavery, yet it is reasonable to suppose that he believed that even slaves would live more happily in his Republic than under the oligarchies or tyrants of Athens, so that, given that he considered slavery a permanent institution, his utopia would make slaves as well off as possible. If we stipulated that all must benefit equally in utopia, we would be in danger of imposing a particular ideal, egalitarianism, on the definition - an improper step in terms of the present attempt to identify the nature of utopian thought and its political role. So we must be content with the stipulation that utopia should aim to benefit everyone, albeit to differing degrees.

To judge whether a so-called utopia truly has, or had, this ideal scope and function, we should not consult our prejudices but should apply an impartial test to determine whether it would benefit people by comparison with the society of which it constitutes, or constituted, a critique. Pareto's optimality criterion (does it make at least one individual better off without making anyone worse off?) will not do, since utopia is often seen as the result of a revolution or social upheaval, not a gradual reshuffling of the positions of particular individuals – though even that process would be bound to displace some privileged people. Admittedly, there are some gradualist utopias which predict that any privileges lost would be voluntarily forgone, as when Godwin argues that rational debate will persuade the rich to give up their wealth.[6] Perhaps a test modelled on that devised by Rawls in his *Theory of Justice*, which circumvents vested interests, might be devised to determine whether a scheme relatively benefited the whole of the population and so counted as utopian.[7] (Is it a society in which I would willingly live, no matter what social role was allocated to me? Does it satisfy the maximin principle?) This would rule out the subjugation of some for the benefit of others, presumably, and thus maintain the universality of utopia. However, this would still not exclude separatist utopias, for if an elect group can select and isolate itself in such a way as not to harm the surrounding population, it can define its own utopia, however strange or perverse, which will fulfil the condition of universality within its own boundaries: indeed, the separatist communities in the USA in the nineteenth century operated on this principle (see Chapter 8). It follows that ultimately there is no watertight test to exclude sectarian or partial utopias realized in isolation, and these too must come within our purview.

Having raised these difficulties, the argument will proceed by using 'utopianism' in its widest sense, to connote utopian elements of theory as well as full-blown utopian plans, and to embrace both schemes which have presented themselves as utopian, recommending an ideal society, and theories labelled utopian by commentators and critics. The major question to be addressed in this chapter is whether utopianism should count as serious political theory. The fact that many utopias appear in the guise of didactic novels appears to remove them from the theoretical and political sphere, as does the fact that relatively few detailed utopian schemes have been even partially implemented. Again, it may be argued that political thought proper does not, and should not, base its analysis on representations of the non-existent, but analyses, codifies and evaluates existing states of affairs. Such points must be debated at some length.

The condemnation of utopianism for dealing with the unverifiable and the unreal stems from an orthodox empiricist and positivist view of social science (including political thought) which is peculiarly deeply rooted in the English academic tradition and may account for the limited attention paid to utopian thought in Britain, a paradoxical neglect since English literature is perhaps the richest source of utopias.[8] Utopian predictions and assertions, even if explicitly extrapolated from recognizable reality, are said to suffer from irremediable unverifiability, and so cannot be seriously regarded. As would-be social science, they can be dismissed in the same way that the logical positivists dismissed evaluative and moral statements. Not only does utopian thought fail to be realistic and verifiable, but it contains a suspicious combination of idealism and imagination. American thinkers, although tinged with the same Anglo-Saxon empiricism, at least accord an important indicative status to utopias, and have produced a body of utopian criticism.[9] French thinkers have never doubted the theoretical importance of utopianism and treat it as a living tradition; a large literature, mostly post-war, tries to locate it sociologically and in relation to politics, psychology, semiology and literature. Ruyer in his influential *L'Utopie et les Utopies* argues that utopias are, despite their fantastic presentation, 'strictly rationalist' and that they constitute 'speculative theory'.[10] The respectability of speculative theory is evidently better established on the continent than in English-speaking countries: it is a genre of thought not susceptible to simple truth-tests or empirical verification, but whose suggestive force is nevertheless undeniable. Utopias have also been regarded as symbolically expressing human verities which could not be written into 'normal' political theory. For example, Servier's analysis of the utopian tradition with respect to Freudian and Jungian symbols produces the conclusion that utopias embody a rejection of the arbitrary authority of the father and a return to the purity of the virgin–mother–provider – *la ville* is the quintessence of the female principle, everyone agrees.[11] Be that as it may, there are clearly aspects of human existence which, while not strictly 'political', are causally important in political life, and which can be emphasized in a utopian scheme but not in the empirical and deductive processes of an orthodox political treatise.

The tradition of such treatises is still dominant, as Rawls's success suggests, although their highly schematic and stereotypical assumptions about human motivation and desire do not comprehend the diversity of men's everyday needs and aspirations. Utopias improve on such explanations of human life, but at the cost of departing from orthodoxy and the principle of Ockham's razor, and so risk dismissal. The academic separation of utopianism from 'realistic' political thought proceeds via the challengeable assumption that imaginative representations do not convey truth, whereas an *abstract* account of reality does so. But often the necessity of abstraction, which distinguishes all political theory from political history or the study of political institutions, *a priori* removes it as far from reality and verifiability as does the invention of an imaginary world. Hobbes's empirico-logical 'deduction' of the necessary powers of the sovereign was in no way a description of existing politics, or verifiable by reference thereto. If it is contended that, like *Leviathan*, most political thinking is fundamentally normative and necessarily unverifiable, then the primary justification for distinguishing this from normative utopian theory set in an imaginary world seems to disappear. Yet surely there *is* a distinction.

Such a debate displays a degree of shadow-boxing on both sides, for the common use of the epithet 'utopian' by political theorists and commentators to describe the idealism even of non-utopians suggests that the rootedness of utopian elements in political thinking is generally, if tacitly, acknowledged. More important than trying to differentiate between utopian and other kinds of political theory is the delineation of the function that these utopian elements have in political thought.

Lateral possibilities and futures

Try to imagine a political theory constructed strictly from abstractions from the immediate present. ('When the executive authority of the state is threatened, the legislative reinforces its power with new laws' and so on.) Unimaginable perhaps. Such a theory would have two dramatic shortcomings: it would lack the explanatory dimension which delves beneath surface phenomena to find root causes, and it would lack any dynamic or historical dimension, being unable to locate the present with regard to past or future or alternative possibilities, and so unable to facilitate change or to make value judgements. Advocates of the normative role of political thought would consider such a theory incapable of this role, since it could only reflect whatever values are embodied in present institutions. In reality, however, there is a multiplicity of devices which enable theory to progress beyond the immediate political present and to pursue a dynamic course without itself being a historical or predictive discipline. The invention of utopia is one such important device which facilitates the escape from brute fact, although not from reality, and its special role can best be examined in relation to similar inventions such as the state of nature and theories of historical progress.

As has been stated, political theory's method is abstract and philosophical and, as a consequence, tends to be non-descriptive and non-historical; furthermore, it aspires to a normative and evaluative mood. The invocation of ideals serves two purposes: often they are used to vindicate the present order of society by proving that it satisfies various moral values or by establishing the principle that what(ever) is, is good. But they can equally serve to transcend present reality and point to a better future. With ideals, we can evaluate the imperfections of the present by reference to notions such as perfect justice and ideal liberty, although this entails problems of method since these are often defined in isolation and are potentially in conflict: many, for instance, see ideal liberty as incompatible with complete equality.[12] There is also considerable controversy about the validity of plucking such absolute ideals from the air for comparison with present reality. Some of these methodological problems are solved by the imaginary creation of a constructive utopia or a harmonious state of nature which supplies an alternative model of society, in which numerous ideals are simultaneously and harmoniously realized, and from which can be derived principles of evaluation detached from present reality, by which present institutions can be judged.

The relationship between a hypothetical model and present society also introduces a dynamic element into the conceptualization, justification and criticism of the present with reference to past, future or 'lateral'[13] possibilities. All would-be predictive or progressive political thinking must free itself in part from the present. By a categorization of the various ways in which this is achieved, the peculiarly constructive and creative role of utopianism can be shown. Many utopias were set in an Elsewhere for the purpose of comparison with Here, especially during the period when exploration was at its height and travellers' tales of strange societies were plentiful. With colonization and the spread of European civilization, the projection or retrojection in time of utopian alternatives became more popular, but both forms of utopia are equally important in terms of theoretical dynamics, allowing the theorist to escape the ever-dominant present. In the analysis which follows, categories 1–6 cover the available range of hypothetical devices of political theory, classified according to their location in time: they illustrate the special critical force and constructive effect of a utopian model, by contrast with other devices.

1   Idealization of the past and criticism of the present

In order to achieve this, various devices are invoked: the Golden Age (every age has one),[14] Arcadia, Eden, prelapsarian states of nature and retrospective or 'back-to-nature' utopias. A wider manifestation of the state of mind which denigrates the present was the 'battle of the books' which raged between the modernists and the classicists in the eighteenth century, the latter asserting that the moderns were immitigably degenerate by comparison with the ancients.[15] As this suggests, this mode of thought is fundamentally fatalistic and unconstructive. It is a lament for the irreversibility of time. Glorification of a lost past renders the thinker impotent with respect to both present and future unless he hopes for a cyclical revival, or believes that social developments can in time be reversed. Evidently, such devices are directly opposed to the theory of Progress, which holds the present to be more glorious than the past, and the future even more so than the present. The utopians Saint-Pierre and Saint-Simon both inverted this mode of thinking when they announced that the Golden Age was still to come.

The idea of a Golden Age is often accompanied by a theory of *progressive decadence*, which entails strong criticism of the present and, *a fortiori*, of the future. Plato's *Republic*, with its account of the decay of the ideal state into timarchy, oligarchy, democracy and tyranny, could be said to exemplify this fear, although it was probably not intended as a historical prediction, but rather as an exhaustion of the hypothetical possibilities. Among other political theories which employ devices for idealizing the past is Rousseau's *Discourse on the Origins of Inequality* (often seen as an Adamist utopia), even though *The Social Contract* suggests that he thought the corruption of man by society was in some sense mitigable. And in the Middle Ages it was a standard premiss of Christian political thought that the Fall had necessitated the coercive apparatus of the state as a corrective for the evil impulses of fallen man: politics was the second curse of Adam.

The implication of all such devices for current political life is that retrenchment and conservation to prevent worse decline are the necessary and only proper forms of political action. Political theory based on such nostalgic premises seems doomed to impotence and quiescence: however, they can provide a basis for critical thought if they illustrate the original state of man, with the constraints and corruptions of present society stripped away. Rousseau's Noble Savage should be seen in this light, rather than as the plea for primitivism which many of his contemporaries took it to be.[16] The prerequisites for a thoroughly constructive or reconstructive political theory are as follows:

1 a conception of society as an artefact (unlike Nature), capable of being purposefully altered by man himself;

2   the conviction that progress, *qua* improvement, is possible;
3   an analysis of socio-political life which is free from fatalism, the *que sera, sera* attitude which negates from the outset human attempts at change, and also free from religious deference ('if God had intended us to fly, He would have given us wings').

Evidently, the purveyors of Eden, Golden Ages and idyllic states of nature lack or reject one or more of these requirements, and the scope of their theory is consequently restricted; they are also devoid of the important quality of optimism.

2   *Justification of the present by reference to a hypothetical past*

In this mode of theorizing, the past is invoked to validate a policy of 'no change', which, many consider, is as important an outcome of political thinking as prescriptions for change.[17] In the case of a social contract theory such as Locke's, the imaginary past is acceptable, even idealized: a contract made under conditions of natural democracy (consent) can therefore justify given dispositions of power and existing institutions. By contrast, Hobbes's theory justifies obedience to the present political regime (the 'sovereign'), however deplorable, by reference to a totally unacceptable warring state of nature which threatens to recur. Thus, whether the imagined past is good or bad, it can be invoked to support the present, irrespective of the independent merits or demerits of present politics. This category contains a dynamic or historical element, implying a necessary and profitable move from past to present, but offers no prospect of a move to the future, since its aim is justificatory.

3   *Justification of the present by reference to a hypothetical present*

This is the effect, if not the intention, of Rawls's theory of justice, which sets out to hypothesize what form an ideally just society, viewed abstractly, would take, and arrives at an abstract, idealized account of Western liberal democracy. The reason for this coincidence of real and hypothetical has, naturally, been located in his choice of premises. Nozick, in *Anarchy, State and Utopia,* could also be seen as justifying current American politics, viewed as the interaction of semi-anarchic groups, constituted by individual choice in a free-market situation. Again, these powerful hypothetical devices provide an important counter-dynamic and validation of the existent, by contrast with utopias.

4 Inversion of the present for critical purposes

This device operates similarly to category 3, but with the reverse effect; although neither entails a time-shift, each achieves the distance which makes it possible to reassess the present, apparently with some objectivity. Inversion, whether utopian, satirical or folkloric, infers serious criticism of existing society, and the need for change or revolution. 'The world turned upside down' is a myth better established in popular than intellectual culture (as the public house of that name on the road to Dover bears witness), but the comic and folk elements disguise a revolutionary intent. Saturnalia in effect constituted a criticism of a slave-based society, even while it operated as a safety-valve, and carnival might be similarly viewed. As for the literary tradition, More set the pattern for one kind of inversion by inventing Greek proper names embodying 'corrosive negatives'.[18] These normally serve to emphasize the nowhereness of Utopia but, more seriously, the name of the prince, Ademos (No-people), overturns contemporary notions of political power. Likewise, Restif de la Bretonne's *Metapatagonia* 'inverts' contemporary France by spelling all names backwards. But the power of inversion goes deeper than the alphabetical and the conceptual: the fourth book of *Gulliver's Travels* provides an archetype of satirical inversion, where men are the servants of horses. Since then, countless other utopias have used the device to demonstrate the absurdity of our own institutions. In some utopias, such as Bulwer-Lytton's, women rule; in Butler's *Erewhon* (*sic*), crime is treated as illness and illness punished as crime. But the constructive possibilities of inversion are strictly limited because the mirror-image of an unsatisfactory world will not necessarily be any more satisfactory. Also, the inversion of a social institution does not lead to one specific alternative: the 'opposite' of privately owned land might be collective farms, or unowned wasteland. However, the subversive effect of inversion can at least provide the impetus for reconstructing the present, if not the blueprint.

5 Constructive criticism of the present via an ideal alternative (future or present)

This is primarily the role of utopias, although other hypothetical devices are also used to the same end. Optimistic Enlightenment theories of progress, including Turgot's three-stage theory of history, depicted existing society as an inferior state and pointed forward to greater social perfection. Marx improved on this approach by providing an explanation of the means of change and by making progress towards an ideal future dialectically necessary. In general, theories of progress have three disadvantages: they are insufficiently specific about the future state and hence unconstructive (*vide* Spencer's idea of the evolution of man to moral and social perfection), they often locate the ideal future at too great a distance to be functional in the criticism or reconstruction of the present, and they encourage quiescence rather than critical analysis, since progress appears as inevitable - a weakness which led to the rifts in the Second International between evolutionary Marxists and activists such as Lenin.●Utopia, by contrast, offers a precise account of an imaginary future susceptible of immediate realization in the present. Although the present classification has emphasized the location of such devices in time, for our purposes utopias which are situated in present time but elsewhere can be assimilated to those projected into the future, since they portray the manners of people more civilized than ourselves (even when they live simpler lives) and so foreshadow our own possible future. Typically, the hope is not that society should evolve slowly towards utopia: what is envisaged is an instant or imminent transition from the present system, a break with history. This renders the utopian idea vulnerable to criticism both from the Burkean right and the Marxian left, yet often this is too glib, for the very idea of rupture is parasitic on a deeply controversial and highly artificial notion of continuous 'history', whereas a conception of history as discontinuous, or as a series of accidents, would make utopia seem less preposterous. Utopianism thus offers a specific programme and immediate hope for improvement and thereby discourages quiescence or fatalism.

Whether utopia is located in time or space, it has a constructive potency which the device of a Golden Age or a state of nature can never offer because time is not reversible. Nearly all utopian authors set out from the three premises mentioned under category 1, which are essential to constructive social theory. Some critics, not least Marx, would deny the dynamic potency of the utopian construct (although others maintain that this is what he also offers), because it so often fails to explain how utopia can be achieved, but this is not a necessary failing common to all utopian thought, nor does it negate the dynamic force of utopianism in political theory, even if it poses problems for political practice. In terms of the present analysis, the creation of a utopia has the double effect of throwing into sharp relief the imperfections of the present and providing a standpoint for criticism - always a difficult process because of the moral imperialism of the existent -

and of offering an accessible replacement, the ideal future.

6 Justification of the present by reference to a worse future

For the sake of completeness, this flourishing genre of literature must be mentioned, since it has considerable import for political theory. Dystopian warnings of future horrors, based on extrapolation and projection of current tendencies or ideas, serve to revalidate the present as the lesser evil, and to promote a 'decision' for no change. This approach parallels that described in category 1, with the *present* now representing a Golden Age which we must strive to preserve. Among the most influential works of this kind have been the literary dystopias, notably *Nineteen Eighty-four, Brave New World* and *We*, but Hayek's *The Road to Serfdom* is a theoretical expression of many of the same fears, which the text of Popper's *The Open Society and its Enemies* also exudes. Evidently, the invocation of a future-shock, like Hobbes's constant invocation of chaos, can at most have a preservative, not a constructive, effect.

The devices just described can be viewed as ways of removing current social restraints and culture-specific elements, and specifying what qualities are necessary for human life and which constraints may be essential to all societies. In this respect, the Golden Age, the state of nature, utopia and the rest can be designated the salient myths of political theory since, like myths, they attempt to portray eternal verities about human nature and ideals, in imaginary or symbolic form. They are not myths in Sorel's sense, for whom a political myth aroused action directly, although Mucchielli has argued for a strong connection between the utopian myth and political action.[19] In fact, such theories operate on several levels simultaneously (of which the mythical is only one), approaching their targets through fictional or hypothetical tricks which serve to entertain the reader and expand his credulity as well as to express human truths and influence political thought.

The purpose of classifying these devices at some length has been to demonstrate that political theory is by no means devoid of hypothetical constructs and myths; on the contrary, they play a pivotal role in the critique of present reality. Utopia is neither aberration nor fantasy, but forms part of this general category. Secondly, as the arguments in category 5 suggested, utopia is in a privileged position, perhaps uniquely so, for generating constructive and dynamic critical thought, with its projection of an alternative or future which is supposedly immediately attainable. Even if it is viewed as the culmination of a historical process, realization in the near future is possible, if the means and the will can be found. This potency rests on the general form of utopia, not on particular contents. Normative concerns, whether justificatory or critical, are central to political theory, and utopian fiction aids and abets these, providing both a critical basis and a source of alternative ideals. In Bauman's phrase, utopias 'relativize' the present, allowing for objective judgements which we could not pass if it were viewed as an absolute.[20] And, although some condemn the static nature of utopian society, Mannheim emphasizes the dynamic and necessary element inherent in utopian theory: 'the disappearance of utopia brings about a static state of affairs in which man himself becomes no more than a thing'.[21] Arguably, then, utopianism contributes an important progressive dimension to the structure of political discourse. While making this claim, that utopia constitutes a hypothetically historical or dynamic element in much political theory, we do not deny that many utopian societies do appear to exist in an ahistorical limbo; nevertheless, the presentation of such societies as 'lateral possibilities' creates a context extending beyond the present in which political theory can be conducted.

The critical and the constructive

In a discussion of the function of utopianism in political theory, should those utopias which only aim at entertainment be excluded by some criterion? The utopian form, after all, has served as a vehicle for many different contents, including straightforward pornographic fantasy such as Restif's, not all of which are politically significant. One criterion might be the political influence which a utopia had: did it evoke counter-utopias, was it discussed in political writings, did it, directly or indirectly, instigate political reforms? The application of this test would exclude a long line of forgotten utopias whose memory is preserved only in bibliographies – but much political theory would also be forgotten but for its quarter-page in histories of political thought. And this criterion would not produce decisive categories of utopia which were not legitimately part of political theory since literary utopias, from More's onwards, have been adopted as political texts, while overtly didactic utopias (such as Dom Deschamps's *La Vérité ou le Vrai Système* (1770), whose manuscript was only published a century later) have been mysteriously forgotten or ignored. Nor can we properly consult the intention of the author to decide whether his text belongs to the political corpus: intention and outcome rarely coincide. Clearly, the reception of a utopian text is the major factor, and this rests on many social preconditions, including organizational methods and the size and nature of the potential literate readership. These matters will be discussed in Part Two, when we shift our attention from utopian theory to utopian practice.

It appears, then, that no criterion regarding form can be specified to test a utopia's right to qualify as political theory. Rather, any utopia fulfilling the condition of social criticism through the depiction of an alternative society must be regarded as the stuff of political theory. However, one criterion might be adopted to exclude the wildest flights of apocalyptic millenarianism and science fiction: any proposal for utopia must be subject to reasoned justification which draws on our experience of man and society. A utopia composed of robots or Martians is not a valid political text for us, unless their behaviour is recognizably human - that is, unless they are human beings in disguise, like Mandeville's bees. This condition would not deny the symbolic and critical force of absurd inventions such as Lilliputians, or emotional computers. Such a criterion may act as a rule of thumb but it too conceals questions about the outer limits of 'human' behaviour, to which no final answers are likely to be established.

The relation between the critical and constructive modes of utopianism must now be elaborated and justified, in order to show more precisely how utopias function as political theory. Every utopia, by its very existence, constitutes an *ad hoc* criticism of existing society. The critical function is pursued in three ways: sometimes, as in Hythlodey's discussion of the causes of crime in England in More's *Utopia*,[22] or as in the King of Brobdingnag's scathing condemnation of English politics to Gulliver,[23] it is reasoned and direct. Sometimes, criticism is effected by a direct inversion of existing institutions which shows them to be absurd, arbitrary and evil. Herein lies the force of inversion, which argues: things might easily be the opposite of what they are (since nothing human is merely natural), yet see how evil, absurd and arbitrary that opposite appears - hence, existing society also shares these characteristics. This logic might be challenged, especially by those who have a Burkean or Hegelian view of our socio-political institutions, believing them to embody, and be sanctified by, reason and necessity. But the utopian starts from other premises, maintaining that social institutions are artefacts, merely the incarnation of reversible choices. Women *could* rule, illness *could* be punished as crime. The absurdity of such institutions would not lie in their content but in their blind exclusion of other equally absurd or equally reasonable alternatives. In this respect, the argument from inversion can be read as a sane plea for political compromise, a plea that all political institutions should be based on an awareness of the available extremes, and should mediate between them: extremity is absurdity. As was said in category 4, the force of inversion is purely destructive - one's face in a mirror will be no less ugly - but this meta-assertion that extreme polarities are ridiculous and harmful constitutes the positive force of the device. The effect of inversion on those who cannot conceive of the social hierarchy and order ever being other than it is, is at least salutary.

A third mode of criticism favoured by utopians is that which bridges the gap between the critical and the constructive - the portrayal of institutions and customs differing from our own which are demonstrably superior to ours. Sometimes the gap remains, since the superior institutions are not always desirable in all respects: More himself would probably have deplored the monotonous symmetry, similarity and regimentation of the cities of Utopia, yet he creates this pattern as an example of prosperity and justice superior in fundamental respects to his own society. Suboptimal institutions can also serve to criticize our own, by their superiority in some dimensions, even if they manifestly lack others, such as the aesthetic, so that one would not wish to realize them literally.

In terms of method, the constructive mode of utopianism is clearly posited on the critical; having diagnosed various social evils, the utopian designs institutions which will eradicate them. From the viewpoint of the reader, the processes may seem simultaneous: generally, he infers social criticism from the description of the perfect society. The determination of the positive by the negative aspect of utopianism is complex. Although logical propositions have contradictions and contraries, there is no such thing as a contradictory institution: even inversion cannot achieve this unambiguously - the opposite of rule by men could be rule by women, children, monkeys or God. Nevertheless, the attempt to negate perceived social evil has led a remarkable number of utopians to hit on similar solutions to major problems, so that one might almost believe that *the* contrary to private property is collective ownership, or that the only alternative to the nuclear family is the collective raising of children, whereas these are drawn from a range of alternatives. Although the will to negate major social evils leads in practice to the choice of a relatively small set of options, utopians differ in the imaginative detail with which they embellish these, and in their treatment of minor social problems for which unique solutions do not prescribe themselves.

Evidently, the truly constructive utopia transcends criticism and mere negation and proclaims its own institutions to be ideal in every respect, a harmonious whole, and does not merely invent piecemeal 'better' institutions to show up the deficiencies of those which exist. Such a perfect society, with its interlocking parts, is clearly the product of an overall design and an innovatory world-view, and thus constitutes a complete reconstruction of society. One could cite Plato's Republic or Fourier's Nouveau Monde as examples of such consummate utopias. From the viewpoint of political thought, the constructive dimension of utopia provides an explicit set of positive imperatives, unlike the critical aspect, and demands revolutionary reconstruction after a specific plan. This plan is unfortunately utopia's undoing, for it provides grounds for disagreement and challenge. Utopia is powerful because we can all concur in its criticisms (short-term ends) and weak because we invariably disagree on the remedies (the long-term ends and the means). In this respect, utopias which chiefly voice discontent are often better received than those which insist on a detailed description of perfection – the success of Marx and the relative failure of the utopian socialists comes to mind.

From reality to ideality

Utopia, the 'good place' which is nevertheless 'no place', helps us to escape from the existent, even if the place of refuge is still determined by the existing consciousness and ideology. This important process need not be branded as escapism, however. We have suggested that it allows political theory to escape from abstract descriptions of the present and to conceptualize modes of change and improvement, by being situated elsewhere in time or space and by operating critically and constructively. A certain number of utopias establish their non-escapist nature by developing theories of history which show the necessary relationship of their ideal societies to the present – relationships that are often said to be dialectical. From Deschamps's perception of three stages of civilization culminating in the 'true system', Condorcet's ten stages of the human mind, Saint-Simon's 'physiological' theory of history and Fourier's fantastic eschatological schema, to Marx's sophisticated dialectical and materialist theory, the same eighteenth-century preoccupation with progress is manifested, a preoccupation originating in the quarrel over the value of the cultures of the ancients and moderns.[24] Such utopias decline to offer an instant escape from reality, and invite the reader to contemplate a historical development which he might accelerate by appropriate action, but which must also ripen to fruition. This approach to utopia is more attuned to our perception of the mental and moral development of the individual - a maturing process rather than sudden conversion - and has the advantage of *not* implying a break with history. Another advantage is that utopia seen as an integral part of a historical process cannot be subjected to the same criticisms as an ahistorical utopia - the *perpetuum immobile* criticized by Dahrendorf.[25]

Apart from serving to distance us from the present, utopias have other, related functions. Those whose emphasis is on social perfection rather than criticism can be viewed as exemplary models of society which lay bare the mechanics of social harmony, having eliminated unnecessary social constraints and defects. In this respect utopianism belongs not just to political thought but to social science. Indeed, utopians of the early nineteenth century considered themselves as social scientists and were so considered by their contemporaries.[26] Conversely, one can argue that the relative lack of utopian writing in this century is a response to the plethora of social and political models produced by the academic industry, which perform the same function in a less imaginative, but some would say more dignified, fashion. Yet this loss is to be deplored because, as was said, a utopian fiction can express powerfully, frugally and figuratively that which cannot be said in systematic, reasoned theorizing. Happily, there remains a backlog of utopias which have significance for us, despite advancing time and progress, and it is tempting to suggest that some utopian models genuinely express quasi-eternal human verities, and so should remain part of our social science and philosophy catalogues. This is the argument of Mucchielli for one, who believes that 'the myth of the ideal city' has always constituted the deep structure of human aspiration and protest.[27]

In the realm of activist, as well as academic, political thinking, utopias have an important role when they are read as manifestos for an alternative society, the expression of lateral possibilities. This role is not limited to the time in which they were written, and ransacking old utopias for signposts to the future is still common practice. In France, disillusionment with organized and orthodox Marxism after the events of May 1968 has led to a strong revival of interest in utopianism for practical purposes, especially in the utopian socialists. The slogans of 1968 - 'soyons réalistes, exigeons l'impossible' and 'l'imagination au pouvoir' - were strongly utopian. Schérer wrote four years later of the danger of the impregnation of Marxism by repressive civilization: utopianism, by contrast, breaks with codified logic, viewing *desire* as a motive force, and thus places personal liberation *before* political revolution.[28] The 'liberation of desire' has created new, even more utopian, slogans – 'tous, et tout de suite' and 'bonheur, aujourd'hui'. Although the plundering of utopias for new insights seems to derogate from their deliberate harmonious integrity, honour is sometimes saved, for there have been attempts to realize utopian schemes in their totality, such as the setting up of a Fourierist colony at Big Sur, near San Francisco (1968–9). The new popularity in France of utopianism, albeit with that small section of the population which is educated, young and gauchiste, has also produced an extensive literature on the significance of utopianism, which is more than ephemeral. But the espousal of utopian ideas in political activity cannot easily be systematically analysed, so various are the associations that are made; Fourier, for example, is heralded as a forerunner of Freud, an unpredictable honour, and a champion of permissive society. The interpretation of the text may diverge widely from the original intention of the author but, as is now argued by the proponents of hermeneutics and semiology, this is the proper treatment of a text, and the healthy proof of its continued vitality.[29] However great the selection or distortion, the rereading process today indicates the important function of utopianism in political activism, as both evidence and inspiration.

Despite this recent utopian revivalism, it has frequently been claimed that the present century has lost the spirit of utopianism, as Mannheim wrote as early as 1929. For him, the accession to political power of the working class, formerly the vehicle for the socialist-communist utopian mentality, and the relative satisfaction of its aspirations, reduced the need for utopianism and left stranded intellectuals who had formerly engendered utopias. Mannheim praises the sociology of knowledge as a critical tool, but still hopes for a revival of utopianism, whose present decline foreshadows 'a decay of the human will', because he thinks of it as a reflection of human aspiration.[30] Shklar's *After Utopia* (subtitled 'The decline of political faith') traces the history of the struggle between the Enlightenment rationalism which propagated utopias and the conservative romanticism succeeding it, which devalued progress, from Rousseau to Camus. She, like Mannheim, argues that the end of revolutions and class wars dictated an end to utopianism, and fears that the dominance of a technological paradigm, supplanting romanticism, will lead to totalitarianism. The hope for utopia is dwindling.[31]

Further reasons can be adduced for the decline of utopianism including the hypothesis suggested above, the take-over of utopia's analytical and model-producing role by a more thorough but more pedestrian academic tradition. The reading public's predilection for scientific and technological, rather than political, panaceas must also be blamed. But although there may be few new fictional utopias, in political theory there is no lack of new utopian models, presented as a cross between analysis and speculation: one need only cite Marcuse's state of erotic liberation, Fromm's socialism, the 'counter-utopias' of Hayeck's catallaxy or Nozick's minimal state[32] to show utopia's continuing popularity with theorists both as a theoretical device and as a vehicle for idealistic content. Its speculative nature still makes it epistemologically suspect for a majority of fellow-theorists, as the criticism of these writers makes clear, and this problem will be raised again in Chapter 3.

Finally, the case for taking utopianism seriously as political theory cannot avoid the discussion of an important conundrum. Readers familiar with utopian literature will have remarked on the minor role, or total absence, of *politics* in most utopias. Utopia seems to exclude politics because, simply, there is nothing left to argue about; also, because its insularity, or a convenient mountain range, eliminates the problem of external political relations.[33] What excuse can there be for asserting the political importance of a genre of thought which seems to abhor politics? Reflection shows that the politics which utopias lack is defined as the expression of differences of opinion and interest, and consequent power struggles: that we identify this as a lack is indicative of our ideological conviction that politics equals argument, competition and the representation of rival interests, and that the successful politician is one who somehow gains power over the others and 'wins'.

Analysis also suggests that utopians do not in fact ignore various aspects of politics which we would consider subsidiary, but make them central. For Plato, the idea of rule by the wise is all-important, and the core of the *Republic* is an elaboration of the provisions for the education and life of the philosopher-rulers which will enable them to take wise decisions by contemplating the absolute Ideas. Another constant theme is that of ideal, impartial laws justly administered, which makes its appearance in Plato's second-best utopia, the *Laws*, and persists through the utopias of More, Morelly and many others. In principle, such laws are those established by the utopian founder, requiring no political debate or further legislation, but merely execution. The lawmaking process is often ignored in these works because the important feature is the fact of the laws' existence. The nineteenth-century distinction between government and administration helps to explain the apparent absence of political debate from the utopias of that time, although we may suspect that the tasks of government are merely transferred to administrators and given a new name. Saint-Simon predicted this change, which was described by Engels as the shift 'from the government of men to the administration of things' (a dictum actually echoed by the anti-socialist Comte), when he argued that in the tranquil industrial utopia the only decisions needed would be the technical ones best taken by experts.[34] Likewise, the hope of Marx and Engels for the withering away of the state is a Saint-Simonian reference. Even Lenin speaks of 'management' rather than 'rule' in a communist society.[35] Other utopias, such as Fourier's, are so ideally composed that the right decisions are taken collectively and spontaneously, and even administration is unnecessary, although Fourier saw that 'intrigue' would continue as a pleasurable activity, but without political consequences. Certainly, there are a number of utopians who lay weight on deliberation, as do some nineteenth-century anarchists, but these refer to a tradition of disinterested and reasoned debate directed towards political truth, rather than to the promotion of interests and exercise of influence which are currently thought to typify politics. Some utopias abolish the ruling class, others happily institute uncontested hierarchies based on expertise or age, or devise rotation systems as did Owen and Herbert Read. But all these methods are a far cry from the adversary procedures which have come to dominate our notion of politics in the West.

This curious divergence between our real and ideal societies also arises partly from the fact that our quotidian politics is, in theory, about finding ways to utopia and, in practice, about compromise between entrenched interests. Both these processes, concerning ends and means, are the subject of hot debate, whereas the goals of a utopia are predetermined by the utopian according to what he perceives as truths about human life, and the means are then 'deduced' from these goals. This state of affairs produces the notorious fixity of utopia, which is an ahistorical snapshot or cross-section of a society whose major political choices have been determined, perhaps for ever, a quality condemned by Lapouge as 'the incarceration of time'.[36] This fixity (which is less attributable to the historical utopias mentioned above) results from the utopian's intellectual confidence that human truths can indeed be discovered (by him) and incarnated in political institutions. But equally, it can be seen as reflecting a new evaluation of politics by the utopian, and the revelation that pleasure is to be found in *living* rather than in arguing about how life should be lived: politics as such is a waste of time. This is true even for Plato, despite the Greek tradition of *homo politicus*, in that he severs politics from ordinary life. The utopian's diminution of the role of politics differs from the liberal commitment to making the political sphere into a narrow, confined element of social activity, so as to maximize the extent of private life and freedom, because utopians almost unanimously have a strongly collective conception of pleasure and fulfilment, which will continue to perform an integrating function in society, even when politics has disappeared. The absence of politics from utopia is not an excuse for what Marx accused liberal societies of, 'the separation of man from man'.[37]

If utopia has politics without policy arguments, can it have politics without power? This question too is redolent of our own conflictual view of the political process, which persists whether we view politics as a class or an interest-group phenomenon, and which sees coercion as ultimately inevitable, even if disguised. Marx, in associating the attainment of a classless society with the abolition of the state, followed a long line of utopians (though also, in a sense, he succeeded Bentham and Adam Smith) in assuming that an identity or harmony of individuals' interests can be achieved which renders political power redundant. Not all utopias are classless, however, for many have emulated Plato in depicting class-based societies; but for utopia to be ideal, it must have ousted internal conflicts and achieved harmony, even organic balance, between classes. But it is a lopsided view which sees power as necessarily conflictual and hence inherently coercive and ignores the aspects of power resting on acquiescence, delegation or agreement. This is the basis of power in utopian societies, which then takes on a co-operative quality: the ruled acquiesce in the rulers' decisions because they have been fairly chosen (as in the theory of ideal democracy) or because of their acknowledged expertise. Such non-coercive power is neither corrupting for the rulers nor degrading to the ruled.

So the utopian model is paradoxically one of power without politics, which raises the old question, 'quis custodiet custodes ipsos?' ('who guards the guards?'), a question which runs counter to the utopian spirit of optimism about human nature. How, without the safeguard of free, adversary politics, can a utopia fail to metamorphose into an authoritarian society? This particular challenge will be faced in Chapter 4, within a general consideration of the hostility of liberal democrats to utopian thinking. Evidently, so many definitions exist of the nature and purpose of politics that a final answer as to whether utopia has politics or not cannot be given. But undeniably, utopia transforms politics into forms which differ in many respects from those recognized and sanctioned by our own ideologies and institutions. Indeed, the absence of the traditional political apparatus from many utopias, and the burning scorn of utopians such as More and Swift for politicking, is food for thought, and should lead to a salutary reconsideration of our own narrow and particular definition of the political process. It might also precipitate a welcome revision of the definition of political theory, which at present circumscribes it so as to exclude most 'social' phenomena.

Arguably, utopianism is more a part of social than political thought because so much space is devoted to social organization, and so little to political. This results not from oversight, but rather from the realization that the social *is* the political. The utopian treats society as an integrated whole whose parts interact analogously to water finding a common level between various vessels. Hostility and resistance to this amalgamation of the social and the political continue, reinforced by our division of social science into a multiplicity of disciplines, but the integrative nature of utopian thought gives some force to the claim of nineteenth-century utopians that they were creating *the* social science. The justification for temporarily annexing utopianism to the narrower field of political thought in this book is that neither political thought nor political action can be understood without a knowledge of the persisting utopian element in politics, which is a source both of critical ideals and of the impetus to change.

Suggested reading

(For full publication details consult the bibliography at the end of the book.) All secondary works on utopia contain definitions of the term, and the sheer variety of approaches can be a source of confusion. A good starting-point is a useful selection of articles edited by F. E. Manuel, *Utopias and Utopian Thought*. K. Mannheim's *Ideology and Utopia* remains a classic statement of the role of utopianism in political thinking and activity. French writers have generally been more inquiring about the place of utopia in conceptual thought. See in particular: R. Mucchielli, *Le Mythe de la Cité Idéale*; R. Ruyer, *L'Utopie et les Utopies*; J. Servier, *L'Histoire de l'Utopie*. E. Bloch (*Geist der Utopie*) associates utopian thought with hope and inspiration. There is an abundance of American secondary works, but these are usually concerned with analysing one particular aspect of the genre (e.g. utopia and the machine, utopia and the family), and do not consider it as a special form of theory, as we do here.

2 Taxonomy and anatomy

While it is seductively easy to generalize about utopias, their nature and their function, the intractable reality remains, that the generic term covers a multitude of works which differ in form, content, intention and degree of seriousness. To attempt a historical survey of utopias is as vain as to attempt to write a history of the English novel from Beowulf to Beckett. The available historical commentaries on utopia take several forms. There are anthologies of utopia, the best known being Negley and Patrick's *The Quest for Utopia*, which sets out to represent the contents of past utopias with welcome brevity. A recent monumental and ambitiously polymathic history is that of the Manuels, who 'avoid the parochialism of exclusive disciplinary discourse by studying the same utopian constellation on different levels' in their *Utopian Thought in the Western World*.[1] A sociological approach is taken in Servier's *Histoire de l'Utopie*, which locates particular utopias in the context of social and economic developments while simultaneously tracing the wider intellectual movements – from affirmation of traditional society to visions of the City of God, and so on – which explain the changing preoccupations of the utopian genre. Finally, there are the commentators who draw selectively on utopias across history to illustrate some thesis, such as the idea that utopia is the quintessence of rebellion against the human condition, or that utopia symbolizes a profound desire for a return to the mother's womb. None of these approaches overcomes the difficulty that a Procrustean degree of pruning must take place in order to fit *Gulliver's Travels* into the same category as the *Republic*, or Morris into the same class as Morelly.

The major problem, however, is one of methodology. One can take a relativist approach, and treat each utopia as an enlightening critique of the society from which it emanated and an expression of the aspirations of men of a certain time, without drawing any conclusions about its relevance to present society, or even while asserting its irrelevance. Alternatively, one can define the genre 'utopianism' as a cross-historical absolute, a form of expression of discontent at the human condition and of aspirations for improvement, and then assert the relevance of

Plato or More to our own predicaments. One of the major theoretical definitions of utopia, that of Mannheim (which is discussed in Chapter 3), that utopias are situation-transcending ideas, has been strongly relativist, but many other thinkers search for an absolute core of meaning, including those for whom utopia is the voice of totalitarianism speaking across the ages. In treating the relation of utopianism to political thought, there is some danger of falling into an absurdly absolutist position. For example, to set out to examine 'liberty in utopia' is a suspect procedure since notions of political liberty for Plato, More or even Fourier differed widely from our own individual-istic notion of freedom. However, we shall start from a modest absolutist assumption, which is that the problem of maintaining order in society is a constant, and is indeed the problem of politics itself. Discontent threatens order, so anyone concerned with the maintenance of order must equally consider the provision of satisfaction in society, or at the very least, the prevention of active dissatisfaction. Although such assumptions do not derive from functionalism, David Easton's analysis of the political system suggests the importance of the relation between satisfaction, support for the political order, and the maintenance of a social system. This is the problem which utopia faces, like all other political theory.

The present chapter attempts a broad chronological survey of utopianism, grouping the best-known utopias into the main periods of their development, in order to show the political dilemmas which they encompass. First, a few words must be said about the multiple and various forms that utopian writing has assumed. There have been political treatises from the *Republic* onwards, dialogues like *Télémache*, straightforwardly didactic accounts of the ideal society such as the Enlightenment philosophers produced, and, since the rise of that new art form, the novel, a vast number of utopian novels which purport to entertain and simultaneously try to convert the reading public. At the end of the eighteenth century, a new genre of utopianism emerged which presented itself as political economy or social science, and this has probably been the most influential form of utopianism in the last two centuries. Utopias can thus be distinguished according to their form, although this is sometimes an accidental property of a work. However, an ideal society presented as a novel seeks to operate on its audience differently (and, indeed, seeks a different audience) from a political treatise which attempts to convert by reason, and differently again from a 'social scientific' utopia, which aims to demonstrate the truth of its ideal by reference to current social phenomena. Again, a quite different appeal is made by political manifestos such as Babeuf's, by *The Communist Manifesto*, and by Owen's millenarian writings, whose appeal is largely emotional and exhortatory. The form which a utopia takes is thus indicative of the effect which the author intends to evoke and of whether he wishes to achieve this by reasoned argument, revelation or appeal to emotion.

Another distinction important for determining the likely effect on an audience and the relevance of the political problems raised is whether a utopia is located in another time or merely another place. The relation of utopianism to time was discussed in Chapter 1, and evidently utopias of the Golden Age or Age of Innocence are self-defeating as far as changing society goes, although they have sometimes generated separatist, 'back-to-nature' movements. Futuristic utopias have more leverage and, even when located in the distant future, can be said to be creating an awareness in their readers of an ideal society which could be realized *now* if they cared to act to bring it about. An allegory of England in a hundred years' time can effectively awake a critical consciousness of the present and, as Horsburgh argues, many utopian ideas have turned out to be merely 'before their time', and have been implemented later. Utopias of place, describing a better present elsewhere, of which More's is the classic example, may seem to teach us a less direct lesson, but they carry the implication that the ideal civilization could exist here and now. The choice of location for utopia has followed fashion, utopias of the Elsewhere being popular in the sixteenth and seventeenth centuries, thanks to the proliferation of travellers' tales at the time; in the nineteenth century, the predominance of theories of history and stadial theories made it more necessary to locate the ideal society in time, and to relate it to the present through a historical narrative, even while implying that the train of events could be hastened by activism; the latter view being shared, in effect, by Fourier and Marx. A further distinction, made in the last chapter, between critical and constructive utopianism, must also be borne in mind when reviewing the history of utopianism, although often the constructive utopian expects his readers to draw critical conclusions, and vice versa.

The utopian past

Utopias of the classical period could form the subject of a dissertation in themselves, and in a sense these provide the most holistic account of utopia as a society in which no distinctions are made between politics and private life, between the individual and his social environment. Among the classical writings which have been labelled utopian (with more or less justice) are parts of Aristotle's *Politics*, Plato's *Laws*, his *Atlantis* and, of course, his *Republic* (?380 BC), which describes a society incarnating absolute justice. Although it consists of three classes (the ruling Guardians, the auxiliaries, the artisans, plus slaves who have no political status), these coexist in perfect harmony thanks to the uncontested rule of the 'philosopher kings' who are freed to contemplate absolute knowledge by the absence of property or family ties. Plato's *Republic* sets precedents for future utopias by defining society as being for the mutual satisfaction of needs, pointing to the close connection between virtue in the individual and in society as a whole, and by basing itself on an epistemological theory which held that absolute, transcendental knowledge about human life was possible, and must guide ideal politics. From Plato and Aristotle derives the notion of the organic nature of society which pervades later utopianism until the rise of egalitarianism.

The utopias produced during Christianity's growth and heyday are equally compartmentalized and perhaps more remote from the sympathies of the modern reader. Given the doctrines of Original Sin and the Second Coming, the notion of a utopia, the ideal society on earth, would have bordered on blasphemy, but between Plato and Thomas More the ascendency of Christianity and theological politics produced the mysterious doctrine of the City of God, which was eternal and extra-terrestrial (and so not a utopia in the usual sense), but also existed immanently on earth in the souls of the faithful. More, concretely, Sir John Mandeville's account of the *Blessed Isles of Prester John* (?1356)[2] portrayed a spiritual, godly people in a state of Adamite innocence, whose virtue doubtless constituted a criticism of the sophistical corruption of organized religion. By contrast, in the same period arose the popular legend of the Land of Cockayne, an anti-spiritual utopia devoted to gastronomic and sensual satisfaction, and notable for the absence of work.[3] Bridging the abyss between the City of God and Cockayne, there emerged in the thirteenth century a plethora of millenarian movements such as Norman Cohn describes in *The Pursuit of the Millennium*. Hard though it is to generalize about these, particularly in the absence of written doctrines, their assertion of egalitarianism against the hierarchical elitism of the Church, their practice of free love and physical indulgence, and their demands for 'heaven now', make them a clear pointer towards later, secular utopianism.

Renaissance and 'early modern' utopias reflect the liberation of thought and political institutions from theological control, the birth of modern experimental science, and rapid changes in economic and social structures. The landmark which More's eponymous *Utopia* (1516) constituted, both in form and content, is well known. The first part is a direct criticism of various social evils of the time, touching on the machinations of court life and the evils of war, arguing for the abolition of the death sentence for theft, and condemning private property. 'Till property is taken away there can be no equitable or just distribution of things, nor can the world be happily governed.'[4] In Book II the island Utopia is described, and is seen to constitute the negation of all these evils. Every detail of life is minutely prescribed and regulated, thanks to the wisdom of the benevolent founder-designer, Utopus, but there are few laws. Criminals become slaves and are obliged to work constantly, but are not otherwise punished. The fifty-four identical towns, whose inhabitants live communally, are centres of production and exchange, but all citizens must spend periods working in the country. There is mutual aid between the towns in case of shortage. The social hierarchy rests on respect and honour, not on property, for there is no possession. All are bound by the duty to work and the result is plenty, enjoyed in moderation. The pursuit of happiness is seen as the highest good – a point reinforced by the various religions of Utopia. As for government, although the system is self-maintaining, representatives are chosen for a national assembly by secret voting: More emphasizes the role of reflection and debate in its proceedings, and the absence of demagogy and sharp practice.

Utopia provided a model for all future well-ordered ideal societies. There were no direct successors for a century, but meanwhile Rabelais's *Gargantua and Pantagruel* (1567) appeared, with its utopian Abbey of Thélème, a humorous inversion of the monastic life depicting a 'monastery' devoted to love, indulgence and luxury. Campanella's *City of the Sun* appeared in 1623, a city of concentric circles (the inverted inferno?) whose inhabitants are dedicated to acquiring knowledge and to pure, pious living. Again, life is communal and closely regulated, and property, with its concomitant vices of greed and envy, is unknown. Bacon's *New Atlantis* (1629), later heralded as the first scientific utopia, takes the ideality of its social arrangements and the virtue of the people for granted, and dwells on the pursuit of knowledge and scientific experiments in the House of Solomon, providing fuel for Swift's satirical account of Laputan experiments a century later. Harrington's *Oceana* (1675) is overtly political, depicting Cromwell as a Platonic ruler, and distinguishing citizens' rights from human rights:

his work influenced the American constitution. Later in the seventeenth century Vairasse's *History of the Sévérambes* (1675) and Fénélon's *Télémache* (1699) depicted just, ascetic, well-regulated communities with property in common, this being achieved in the first instance by an enlightened despot, a recurring dream of that period. Mandeville's *Fable of the Bees* (1714), a satire of the symbiotic relationship between private vice and public prosperity, has been viewed by some as the first *laissez-faire* utopia.

Gulliver's *Travels* (1726) constituted the apotheosis of the utopian form as savage and entertaining satire. Thereafter the focus of utopianism shifted to France, where the Enlightenment produced relatively solemn and didactic utopias – ideal constitutions and codes of law – redolent of the philosophical preoccupations with Reason and Nature. The development of the ideas of progress and perfectibility, which were to dominate the second half of the century, had particular consequences for utopianism. The belief that the human race was progressing to even higher levels of civilization, together with the three-stage theory of Turgot and his imitators, located the Golden Age firmly in the future, while the hope that human beings were, individually and collectively, perfectible made a secular heaven on earth attainable, abolishing the stain of Original Sin. During this century the Abbé de Saint-Pierre's *Project for Everlasting Peace in Europe* (1713) provided the first internationalist utopia. Appearing at the height of the Enlightenment, Rousseau's *Discourse on the Origins of Inequality* (1755) might appear a surprisingly primitivist utopia, as it did to his contemporaries, but it should rather be read as the prelude to his account of the moral nature of socio-political life in an ideal democracy which appeared in his *Social Contract* (1762). This does not fall into the communistic tradition of the utopias of the time, but argues for a modest level of living with a minimum of inequalities.

Morelly's *Code de la Nature* (1755) is a typical product of the time; purporting to describe a code of laws and morality which are ideal because attuned to nature's purposes, it depicts a simple, aesthetic, communistic society centred on knowledge and rational education, with incongruously strict conjugal laws 'which would prevent all debauchery'. Like many *philosophes*, Morelly found it hard to decide whether Nature was a rationalist or a sensualist, and his *Basiliade* (1753) offered a more natural account of free love, enhanced by the enjoyment of abundant resources. The theme of sexual utopia recurred in Diderot's *Supplement to Bougainville's Voyage* (1772, published in 1796), a mock traveller's tale, where the innocence and healthy eugenic motives of free love in Tahiti are extolled; but Restif de la Bretonne's *Andrographe* (1782) describes sexual life in a communist society regulated in the minutest detail, with strict penalties for deviance. These anti-sensualist, pro-marriage fantasies found their inversion in the writings of Sade and in Fourier's *Nouveau Monde Amoureux*. Another free-love utopia was that of Dom Deschamps's *La Vérité ou le Vrai Système* (written 1770). This typical three-stage theory looked forward to the third, communistic stage without property or luxury, and with total equality and freedom, the manifestation of both moral and metaphysical truths. The political content of Enlightenment utopias is usually their least interesting aspect. Egalitarian in principle (though often not with respect to women), communistic with respect to economic organization, they rest on fixed natural moral laws, enforced by fairly-chosen magistrates. Nature has, as it were, taken politics into her own moral hands.

Overtly political and contentious utopianism begins, of course, with the French Revolution, and Babeuf's *Manifesto of the Equals* (written 1790–5) is a forthright polemical statement of extreme egalitarianism which maintains the equal right to life and equal obligation to work, both established by Nature, and the wrongness of appropriation of property. Babeuf's 'utopia' consisted of equality of treatment for all, in every respect. From the same turbulent period emerged Godwin's *Enquiry Concerning Political Justice* (1793), a strong attack on government authority, law, punishment and property which advocated free autonomous communities ('parishes') and a simple, reflective life. Condorcet's *Sketch for a Historical Picture of the Progress of the Human Mind* (1795) is an account of man's progress through knowledge towards freedom in various stages; the future, tenth stage has the utopian qualities of complete freedom, abolition of poverty and of ignorance. Such works as these derive from the revolutionary period when even the most utopian works were read polemically and often considered seditious, however innocently idealistic their content.

The nineteenth-century utopian mode is altogether more familiar to us. The vehicle of the voyage to an imaginary land disappears, often being replaced by a less or more sophisticated theory of history which locates utopia in the near future. The meaning of 'utopian' shifts slightly to connote 'a proponent of an ideal society', a usage which derives from More but which has a different emphasis. Utopias of this period and of the early part of the twentieth century can properly be called 'modern', being utopias based on science, technology, modern industry and the hope of material abundance. Reactions to the complexities of industrialism dictate more elaborate forms of collective ownership than the simple communism of earlier utopias, and the promise of machine-produced plenty evokes the prospect of consumer utopias with luxury for all. Saint-Simon's utopian socialism (*floruit* 1800–25) depends on the attainment of full industrial development accompanied by advanced scientific knowledge and appropriate political institutions. A parliament of industrialists, engineers and scientists will take decisions which produce prosperity for all. Saint-Simon left the issue of ownership somewhat vague but his disciples, the Saint-Simonians, firmly decreed the abolition of inheritance, so that the state could determine who should have the use of productive property; they also coined the maxim 'from each according to his ability, to each ability according to its work', which, in a modified form, became the slogan of the Marxist utopia – if utopia it be. Owen's scheme for industrial communities with common ownership, developed in the same period, likewise aimed to separate the material benefits of mechanization from the correlative social evils and guarantee prosperity. His democratically-run, self-sufficient communities were to rest on the communal upbringing and massive moral education of children, to the extent that few rules would be necessary for adults. Fourier's 'phalanstery' (contemporary with the ideas of the aforementioned 'utopian socialists') is based on the principle of providing everyone with attractive work, and on the complete satisfaction of instinctual needs ('passions'), but does not entirely collectivize ownership, although property is separated from its usual accompaniments of power and honour, and so rendered harmless. Fourier's is a utopia of spontaneous order and harmony, based directly on human nature without the intervention of law and politics. Cabet's *Voyage en Icarie* (1840) was a full-scale utopian novel, but its fictional form did not prevent it from stimulating a remarkably active political movement. Its promise of a thoroughly industrialized and thoroughly communistic nation-state utopia reappeared in the later works of the German socialist pioneer, Weitling, but whereas Cabet advocated a peaceful path to utopia, Weitling regarded a revolutionary rising of the proletariat as a necessary precondition for social transformation.

It may well be asked why so many 'modern' utopias are socialist – indeed, the two categories almost became coextensive during the nineteenth century. A sociological account would connect the proliferation of socialist theories with the inception and development of capitalism and the visible injustices which resulted. There is also a strong connection with the romanticism of the late Enlightenment, with its assertions of equality and its resistance to political injustice and coercion. But there is also a distinctive non-socialist utopian tradition to be traced through Comte and later positivists. The author of the voluminous *Cours de Philosophie Positive* (1830–42) subsequently employed his new science of *sociologie* to outline a complete 'system of positive politics', combining the scientific rationalism of technocracy with a neo-Catholic religious hierarchy. Neither socialist nor liberal in outlook, Comte described himself as *un conservateur*, but his radical proposals had little in common with conservatism in any orthodox sense. Rather his 'positive polity' looked forward to twentieth-century notions of scientific-technological society, although the strongly religious element in his thought added a dimension to his utopianism which few of his technocratic successors have imitated.

The nineteenth-century anarchist ideal (if indeed such a distinction can properly be made in the early days of anarchism and socialism) generally pointed to utopias based on collective ownership and small-scale production, but placed greater emphasis than did socialism on the autonomy of the productive units and the absence of any overall national structure. Proudhon idealized both craft-based workshop production and a system of peasant shareholdings within a general setting of mutual aid. *Mutual Aid* (1902) was also the title of Kropotkin's quasi-scientific work showing the natural tendency to such aid within animal species and primitive tribes, and drawing optimistic conclusions about the possibilities of benign social organization. We are inclined to see the shortcomings of both anarchism and early socialism through Marx's eyes, and his pejorative definition of utopianism will be discussed in the next chapter. But the case for calling Marx's own theory utopian has often been stated, resting on the apocalyptic role of the revolution, and his idealization of the stage of higher communism.[5] Marx's analysis was certainly more rigorous, perhaps more scientific, but the ideal solutions which he proposed (although sketchily) shared much with utopias from More onwards.

The latter half of the nineteenth century was also rich in socialist theories so idealistic that they might well be called utopian: the idealistic socialism of Péguy, the revolutionary theory of Déjacque and the theory of the welfare state of Popper-Lynkeus would merit discussion in a longer survey.[6] There were also attempts at more practical, less political utopianism which took the form of writings on planning and the creation of model towns. Such 'design utopias' had links with the earlier communitarianism of Owen and Fourier, but attempted to show how the notion of utopia could be accommodated in a more urbanized and more industrial society. This was the aim, for example, of Ebenezer Howard in his proposals for garden cities (*Tomorrow: A Peaceful Path to Real Reform*, 1898).

The end of the century also saw a widespread reversion to the fictional utopian form as a vehicle for political propaganda, most notably in Samuel Butler's *Erewhon* (1872), Edward Bellamy's *Looking Backward* (1888) and its sequel *Equality* (1897), and William Morris's *News from Nowhere* (1891). The popularity of such works (and especially of *Looking Backward*, probably the most widely read fictional utopia ever written), testifies to the upsurge in literacy which was occurring at this time, and which greatly enhanced the novel's significance as a medium of mass communication. Butler employed the time-honoured method of satirical inversion to show the injustices of the legal system and the evils of mechanization. Both Bellamy and Morris depicted the practical implementation of socialism in future utopias. Bellamy's United States of AD 2000, a highly scientific and technological society, caught the public imagination sufficiently to provoke a voluminous pro- and anti-Bellamy literature as well as an active 'Nationalist' movement in America (Bellamy preferred this designation to socialism because he considered the latter to be unlikely to succeed in America). Morris took issue with Bellamy's vision of a fully industrialized society by depicting an agricultural and craft community with bucolic and aesthetic, though not intellectual, pleasures, a community established in the wake of a successful Marxist revolution in the Britain of the early 1950s. It is the combination of constructive utopianism and Marxist theory which has earned for Morris a particularly distinctive place in the history of socialist thought. To this day his work continues to stimulate lively debate on the issue of what role utopianism ought to play in the Marxist concept of future socialist and communist society.

In the early twentieth century the Russian Revolution diverted socialist dreams from utopianism to the observation and eulogization of Soviet reality, and then to the criticism and justification of Soviet shortcomings, which may account for the relative paucity of utopian writing at this time. However, writers such as H. G. Wells indefatigably employed the utopian novel to make didactic and satirical points about society, and some of Shaw's plays, such as *Man and Superman*, are also of the genre.[7] (Both writers were active members of the Fabian Society.) In the Western world socialist utopianism now had to accommodate itself to the changed conditions in which, for the first time, large socialist parties found themselves in possession of effective national organization. As opportunities for socialist influence and access to political power spread, utopian discussion of how socialism was actually to be achieved declined in favour of notions of gradualism and parliamentary reformism through the use of legislation. Other factors conspired, in the 1920s and 1930s, to alter the prevailing mood from optimism to despair: widespread economic depression, the constant threat of war, the instability of liberal democracy, the rise of Fascism. Not surprisingly dystopian texts figured prominently in the literature of this period, the most notable examples being Zamyatin's *We* (1920), Huxley's *Brave New World* (1932) and Orwell's *Nineteen Eighty-four* (1949). The realities of Fascism and Stalinism were taken as warnings of what a modern scientific-technological system, established in the name of utopianism, might be like.

The living tradition

In the 1950s and 1960s it was widely argued that utopias were a thing of the past, that political theory in the orthodox sense was 'dead', that ideological differences were being submerged in new concepts of rationalism and scientific planning, and in party competition to win over voters of the middle ground. Such an outlook was certainly premature, and what is noteworthy from our point of view is that the post-war years have produced a large number of writings which might be labelled 'utopian', together with a corpus of academic commentaries on utopianism, particularly in France and the USA. These have grown from a mixture of social, economic and intellectual conditions containing contradictions which lead would-be utopians in various directions. The reaction against totalitarianism, against the inhumanity and horrors of total war and destruction has created the *sine qua non* for the new utopias, which must find ways of averting these evils. Meanwhile, the prospect of a super-automated society suggested (before the recession of the 1970s) the possibility of material abundance beyond our dreams, while the essential barrenness of a materialistic way of life, and the failure of capitalism to fulfil our deepest needs, simultaneously caused idealists to search for utopias of greater simplicity and asceticism. In another dimension, the breaking down of disciplinary barriers in the academic world has facilitated the treatment of the utopian idea in areas such as planning, architecture and psychology, with a consequent enrichment of our conception of the breadth and scope of utopianism. Modern developments in psychology, both Freudian and behaviourist, have provided new theories of human need and motivation on which entirely new social structures can be built. However, the theories to be treated here fall, more or less, under the heading of political theory. But they show the same eclectic tendencies as utopias of the past which, even while rejecting their social heritage, incorporated the intellectual achievements of their time and current fashionable ideas into their theorizing. In this respect, each utopia is a mirror of its time, despite its critical orientation. The interest in Marx's early writings shows how even an earlier utopian thinker can be reinterpreted to fit in with modern conditions and to appear relevant. The utopias of Marcuse, Nozick, Friedman and Skinner will be analysed in some detail, as exemplars of forms of utopianism which evolve from our own problems and follow current rules of thought and intellectual fashions.

Herbert Marcuse's role as a utopian with 'New Left' leanings is well established, and his efforts to associate himself with revolutionary movements, in particular that of 1968, made him an influential, if ambiguous, figure. But the most utopian of his writings, *Eros and Civilization*, dates from 1956 when he embarked on the grandiose venture of amalgamating the two revolutionizing (and incompatible) theories of this century, Marxism and Freudianism. He offers an analysis of the domination and repression of advanced capitalism in psychological terms, calling frequently on Freud's *Civilization and its Discontents* (1930) for supporting evidence. Like Freud (and Fourier before him), he maintains that society is based on sexual represssion, but unlike Freud, he maintains that libidinal liberation could take place without the destruction of civilization. Capitalism rests on the dominance of the 'performance principle', which dictates delayed gratification and sublimation of libidinal energy in productive labour. Surveying the achievements of advanced technology, Marcuse argues that the techniques for super-automation are available, which would virtually abolish labour, leaving man free to develop himself in extensive leisure time. In fact, the breakthrough has not occurred because the 'system', the capitalist collective, prefers to dominate workers by keeping them safely at work and consuming their energies in alienating labour, which diverts them from political radicalization. This unnecessary labour extracted by the system Marcuse designates 'surplus-repression'. As is well known, he departs from Marxist orthodoxy by rejecting the determining role of the basic productive process and contending that domination occurs separately in all the various linked but independent sectors of the social economy: domination and alienation are omnipresent in consumption and leisure as well as at work. His *Essay on Liberation* (1971) is a plea for liberation from the 'quasi-biological needs' for consumption which capitalism has implanted in us, thereby enslaving us to its processes.

Marcuse is one utopian who does not shirk consideration of the means to utopia: he contends that revolution is essential. But because of the all-pervasiveness of the state apparatus and the loss of revolutionary potential by the working class through consumerism and embourgeoisement, he seeks an alliance between students, marginals, engagé intellectuals and the impoverished workers of the Third World. His solution has evoked various degrees of enthusiasm, scorn and irritation at this wildly unorthodox reconstitution of the revolutionary class.

As for the content of utopia, he advocates, in highly abstract terms, a return to the pleasure principle, the principle of immediate, 'polymorphous' gratification which Freud considered to be typical only of the early years of life and quickly superseded. In terms of Eros, this would dictate the desublimation and degenitalization of sex, and free enjoyment of 'polymorphous perversity'; but sexual liberation is also bound up with spiritual development, a return to aesthetic awareness and to the 'play principle', considered to be fundamental to the aesthetic dimension by Schiller and others.[8] The organizational consequences of this form of personal idyll are barely discussed: Marcuse is in essence recommending a life of anarchic individual enjoyment, a complete negation of the dominating structures of existing society - a critical role in which he rivals the utopians of the past. The vision of *Eros and Civilization* may fairly be called a modern utopia in that it depicts a pinnacle of individual development and pleasure within a vaguely defined, socialistic, libertarian social framework. Where previous utopians have defined happiness in terms of material satisfaction, moral virtue, fulfilment of the 'passions' and so on, Marcuse projects it on to a psychological plane (as defined by Our Freud), suitably matching his utopian remedy to contemporary preoccupations. The violence which he does to Freud, who believed repression a *sine qua non* of anything worth calling civilization, and to Marx, need not be discussed here as it is not the 'correctness' of his theory which is of interest, but its role. The adoption by some New Left thinkers, student radicals and fringe groups of his terminology is perhaps sufficient evidence of its influence: the idea of 'the Great Refusal' (that is, a refusal by individuals to validate in any way the dystopian present) and the omnipresence of the word 'liberation' are examples. But Marcuse's activities also bear out Friedman's comment that utopians do not innovate but verbalize an existing climate of ideas,[9] for liberation was in the air long before Marcuse's *Essay*, and he may be said to have elaborated the consequences of *l'imagination au pouvoir* rather than invented the idea.

By contrast, Robert Nozick in *Anarchy, State and Utopia* (1974) provides an up-to-date example of a conservative 'utopia' (or 'counter-utopia') and some observations on the nature of utopianism. His problematic is the construction of a minimal state which does not violate anyone's 'natural' rights. He starts with a premiss of human variety and differentiation of tastes, and with the pessimistic assumption of a warring, Hobbesian state of nature in which everyone has, however, natural freedom. The absolute primacy of individual rights is asserted, requiring that developments be justified by Kantian, rather than utilitarian, standards. He hypothesizes that *without mutual consent* (that is, even with no social contract) the use of money would be accepted for convenience and private protection agencies would be set up. Individuals could freely join or leave these at first, but the supply-and-demand process and the greater efficiency of some protection agencies would result in the development of a dominant protection agency in a particular area, which would punish anyone using force without its permission, and would satisfy the minimal conditions for being a state, yet would have arisen without violating anyone's rights.[10] Thus, starting from a conflictual model and by the consistent application of non-intentional, 'invisible hand' explanations, with individual self-interest and free will as the motivating factors, Nozick justifies the institution of a no-more-than-minimal state, and goes on to explain the principles of social justice and government therein on similar lines.

The last part of the book sets out to explore the idea of utopia, and asserts that the minimal state is not utopia but that, by exploring the utopian idea, the defects of the minimal state will come to light. 'The utopian tradition is maximax',[11] the best of all possible worlds, but there are limiting conditions: all possible goods cannot be realized simultaneously, and there is no *one unique* way of life which is objectively best for everyone, although for each individual there is one life which is best for him.[12] Again, Nozick assumes human diversity, and argues that the form which utopia would logically have to take would be a market-place of associations with free exit and entry, which would eventually constitute a 'stable world' since each individual would experiment until he established himself permanently in a suitable community which also needed his contribution. Stable associations would consist of different, not similar and hence competing, individuals, and pleasure would be achieved through the full development of diverse capacities. He is thus able to assert that 'Utopia will consist of utopias ... communities will wax and wane';[13] utopia is, then, a meta-utopia, a framework for the birth of trial communities, with a minimal central authority to arbitrate between the communities if necessary. Nozick concludes that his analysis of utopia, starting from independent assumptions, has nevertheless converged with his earlier analysis, showing the minimal state to be utopia itself.

Particularly interesting is the fact that Nozick is conversant with the problems usually encountered by utopianism and counters them at every stage in his analysis, as in his rejection of the idea of one absolute good for all men. He discusses the problem of utopian majorities' enforcing conformity on their fellows and the obstacle which a fixed, unchanging plan presents to any belief in or enthusiasm for utopia; also, the desperate reliance of the utopian theorist on human beings' behaving as predicted.[14] He also evades the problem of optimism by proceeding from 'minimin', Hobbesian assumptions about human nature and the likelihood of conflict. His own framework prevents enforced conformity because of the exit option, is so fluid as to hardly constitute a plan at all, and does not require people to behave in any particular way, except as their desires or self-interest dictate. A reading of Nozick poses certain problems: by his own admission, his framework is libertarian and *laissez-faire*, and earlier in the book he advances a theory of social justice based on historical entitlement to goods, to the exclusion of any 'pattern' such as need or desert.[15] To those accustomed to thinking of utopia as a milestone in the pursuit of social justice, his model is not utopia but anathema. The present status of *laissez-faire* as the prevailing ideology, in opposition to which socialistic utopias are projected, has made many sceptical commentators reclassify Nozick's theory as reactionary classical liberal ideology. Yet undoubtedly Nozick's ideal retains a strong flavour of the would-be-utopian United States in the days of the pioneers, Shakers and Rappites, and also of Californian life since 1968, with its multitude of communal experiments.

But from the viewpoint of the study of utopian form, this ambiguous creation interestingly demonstrates that if *realistic* limiting conditions are fulfilled, such as the diversity of desires and the unpredictability of human behaviour, the only utopia logically possible is a *meta-utopia*, a framework without content which begs the question of what constitutes the Good Life, leaving individuals to define it for themselves. Or perhaps one could say that the Good Life consists of being free to define the Good Life .... Nozick's utopia is also remarkable, perhaps unique, in satisfying Popperian conditions for the trial-and-error method of constructing an ideal society; it is the only truly empiricist utopia and, as such, must be dear to liberals' hearts. In a way, the strong hostile reaction among non-liberals to Nozick's utopia suggests how close we have now come to defining a determinate ideal content for utopia in terms of socialist justice, welfare and the satisfaction of need, matters which Nozick leaves to choice and chance – although no doubt some enterprising fellow in his utopia would set up a profitable association for social marginals and rejects! Nozick may not be the best evidence for the proposition that utopia is not dead, but he is good proof that the problems set up by the utopian mode of theorizing still have a determining importance in political thought.

In *Utopies Réalisables* (1975), Yona Friedman, a planner who also writes on ideal architecture, argues that our social problems stem from organizations which have grown beyond natural dimensions. By axiomatically showing the necessary properties and the limiting size of a 'realizable utopia', he demonstrates the imperfections of existing society. His axiomatic conditions for the realization of a utopia turn on shared dissatisfaction, the availability of remedies and the achievement of collective consent by the utopian inventor, which prevents paternalistic or imposed utopias. Non-paternalistic utopias are superior because there the decision-makers are also the risk-bearers. Adding axiom to axiom, Friedman shows the essentially *social* nature of utopia: communication and influence determine dependency and hierarchy. The critical size of a utopian group is determined by a number of factors,[16] and particularly by the brain's ability to receive and transmit messages, and by the tendency of repeated messages to deteriorate. These natural limitations make the originally Christian dream of the universal utopia impossible: 'unity in diversity' is the best we can hope for.[17] Friedman considers non-competitive society the utopia of our time, and thinks it can be attained by the management of scarcity with stocks and rationing systems; we must at all costs combat 'fictional scarcity', the corrupting artifice which currently promotes inequality. He defines an egalitarian structure as one where the departure of a member leaves the scheme of interpersonal dependencies unchanged, and then discusses the need to achieve both objective and subjective equality, and to find a happy solution to the human desire for personal distinction.

Because of its communicative nature, utopia is ideally located in a *town* which regulates itself so as not to exceed the ideal size. Friedman does not propose uniformity for the members of his ideal community, but equality between differentiated individuals, perhaps non-interchangeable craftsmen. Globally the world's agricultural and demographic patterns should be changed for more efficient use of resources and greater enjoyment of the sunny climate, and a network of egalitarian urban villages, weakly linked, should be set up with free immigration between them in cases of discontent.[18] Despite his emphasis on equality, Friedman appears to be recommending a basically free-enterprise organization, with 'taxes' being paid by service for the community. His conclusion recommends *auto-défense* against the many mafias of our own overgrown society.

Friedman's theory is clearly born of the modern preoccupations with size and overgrowth, and the fear that human beings will end in a 'behavioural sink', acting as rats do under such conditions, or lemmings. These apprehensions constitute the framework for a utopian model which is constructed painstakingly with deliberate simplicity, since Friedman thinks theory should be available to everyman, using premises which seem self-evident, and devices such as exhaustive cataloguing of possibilities (as in his Chapter 5, with regard to the relationship of possession) and selection of the choice uniquely appropriate to the previously accumulated axioms. The theory consequently has an engaging air of inevitability and logicality, although some crucial definitions and evaluations have been quietly inserted *en route* – for example, the presumption that the ideal is a face-to-face community without intervening institutions. In some respects, Friedman's utopia surprisingly resembles that of Nozick, but in an important or defining respect it differs, for with Friedman the emphasis is always on the collective, consent-based nature of communication and language: Friedman writes little of individual desire or happiness, since the path to this goal is through a *social* ideal, whereas Nozick focuses on the freewheeling individual primarily motivated by the jealous protection of his personal, anti-social rights. Friedman suggests that most tentative utopias have failed because they do not meet his conditions: for instance, the traditional 'one-man' utopia never succeeds in gaining the consent of other members of the collectivity. Again, utopias which are initially successful attract too many adherents and grow beyond the critical size, which precipitates their downfall, although it would be possible to institute feedback and auto-regulation, perhaps by splitting off into subsections, so that in principle utopias *can* be realized.[19] For us, Friedman's own theory is of special interest because it is simultaneously a theory about the necessary nature of utopia, a theory about the proper nature of theory (which must be lucid, linear and deductive), *and* a utopia conforming to the conditions of the meta-theory, the self-validating whole being designed to suggest, in the best utopian tradition, that there is *one* ideal solution which is logically deduced before one's eyes. Needless to say, the secret of this achievement lies in the original premisses, which would be the starting-point for any criticism. It is noticeable that, despite its theoretical perfection, Friedman's suggestions for applying his model exhibit the same problems of the leap between theory and practice which haunts all utopias: the concrete solutions proposed for society here and now never seem to follow *necessarily* from the theory.

One modern utopia which explicitly sets out to apply contemporary scientific discoveries is B. F. Skinner's *Walden Two* (1962), the fictional account of an experimental community based on his own psychological theory of reinforcement, a behavioural explanation of human action. Elsewhere[20] he argues that man is almost infinitely conditionable, to the extent that even supposedly basic or absolute needs such as appetite can be changed or diverted by the use of reinforcement. For Skinner then, human nature does not represent the absolute imperative that it was for earlier utopians. His ideal community, inappropriately named after Thoreau's solitary paradise, is run by behavioural psychologists, experts in human conditioning who devise complicated methods to form the inhabitants from early youth (a notion which reminds readers uneasily of the so-called Pavlovian conditioning of *Brave New World*) to produce sociable and public-spirited adults. All 'spurious' communication, such as 'please' and 'thank you' is eliminated, as is a lot of the rationalization which accompanies our own elaborate conditioning processes in the guise of education. Some visitors to Walden Two, if they do not leave in horror at once, find it so alluring that they stay and join. In *Beyond Freedom and Dignity* (1972) Skinner supplies the explicit political theory which would support his vision of utopia and justify him against some harsh critics, who include Noam Chomsky. He argues that, just as the environment acting on an organism in a certain, controlling fashion, will call forth defensive devices, so overtly coercive procedures in society evoke behaviour in men which he characterizes as 'counter-control'.[21] The doctrines of free will, freedom and dignity are among the ideological counter-controls by which men have resisted cruel, conspicuous or aversive control by rulers. But today's more subtle, less brutalizing forms of manipulation render such doctrines irrelevant and functionless: after all, to most appearances, we (in the Western democracies at least) *are* free. Freedom and dignity can therefore no longer serve as guiding ideals, Skinner asserts, and must be replaced by some supra-individual value such as 'the survival of cultures'.[22] A society such as Walden Two with a strong communal identity would clearly be well placed to propagate such values and is, for Skinner, a model which illustrates that human life can be tranquil and pleasurable without the contentious individualistic notion of freedom.

Much has been made of the fact that Skinner's theory of reinforcement was developed through work with rats and pigeons and is inadequate to describe the complex reactions of the human organism to the social environment. Critics have not been slow to draw the sinister pro-totalitarian conclusions of his arguments. Yet from another viewpoint, Skinner presents an impeccable example of utopian activity: he discovers an idea which seems to point to a fundamental truth about human nature and existence, and goes on to elaborate logically how a new model of the Good Life can be constructed round this discovery. His choice of the fictional vehicle, unlike other contemporary utopians, is indicative. Presumably he allows himself this imaginative licence because the 'proof' of his utopia is clearly explained in scientific terms in his other books such as *Contingencies of Reinforcement* (1969), so that he is not obliged to demonstrate the truth of his inspiration formally in his utopia. Nevertheless, his utopia has the traditional small-community form and raises exactly the same non-scientific problems as to how the rulers themselves can be controlled, especially when they possess the expertise to manipulate everyone else, and how in the midst of perfection stifling monotony can be avoided.

Walden Two constitutes in its form a more orthodox utopia than the other theories discussed in this chapter, of which we might be more inclined to say that they are in the realm of utopian discourse, or, with Mannheim, that they are expressions of the utopian mentality. But the notable feature that all these modern utopias have in common is a concern with the proper presentation and validation of their theory: whether it is by appeal to well-established doctrines, as in Marcuse's case, by conformity with philosophical criteria, as with Nozick and Friedman, or by the application of a scientific hypothesis as in Skinner's utopia, the intention is the same. Utopia can no longer risk being based merely on an imaginative inspiration or on casual observation of human nature, but must appear clad in respectable method. This discovery is not new – Saint-Simon, Owen and Fourier traded on the cachet of social science long ago. But the choice of a non-fictional form for a utopian model need not diminish its utopian essence: it is largely a matter of choosing the best vehicle for reaching and impressing the literate public. The fact that utopias often now wear the mantle of social science or are disguised as handbooks of revolution is chiefly an indicator of intellectual fashion – and, whatever the disguise, readers are quick to seize on and criticize the utopian elements in a theory.

Despite those commentators who maintain that our age produces no utopias, a considerable list of theories with strong utopian elements could be compiled, even leaving aside science fiction and futurology, which tend to lack analytical, normative and recommendatory elements constitutive of utopia. Hayek's catallaxy has been mentioned as an attempt to revive the classic *laissez-faire* liberal utopia. On the socialist side are the Freudian psychologist, Fromm, and many New Left thinkers; and outside this major ideological division are thinkers such as Ivan Illich, who departs from the essentially occidental tradition and delineates a Third World utopia, and the communards and the ever-growing number of exponents of alternative technology headed by the author of *Small is Beautiful* (1963), Schumacher. This muster suggests that the utopian tradition persists with diversity and vigour.

Although a future generation must decide conclusively what significance these modern utopias had, we can see them as representing strong scepticism about the ability of large-scale industrialism and its corollaries (finance, capitalism, city life, high consumption, etc.) to provide human happiness, and a corresponding denial that a straightforward capture and socialization of the means of production would provide a better solution. The emphasis has shifted to a diminution of the size of the social unit and a decrease in material satisfaction with the conservation of resources – not surprisingly. The new utopias are more anarchic or voluntaristic than those of the past, and constitute a clear rejection of ever more centralized, ever less accountable government. In this respect, these works taken together offer as clear an indictment of modern Western society and its tentacles as More's utopia did of England in 1516.

Utopian essence

Even such a brief survey as this suggests that there is supporting evidence for the 'eternal human aspiration' brand of utopian analysis, and also for those who hold that utopia is 'necessarily socialist', such as Marin.[23] Having sketched the length and the limits of what is commonly considered the utopian tradition, it is possible to consider the various typologies of utopia that have been proposed. First, it should be noted that the activity of classification in this context is something of an artifice and imposes the interests of the classifier on ideas whose original purpose or intention had little in common with his. There are, it might be said, as many dimensions of classification as we have theoretical interests. There is also the danger that the chosen categories will assert the principle of the excluded middle ('all utopias are EITHER egalitarian OR elitist . . .') and so disguise important but subtle variations.

The analysts of utopia have approached the subject via four general categories:

1 Form;
2 Overt content;
3 Disguised, for example symbolic, content; and
4 Effect.

Under the heading 'form' comes the question of whether a utopia is fictional or directly didactic, which may in turn have repercussions on its effectiveness. But this distinction is not of great importance for the present analysis, since political propositions have successfully been conveyed in utopias of many forms. An analysis of the overt content of utopias turns into a rather barren phenomenology describing and categorizing the various institutions and customs of the ideal societies. Most popular and fruitful is the analysis and classification of utopias according to some covert content, such as Marin's semiological analysis of *Utopia*, or according to various categories of interest to us which are projected on to the content of utopias. Bauman, for example, distinguishes those utopias which embrace progress and hope to proceed thereby to a better order from those which advocate a return to a 'natural' order, sacrificing technological benefits, the 'utopias of simplification'.[24] He then suggests that the latter are utopias of passive enjoyment, a middle-class dream not experienced by those at the top or bottom of society. Parallels with ecology and alternative technology movements need no emphasis, but this classification incongruously puts capitalists and workers into the same bracket – and indeed, Bauman labels both Marx and Marx's *bête noire*, Bentham, as 'progressive utopians'. This example is typical of the suggestive use but fallacious one-dimensionality of most classifications of utopia.

The classification of utopias according to their effects has been touched on already, when it was argued that it is a contingent matter whether or not a utopia generates political responses, depending not so much on the utopia's intrinsic qualities as on the social conditions and outcome of the tensions to which it is witness and gives expression. But if, as Servier and others argue, all utopias mark turning points, why are some 'effective' and others not? Critics of utopianism such as Marx would argue that it is the defining property of utopia to be politically ineffective – if he were right, this category could not serve to differentiate between individual utopias, but only to distinguish them from more potent types of political doctrine. As Horsburgh argues, in general, utopias lack a political power base at first, and only gradually invade the centre of politics from their original, peripheral position.[25] There have also been attempts by Ruyer, Duveau and others to classify the personalities of utopians in such a way as to distinguish their work from other political theory because of their personal ineffectiveness.[26] Thus, the 'man who dreams of islands' is said to be schizoid and introverted, compensating for his impotence and alienation from the world by playing God in a personal paradise. There is a parallel literature on the 'psychology of socialism'. Analysts less hostile to utopianism have maintained that despite the 'private world' element, utopias are not solipsistic: Mucchielli refers to the common inspirational core of all utopias, while Manuel points out that the very fact of publication makes utopia 'at the very least, *folie à deux* - of the writer and printer'.[27] Although the 'personality' approach is dismissive of utopian authors and their free will and intentions, it is a rare and therefore interesting attempt to explain why particular individuals choose to write utopias rather than political tracts.

Among the supposedly disjunctive categories of analysis which commentators have found fruitful are the ascetic/abundant (indulgent), aesthetic/functional, scientific/primitivist, sensual/spiritual and religious/ secular. Most recently the introduction of the term 'sexist' to academic circles has given rise to analysis of the role of women and the function of the family in utopias. From the standpoint of political thought to-day, the following dichotomies are the most important: egalitarian/ inegalitarian (or elitist), 'open'/totalitarian, libertarian/coercive, demo-cratic/undemocratic and optimistic (with regard to human nature)/ pessimistic, and these will be discussed in the next section.

The political content of utopia

Utopias approach the same problem as most other political theory - that is, what form the 'ideally best polity' should take - but usually differ in devoting more attention to the social conditions which support the political structure, because they treat society as an integrated totality. In this respect, political theorists are only just catching up with utopians. The major area in which utopia is surprisingly silent is that of war, nationalism and international relations. The reasons for the omission are significant. Plato, More and Campanella assumed the likelihood of continued external aggression towards such ideal states as their utopias, and either included elaborate military training in their schemes, or, in More's case, sanctioned the use of mercenaries so that the utopians should not be corrupted by the slaughter of their fellows – a *sauve-qui-peut* arrangement inviting ironic comment. Cyrano de Bergerac's *Comic History of the States of the Moon* (1657) is the first strong utopian expression, by inversion, of doubt about the propriety of war. When Moon princes go to war, they select umpires and match all combatants in strength and skill; the battle then proceeds and losses are counted. If they are equal, lots are drawn for the winner. One eccentric Lunar philosopher still disputed the justice of these arrangements, arguing that if a combatant won in these ultra-fair circumstances it must be by skill (deception) or overwhelming strength (unfair) or by chance, in which case only Fortune wins! A Lunar lady naively asks the narrator why, if princes on Earth always go to war for just causes, they do not merely submit their cases to a judge for arbitration.[28]

Utopia is often shielded from war by natural barriers, or else the utopians' child-like innocence and lack of possessions make them incapable of war and unworthy of being warred against. But a new rationalist justification for the absence of war from the ideal city was generated by Saint-Pierre's *Project* and utopians thereafter usually followed him in presenting their ideal societies as parts of a world-wide federation of similar, amicable communities: Fourier describes this organization in detail and the same sort of arrangements are proposed by anarchists like Bakunin and Godwin, for whom the existence of a central state with territorial ambitions was anathema. The utopian quite logically eliminates by his prior assumptions three of the primary causes of war: since all citizens are utopians, and happy to be such, there can be no ethnic minorities appealing for the help of outside forces. And since each utopia represents the perfect autarchic economy, or has the upper hand in any necessary trading partnership, as in *Utopia*, there is no reason for territorial aggrandizement. The missionary impulse of utopian citizens is generally limited to generous hospitality to travellers and to the hope that the world will eventually follow their example. So while utopians are intensely patriotic, there is no scope or need for nationalism as it is generally understood – that is, as the aggressive assertion of self-interest.

Earlier in this chapter, the 'constant' of politics was defined as the problem of maintaining order, which is usually synonymous with maintaining the existing socio-political order. The people make demands on the system which are satisfied, or not, and consequently accord to the system the support necessary for its continuance, or assail it with dissatisfaction which will precipitate change.[29] It can be seen then that the main endeavour of the utopian political system must be to provide satisfaction in the form of a comfortable minimum of welfare, or more, for its citizens, in exchange for which they will automatically offer their support. The provision of consumer satisfaction is a particular feature of the later utopias which envisage abundance, but even the so-called ascetic utopias provide everything needed for an agreeable life. Today's scepticism about this ideal solution rests firstly on the supposition that needs are, in fact, unlimited and always outreach available satisfactions, so that it is impossible to create a population which is satiated and content. The possessive individualist account of human nature attributed to liberal theorists by C. B. Macpherson,[30] which emphasizes infinite acquisition, is particularly antagonistic to the utopian solution. Secondly, it may be that men want things which utopia simply cannot provide such as uncertainty, adventure and novelty. Erich Fromm, sketching a modern socialist utopia,[31] emphasizes free man's need for uncertainty and this argument relates to the older one of man's free will, a faculty which utopia appears to threaten or deny unwittingly, or wittingly, as does Skinner. So there are at least two reasons for doubting that utopia could deliver adequate satisfaction to guarantee social order, although these vanish if one accepts assumptions about the modesty of need and lack of greed of ideal human beings.

The forms of obedience required from the citizens are usually set out succinctly in a body of rational and wise laws. The rule of law connotes a fairness and impartiality unattainable under the rule of men, which is why many people would prefer to live under Plato's Laws than in his Republic; this idea is joined with the natural law tradition in Morelly's Code to produce a set of wise and fair laws which no 'natural' man would wish to transgress. (Many utopians, such as Owen, blamed existing laws for running contrary to human nature, with inevitable perverse effects.)[32] The legitimacy of such laws is founded on their self-evident truth, not on a due process of legislation, though sometimes a semi-divine founder such as Utopus is cited as the source, or else the agreement of an ultra-democratic assembly. Even in utopia the existence of law must rest on penal sanctions which in turn reflect the utopian's perception of deviance. In many utopias the severest penalty is banishment – a new expulsion from Eden – which is made possible by utopia's position as an enclave in an uncivilized world, while lesser punishments are usually humane if somewhat harsh (as in Morelly's and Restif's societies). But utopias from the later eighteenth century onwards reflected the humaner influence of Beccaria's *Crimes and Punishment* (1764) and of Enlightenment psychology, which argued that the character, and hence the criminal personality, is formed by the environment: they therefore take a more compassionate view of crime, especially Godwin, Owen and, later, Butler. The logical inference from the environmentalist account is that an ideally constituted society will eradicate crime altogether. The idea of human perfectibility, widely canvassed in the eighteenth century, strengthened this optimism and was the source of the belief that crime could be entirely eliminated. Later utopias, then, expect rational adherence to just laws by moral men, and the coercive arm of the political apparatus atrophies, or abdicates.

However, utopians' faith in the power of truth and rationality to procure obedience has always been shaky, and scarcely any utopia lacks a propaganda machine to reinforce natural morality. Plato's foundation myth, the 'noble lie', is often hailed as the origin of political propaganda, and later utopias devote much of their elaborate education programmes to the inculcation of respect for the laws, morality towards fellow citizens, and self-control. Indoctrination of this kind seems inevitable in any society, and perhaps a lesser evil compared with the brutalizing effect of punishment. But can one really be sanguine about B. F. Skinner's use of psychological conditioning in *Walden Two*? More attractive is the alternative approach which makes obedience instinctual because society's laws so closely follow men's desires: primitive utopians such as Diderot's Tahitians obey the laws by acting instinctively, and Fourier sets out to achieve the same spontaneous order in the sophisticated phalanstery by designing possibilities to suit every temperament. This represents an ideal solution to the problem of order.

All utopias rely to some extent on a traditional method of keeping order virtually unknown in modern individualistic society, that of mutual control. Whereas political states including and since the Roman Empire have increasingly specialized the judicial apparatus and separated it from the people so that the committing and punishing of crime becomes a sort of esoteric ritual,[33] traditional or natural societies accepted everyone's right to intervene to prevent disobedience or anti-social activity. Examples are the Athenian citizens' right to prosecute each other, which led to Socrates's trial, or Locke's right of every man in the state of nature to punish transgressors. By comparison, the citizen's right today to bring private prosecutions is limited and almost in disuse (in British law at least). Utopias institutionalize this interpersonal intervention and mutual correction by encouraging citizens to bring moral pressure to bear on each other and by denying that this constitutes any encroachment on individual rights or privacy. Even such an individualistic anarchist as Godwin welcomed the idea that one's neighbours would constitute a moral inquisition.[34] Such solutions seem sacrilege to the twentieth-century Western individualist, but they are fully justified in terms of the utopian's conception of society as a communal enterprise in which anti-social and criminal behaviour directly harm everyone else.

Commentators on the utopias of More and Campanella have remarked on the 'transparency' of their societies.[35] The buildings contain exceptional numbers of windows and communicating doors, so that private life is virtually lived in public and the pressure to conform is maximized. Many other utopias emphasize the transparent quality of utopian life, which is a fundamental ingredient of order in that it facilitates mutual criticism and induces self-control. Likewise, one can identify the uniformity of the buildings, dress and customs in many utopias as a feature which aids the swift identification of egoistic differences which may prove socially dangerous. From the standpoint of preserving society, maintaining the system, all such devices are justifiable. Indeed, the respect in which utopia most differs from a liberal-democratic model of the political system is that the political apparatus of utopia is not distinct from the people of utopia but is constituted by them. So our current separation and reification of the political function, which then ministers to and provides for the people, does not resemble utopian ideality where the people provide for and regulate themselves.

Apart from providing total satisfaction for citizens and imbuing them with strong legal and moral sensibilities, the utopian's third way of promoting order, which utopians themselves considered their most vital innovation, is the prior removal from utopia of all sources of social disruption and all temptations to disobedience. The major cause of social evil, utopians almost unanimously agree, is private property, which produces a variety of disruptive sentiments and desires; often money and gold, symbols of possession and accumulation, are ceremoniously abolished. Few utopians go as far as Babeuf in their egalitarianism, but all ensure that social distinctions and hierarchies (which many of them consider natural) are based on genuine merit or respect for age or achievement, sources of distinction supposedly incapable of arousing jealousy because accessible to all. The eradication of social causes of discontent thus creates the prior conditions for satisfaction and obedience.

Liberty and equality in utopia

The problem of order and control in utopia leads directly to the question of freedom. But freedom in utopia must be measured along a different axis from that constituted by our present preoccupations. Almost every modern critique of utopianism, even if less forthright in its criticisms than is Popper concerning Plato, emphasizes that utopias forfeit freedom in order to achieve equality: they rob us of the right to own property and to bring up our children, and clutter daily life with detailed, oppressive regulations. The dimensions of today's dominant conception of freedom are well known, comprising freedom to an extensive private (social and economic) life for the individual, freedom to rise by merit, and freedom from politics. The 'free society' has been equated with that in which the aggregate of individual freedoms is maximized. Evidently, the development of our notion of freedom and its conflation with political individualism has an extensive history whose roots are to be discovered in the Christian doctrine of free will. But there is a dichotomic tradition with regard to free will: many, rather than rejoicing in it, have regarded it as an intolerable burden, a faculty whose misuse can precipitate eternal damnation, but for whose proper use all too few guidelines are given. A celebrated restatement of these fears is the argument of the Grand Inquisitor in Dostoevsky's *Brothers Karamazov*, a seductive invitation to man to lay aside this burden and follow the dictates of a stronger, wiser being.[36] The psychologist Fromm admits the force of this exhortation in *The Fear of Freedom* (1942), which deals with the Nazi phenomenon, and counters it with his own definition of freedom and uncertainty as constitutive of full human life. But the inverted utopia of uncertainty described in Borges's story 'The lottery in Babylon' (where one's life and fate for the next two months are determined by the secret casting of multiple ballots) would clearly not satisfy Fromm's requirements, for the precondition for his ideal is self-mastery and the mastery of one's environment. In fact, taken to its extreme, the idea of freedom dictates a solipsism unattainable in the social context, and so, unattainable.

The first priority of utopia is that of *freedom from*. Need, unemployment, illness, war, oppression, envy: these and many other social evils are stigmatized in the critical preambles of utopias (*vide* Fourier's list of the 144 evils of 'civilization') and eradicated in their positive proposals. Only a tiny and privileged percentage of the current world population can afford to be blasé or dismissive about this goal. As for individual freedom, the topic is not widely debated in most utopian texts. Most utopias purport to offer a formula for the 'natural' life, a way of life which would be freely chosen by men who preferred it to others because it was attuned to their instinctive needs and best satisfied their subjective desires. If this is so, utopia does not *consciously* follow in the footsteps of the Grand Inquisitor, because the idea of the natural life is out of the range of the free-will debate altogether. This characterization of life in utopia as 'natural' does not exclude those more sophisticated utopias which rest on historical theories and aim towards 'higher' stages of civilization, for these envisage a changing or increasingly perfect human nature which can be expressed in a higher society; Deschamps and Saint-Simon both made it clear that their utopias would cater for a new type of man with new capacities. The Rawlsian model of hypothetical choice might be invoked here to illustrate in what sense utopias are free: they are societies such that 'natural' free men in an Original Position behind a Veil of Ignorance would choose to live in them. The problem is that the critics of utopia bring to bear their own particular knowledge, ideology and interests (which Rousseau and others would consider as witnesses of the corruption of society) and cannot make this innocent choice or judgement.

It cannot be denied that freedom in the sense of uncertainty and branching opportunities is absent from most utopias. Often, a utopia has no institutional arrangements for changing its own constitution because it is considered the best, which has provoked criticisms from Dahrendorf and others, but some utopians such as Cabet and Weitling anticipated these and provided indigenous means for reform and change. But fundamentally, utopia's claim to be a free society rests on the adage that if you are not free to do what you don't want to do, you are still free. In this connection, the laws prohibiting murder come to mind: they are said not to restrict our freedom because we ought not to want to commit murder. It is the introduction of 'ought' into the formula which causes the problem. Does utopia only permit us to do what we ought to want to do? We would argue that most utopias do not make this moral imposition but seek to draw on natural morality, particularly utopias of the Enlightenment and after. They play many variations on the tune 'altruism is enlightened self-interest', and illustrate through reason and instinct that what is good for the community as a whole is also best for the individual. Whether we define the utopian end-product as free or not depends on our own ideology, but it cannot be denied that utopias are *intended* to be free. In so far as they provide the best form of social life, the impossibility of a change for the worse is not an infringement of freedom.

If utopias do not dwell overmuch on civil or political rights, it is because these safeguards against a growing state apparatus would be superfluous in a society without a state, or where the state coincides with society. The utopian socialists made a point of castigating the hollowness of such rights in situations of economic inequality, as did Marx, and offered instead a romantically-influenced version of 'positive' freedom in the sense of self-fulfilment: Fourier's phalanx is an exemplar of this even though it lacks the intellectual dimension which someone like J. S. Mill would associate with fulfilment, in that it offers every chance for the individual to satisfy and develop each of his many talents or passions. This process does not, as is sometimes argued, require multiple choices for the individual, but merely that the appropriate opportunity should be there for him at the right time. In this respect, utopias can make better provision than our own haphazard *laissez-faire* society. The best conclusion is that the question 'Is utopia a free society?' is wrongly posed – or rather, is posed from a very particular viewpoint of freedom, which stigmatizes as unfree anything which involves planning or which takes into account macro as well as individual considerations. Utopia cannot be dismissed outright for departing from this model.

The egalitarian/inegalitarian and egalitarian/elitist disjunctions are of particular interest in the utopian context, since many authors show an inclination to reconcile the two. The general policy of abolishing private property gives all utopias a claim to be considered at least more egalitarian than any real society, but within the general category of egalitarianism various forms of equality are promoted. The more ascetic and less attuned to consumption the utopia, the more uniformly egalitarian is the treatment of citizens; in this respect, Babeuf's *Manifesto* represents the culmination of tendencies manifested in the so-called ascetic communistic utopias of the sixteenth to the eighteenth centuries.[37] The unprecedented prospect of abundant resources which industrialization and the development of techniques of mass production seemed to hold out, combined with a growing cult of individuality, made it possible for the utopian socialists to envisage differential treatment of individuals according to their special needs and talents: affluence promotes individuality, as our own society demonstrates. Yet these utopias remain egalitarian in principle because the procedural formula 'to each according to his needs' is being fairly applied, even though the result may not be a numerically equal distribution of goods: the important point is that nobody is deprived of goods or opportunities in order to benefit someone else. The underlying principles of utopian egalitarianism are, first, equality of satisfaction for all, achieved by whatever distribution is appropriate, and second, special roles or powers distributed according to *aptitude*, a term lacking the honorific connotations of 'merit'. By contrast, inegalitarian and class-based utopias invariably rest on hypotheses about the organic nature of society, which justifies differentiation. So much for economic equality – but what about political equality, so often parasitic on the economic conditions?

A number of utopias have democratic institutions for the choice of ruler in each communal group or town. The tasks of such leaders are administration and arbitration, rather than policy-making; therefore they do not have power over their fellows' lives in the sense which 'politics' usually connotes. Furthermore, when the political role is treated as a rotating duty and does not attract special socio-economic privileges, the leaders can hardly be said to constitute an elite. But can the egalitarian impulse in some utopias be made compatible with the elitist political institutions which they also favour? The idea of elites naturally equipped to rule makes its appearance with Plato's race of intellectual Guardians, and persists throughout the tradition; for Fourier, the multi-talented individual, the *omnigyne*, is a natural leader, while for Saint-Simon industrialists, scientists and artists have the special knowledge necessary to run the industrial utopia. In our own time, B. F. Skinner has similarly elevated the role of psychologists, experts in human behaviour. All such elitism rests on the axiom that knowledge is good and that, since knowledge dictates its own benign application (a hope especially associated with the eighteenth century), the rule of experts is not inherently risky. If such elites contribute their leadership skills to society without taking an extra share of social goods in return, the principle ceases to be incompatible with egalitarianism – unless, that is, one assumes that political power is itself a good which all men want, which utopians do not. The principle of the natural elite, whatever its basis, cannot *per se* be endorsed, since its logical extension into the idea of the super-race has led to objectionable utopias such as Wells's *Men Like Gods*, and in our own time to a nightmare reality. But elitism, promoted by human variety and specialization, is likely to be with us always, and the utopian solution of an elite *with open access*, held in check by strongly egalitarian social arrangements, is a passably good solution.

So far utopia has been anatomized in terms of the organs common to most political theory. The unusual atrophy of the political function itself has been shown to be a consequence of the claim that utopia is the ideal society. Furthermore, while early utopias located political power in benign kings or magistrates, emulating the forms of government best known to them, from the eighteenth century onwards politics began to be viewed as a natural order: reason would lead the citizen into a state of harmony with his fellows, and there was no justification therefore for isolating political power and bestowing it on one man or group, even if it was useful to codify the dictates of reason in a body of laws for guidance. Hence the apparent disappearance of politics from utopian thought, although it would be more accurate to say that we must read the *whole* of a utopian scheme as political.

But if by contrast we regard utopian theory as a corpus, we find throughout the hypertrophy of elements which normal political theory tends to ignore or treat summarily. In a genre of thought explicitly devoted to the production of human happiness, it is not surprising that close attention is paid to human desires, since the simplest non-paternalistic, non-moralistic definition of happiness is 'the satisfaction of desires'. The question of desire leads in turn to the subject of human nature. Although many theorists would now contend that 'human essence', 'motives', 'natural laws' and other similar abstract absolutes are theoretical artifices with little relation to human reality, which is relative and ever-changing, they have yet to show that a normative theory can be erected without such props, since ideals must have some human reference point. Utopians were not afflicted by such doubts, and set out to find the path to happiness equipped with contour maps of human desire.[38]

Where normal political theory has perforce to come to terms with desire, it usually does so by making scanty, stereotypical assumptions which express inadequately the complexities of human life, such as Hobbes's first law of nature, the law of self-preservation, or Locke's life, liberty and estate. Even democratic theory, which proclaims democracy to be the expression of the will of the people, is content that this 'will' should be expressed in the form of acquiescent choice between predetermined or totally vacuous manifestos or, on the Burkean theory of representation, between personalities. The postulate of infinite acquisitiveness and so, in the context of scarce resources, of competitiveness, which underlies liberal thinking, is not subscribed to by utopians of any period, who generally have a more elaborate, compassionate and rich conception of what constitutes human motivation. The early pre-capitalist utopias prescribe a modest sufficiency of material satisfaction combined with extensive intellectual and spiritual satisfaction in the form of publicly provided culture. Utopia after utopia emphasizes the pleasures of knowledge and skill, and the enjoyments to be derived from varied and co-operative work. A number hypothesize that all men's material needs can be met even with a shorter working day: for More, six hours, for Owen four hours, for Godwin only half an hour. Implicit in such predictions is the assumption that material needs or desires are limited and that full satiation can be attained, with surplus time then being committed to other forms of satisfaction. Utopias which give greater weight to consumption postulate manufactured abundance, which leaves personal leisure intact, or else develop a theory of pleasure in work, such as Fourier elaborates, but which is also implicit in Marx's account of unalienated, creative 'social' labour.

Through the institutions of utopia we can read each utopian's conception of human nature. A surprising number, if not all, are optimistic that man will be a sociable, peaceful, co-operative creature in the absence of provocations such as poverty, oppression and hard labour, even those writing before Rousseau's classic exposition of the corruption of men by society. The Enlightenment obsession with human perfectibility and progress derived from the sensualist philosophy emanating from Locke and Condillac, which drew attention to the importance of external factors and environment in forming human character, and led to an appreciation of the potential of education for improving human behaviour and sociability, a view expressed most forcefully by Owen. This outlook implied a dynamically evolving human nature which utopians catered for by locating their ideal societies in a future higher stage, although often overlooking the logical point that unending perfectibility entails a series of ever more utopian utopias. The static, mechanical quality of pre-eighteenth-century utopias must be understood in the light of the absence of concepts of progress, the ideal then being the refinement and perfection of a human life whose elements were already known. The notion that human behaviour can change and that men can improve either by evolution or by the absence of factors which oppress and pervert is largely absent from other political thought, which is the chief reason for the divergence between the typically pessimistic theory which is called 'realistic' and the species called 'utopian'. We have come some way from Original Sin, but the conviction that man is basically egoistic and so potentially anti-social remains the starting-point for even idealistic theorists of the political order, and the basis for their suspicion of and antagonism to the utopian mode.

Finally, we might consider whether there is a common structure to utopianism which makes it a distinct subspecies within political thought. The fictional distancing device cannot serve as a defining characteristic, for it is by no means common to all utopianism, and does not have great significance other than to indicate that the enclosed theory is normative and critical of existing reality. If one is prepared to take an absolutist or universalist approach, one might argue as does Mucchielli that all utopias express a universal aspiration, the myth of the ideal city. But the attempt to generalize amid such diversity produces somewhat platitudinous formulae which give no precise idea of the special nature of utopian theory. More specifically, we would argue that while both utopianism and other political thought set out to treat of ideals, the utopian enterprise is an attempt to depict the complete and concrete instantiation of these ideals in their society and the social consequences which this entails: this differs significantly from the approach which uses ideals as the light at the end of the tunnel, incapable of realization but useful to guide us in our choice of political means. The difference is not merely that between optimism and pessimism, but has its roots in a divergence of theoretical method, as Chapter 4 will argue. And it is this endeavour to concretize ideals which produces the special characteristics of utopian thought, such as the totalistic approach (necessary so that no disharmonious element of society should undermine the chosen ideals) and the curious, often absurd, insistence on tying up the ends which conventional political theory would leave loose. The totalistic approach itself appears as the most prominent characteristic which distinguishes utopian from other forms of political theory, and is evidence of a conception of society as an integrated whole whose parts cannot be treated separately, but must be brought into harmony. This emphasis in turn produces a phenomenology of utopia which differs so widely in its content from that of most political theory, which restricts itself to political phenomena, that utopianism is erroneously relegated to an entirely different category.

Suggested reading

Detailed commentary on utopias and quasi-utopias throughout history can be found in the encyclopaedic *Utopian Thought in the Western World* by F. E. and F. P. Manuel. An earlier general account of the form is offered by L. Mumford, *The Story of Utopias*. But the flavour of particular utopias is better captured at first hand in the collection of extracts edited by G. Negley and J. Patrick, *The Quest for Utopia*, and in *French Utopias*, edited by F. E. and F. P. Manuel. A. L. Morton's *The English Utopia* shows utopianism to be part of an indigenous tradition of radical thought. J. Servier's *Histoire de l'Utopie* is another historical survey with a strongly analytical bias, and it contains many original perceptions. The full range of primary sources can be found listed in two recent bibliographies: G. Negley, *Utopian Literature: A Bibliography*, and L. T. Sargent, *British and American Utopian Literature 1516-1975*. There is no better way to understand the peculiarities and virtues of utopian thinking than to read some of the original texts, but the survey works mentioned here offer a swifter route into the subject.

3 Ideology, science or symbol?

This chapter sets out to discuss and evaluate the many claims that have been made concerning the epistemological status and the functions of utopian thought. The major distinction, made by thinkers of differing persuasions, is that 'utopian' and 'scientific' are mutually exclusive terms, and this must be reviewed in the light of the fact that many thinkers here classified as utopian actually claimed to be scientists, especially the early socialists.[1] First, the relation of utopianism to science and ideology will be considered from the standpoint of Marx, and then the validity of various attempts to give utopianism a quasi-scientific status will be assessed; finally, we examine some interpretations which assign a purely symbolic or expressive role to utopia.

The Marxist critique

The critical analysis of utopian socialism offered by Marx and Engels inevitably provides the starting-point for the debate on science, ideology and utopia. But it should be borne in mind that Engels's evaluation of Owen and Fourier was less hostile than that of Marx: in 1846 he published 'A fragment of Fourier's on trade', adding an approving introduction which favourably compared Fourier with the German idealists of the time, and he took a lenient, almost friendly, view of Owen's communities in his 'Description of some recently founded communist colonies' (1845).[2] There is some reason to think that the acerbity of the criticism in Marx's early writings was due to the success which Owenism was enjoying in the 1840s in England, for Marx saw the Owenite centres, with their programmes for education and self-betterment, and other, similar organizations as devices which bour-geoisified and divided the working class, and indeed the accounts of the proceedings of such institutions suggest that the inculcation of bourgeois morality and discipline was an important activity.[3] Engels argued that because Owen, 'the founder of English socialism', was a manufacturer, the movement 'proceeds therefore with greater con-sideration towards the bourgeoisie and great injustice towards the proletariat in its methods'.[4] The Saint-Simonian and Fourierist movements were decried for similar reasons. In *The Holy Family*, the prevalent, 'diluted' version of Fourierism was dismissed as 'nothing but the social doctrine of a section of the philanthropic bourgeoisie';[5] elsewhere, Marx complained that the Saint-Simonians' glorification of the productive powers of industry, falsely credited to modern capitalism alone, leads to 'the illusion of seeing the dirty bourgeois as a priest'.[6]

Certainly, the critique of utopian socialism appeared largely in the early works of Marx, written while disciples of the utopians were still active (with the exception of Engels's reworking of the relevant section of *The Communist Manifesto* in his *Socialism: Utopian and Scientific*, 1880), while the later Marx quotes More approvingly in *Capital.*[7] There is therefore no reason to think that Marx saw himself as offering a universal analysis or indictment of utopianism in general, although he certainly helped give the word its pejorative connotations. It should, however, be noted that there were also many bourgeois critics of the utopian socialists, and Abensour characterizes the years 1830–48 as a period of gradual ejection of utopianism from the realm of liberal respectability.[8] Marx himself only followed others in labelling the early socialists 'utopian'.

Marx's analysis of the utopian socialists, though particular and polemical, may nevertheless provide pointers for a definition and location of utopianism in general. *The Holy Family* praises the critical power of these utopians, who

declared *progress* (see Fourier) to be an inadequate, abstract *phrase* because it always ends in progress against the mass of mankind; they assumed (see *Owen* among others) a fundamental flaw in the civilized world; that is why they subjected the *real* foundations of contemporary society to incisive criticism.[9]

And *The Communist Manifesto* declares 'They attack every principle of existing society. Hence they are full of the most valuable materials for the enlightenment of the working class'.[10] Marx did not quibble with the utopians' identification of social evils but with the inadequacy of their diagnosis of causes. They lack a perception of the economic basis of capitalism: the industrial revolution was only incipient in France when Fourier and Saint-Simon wrote, but this deficiency is more culpable in the case of Owen. The absence of a historical perspective is another major defect, particularly since it leaves these theories devoid of any plausible methods whereby socialism can be achieved. And they neglect that most important dimension, a class analysis, for they think themselves 'superior to all class antagonisms', and seek to emancipate 'all humanity at once'.[11] Of course, class analysis and the historical perspective were the key elements in *The Communist Manifesto* and were Marx's chief preoccupation at that time.

To say that the utopians lacked a historical theory was factually incorrect, for Saint-Simon at least had a well-developed stadial theory of historical progress (as had many Enlightenment philosophers) which had in fact influenced Marx himself, although he did not care to admit it.[12] Curiously, Engels is more enamoured of Fourier's bizarre historical eschatology. 'Fourier is at his greatest in his conception of the history of society' and 'Fourier, as we see, uses the dialectical method in the same masterly way as his contemporary, Hegel'.[13] Praise indeed! However, Engels also noted that some socialists take no account of historical development and wish to produce communism overnight. 'They acknowledge only a psychological development, a development of man in the abstract, out of all relation to the Past.'[14] For the utopian, his own appearance on the scene 'is not an inevitable event, following of necessity in the chain of historical development, but a mere happy accident. He might just as well have been born 500 years earlier'.[15] The criticisms which Marx and Engels make are substantially correct in terms of their own categories: there are, for example, elements of historical theory and of dialectical method in both Fourier and Saint-Simon, but they are never combined so as to analyse convincingly the determination of a historical sequence of events. But the extent to which this detracts from a would-be operational social theory is disputable.

The absence from the utopians' theories of any conception of the self-conscious revolutionary proletariat provoked Marx's strongest objections, for he thought that gradualist or inevitabilist theories would succumb to political quietism. His perception of history as the history of class struggles naturally made it impossible for Marx to accept the one-man utopia as operational, and made him reject experimental communities and planned reform as feasible means of change. Any overt attack which he might have felt inclined to make on the utopians' personal class position would have applied *a fortiori* to Marx himself, so he contented himself with blaming their disciples for the infusion of bourgeois ideology into their ideas. The utopians themselves he condemned for their lack of a conception of the proletariat and for their aspiration to universal, rather than class, emancipation, often expressed as a pious hope for co-operation between the classes. This would be *a priori* unattainable since the emancipation of one class entails the suppression of the other. Marx certainly follows impeccable logic here, since the mechanics of any revolutionary change would undoubtedly reduce the relative, if not the absolute, well-being of some individuals, so that for a utopian to claim to emancipate everyone simultaneously would be tantamount to claiming that he was liberating the wealthy from their riches. In denigrating the idea of universal emancipation, Marx was perhaps also indirectly chiding the utopians for their adherence to remnants of the Enlightenment morality of universal humanism, which in the capitalist context was transformed into a blatantly apologetic ideology and so had to be rejected. The absence of a class dimension from utopian socialism, then, suggested to Marx that the utopians were victims of bourgeois ideology in their concepts if not in their analysis of society.

A more methodological criticism of the utopian socialists, further developed by Engels, was that their method was idealist: that they sought solutions via pure reason without adequate study of material conditions, and expected their utopias to instantiate a series of idealistic absolutes – justice, equality and reason. As Engels said, 'We know today that this kingdom of reason was nothing more than the idealised kingdom of the bourgeoisie; that this eternal Right found its realisation in bourgeois justice' and so on.[16] Idealism is bound up with other utopian defects, such as the neglect of history. 'To all these socialism is the expression of absolute truth, reason and justice . . . absolute truth is independent of time, space, and of the historical development of man.'[17] In these respects, the socialists were as culpable as the German idealists, but Engels had a word to say in their defence: 'French nonsense is at least cheerful.'[18] The failings of the utopian socialists are most plainly seen through Marx's positive evaluation of his own method. His materialism was a deliberate counterpoint to the eighteenth-century rationalist method and to Hegelian and neo-Hegelian idealism – although he recognized Hegel's influence on the formation of his own ideas. The all-important innovation was the application of the dialectical method to the materialist and historical approach: by contrast Owen, for example, was materialist in his appreciation of the impact of environment on character, but still hopelessly ahistorical and abstract in his conclusions. The resulting method of dialectical and historical materialism (as commentators have since labelled it) was, Marx considered, superior in its grasp of reality and its power to precipitate action. In addition, Marx systematically equipped himself with an epistemology which validated his own method of political theorizing while invalidating that of others, including the utopians. Needless to say, the question of whether Marxism is itself utopian can only be answered in the negative in terms of his own criteria - although many writers since have considered it to be so, and we will ourselves give further consideration to this assertion in Chapter 7.

Despite all this, one could cite rival patterns of thought which make the supposedly idealist and ahistorical approach of Owen *et al.* appear less misguided or irrelevant. The architect's blueprint and the economic plan are just as respectable models for change as the revolutionary's dialectical manual, and circumvent the problem of the break with history - as did the socialist utopians who hoped to effect change by reason and persuasion. While conceding that idealism is liable to be the hallmark of all utopias, since they are produced by one individual's imagination and since his ability to experience all the relevant material circumstances and to supply a synthesis is limited, one could argue that idealism is not a defect in utopian thinking since any model of a better future society must abandon the extrapolation of trends in order to project improving ideas. It could be said that a materialist analysis such as Marx's is severely limited in what future possibilities it can countenance by the dead hand of the present, and in fact Marx's own rare pronouncements on the likely form of higher communism largely followed suggestions which the utopians had already articulated, and so partook of their idealism. With respect to idealism, the Marxist view of utopianism in general must depend on how it is conceptualized: if seen as the eternal aspiration for the ideal city, it is irremediably idealist (in every sense), but if seen as a purposeful negation of current social evils, it can be methodologically vindicated.

Marx's criticisms, then, are in part theoretical, because the utopian socialists were not scientific (materialist), and in part concern their practical failings and their inevitable impotence - the matter of correct theory and successful practice being closely linked for Marx. This particular criticism Marx would evidently extend to any utopia, since utopias have proved historically to be politically ineffective. But since Marx set out to define and dismiss utopian socialism rather than utopianism as such, it would be misleading to apply his critique wholesale to the genre. In any case, the criticisms do not lead to an equation of utopianism with ideology as Marx himself defined it, for utopianism is usually not the sympathetic explanation of the mechanisms of existing society, or a justification and apology for the ruling class - even if some versions of Owenism or Fourierism were seen as such by Marx.

For Marx, utopia falls somewhere between materialism and ideology, into an idealist limbo. However, those Marxists who still insist on a strict disjunction between ideology and science would doubtless classify all utopias as ideology because they present deluded or partial world-views, conceived of by suspect intellectuals, and based on imperfect information and unscientific analysis. Yet it would be a mistake to call the constructive, speculative and futuristic elements of utopian thought ideological, partly because there is no proper way of applying the materialist criterion to these, partly because certain passages of ortho-dox Marxism would themselves fall prey to the same criticisms, which presumably Marxists would wish to avoid.

In trying to evaluate the role of utopianism in political thought, one is quickly led to the conclusion that Marx's utopia/science distinction is a false dichotomy which merely serves to exclude non-favoured theories from the charmed circle. The 'imperialism' of the dichotomy is criticized by Abensour, who argues that a new reading of Marx casts doubt on this antinomy. In *The Holy Family* 'doctrinaire science' is actually seen as a fault of the utopians: Proudhon is described as 'scientific' and Owen is acknowledged as a materialist. Abensour contends that the real split is between total revolution and partial revolution (utopianism), not between science and utopia:[19] utopia was for Marx a partial project, attacking secondary phenomena, not essences. He detects a new libertarian utopianism in the margins of Marxism from the end of the nineteenth century onwards, in the works of Morris, Bloch and Benjamin. The 'utopianization' of Marx is heterogeneous and non-coercive and makes use of utopia's energy and its 'positive intentionality'.[20] Such developments shatter the old opposition and provide new answers to the question of how utopianism and communism relate: thus Abensour's main thesis is the recon-cilability of Marxism and utopianism at many levels.

Utopia's transcendence

If one accepts Marx's account of ideology as a part of the superstructure reflecting dominant class interests, and his hope for the generation of a counter-doctrine through the growth of a class movement (whose epistemological status varies according to whether one consults Marx, Lenin or others),[21] the anomalous position of that isolated, alienated, individualistic intellectual, the utopian, needs special explanation. This is attempted in Mannheim's *Ideology and Utopia* (1929) which sub-sequently had a formative effect on the theoretical analysis of utopianism.

Mannheim employs a generalized, non-doctrinaire version of Marx's materialist explanation of social consciousness as the basis of a new discipline, the sociology of knowledge, which is to replace past ideological and utopian distortions and to give an accurate account of the relation of ideas to reality in their own time. Mannheim, as is well known, defines ideology as ideas and representations not congruent with reality: he distinguishes the 'particular' conception of ideology, where this incongruency disguises the true nature of a situation to someone's advantage, from the 'total' conception, which is a complete thought-system, the property of a concrete socio-historical group or of an epoch.[22] Marxism, he says, wrongly fused the two conceptions so that a particular (deceptive) ideology was also viewed as a total ideology, creating false consciousness in those whom it deceives.[23] He recommends a sociology of knowledge approach which would replace the analysis of ideas as ideology and locate them in their socio-historical environment without falling into unbounded relativism – although Mannheim's book has been criticized for just such relativism.

A state of mind is utopian when it is incongruous with the state of reality within which it occurs . . . . In limiting the meaning of the term 'utopia' to that type of orientation which transcends reality and which at the same time breaks the bonds of the existing order, a distinction is set up between the utopian and the ideological states of mind.[24]

According to Mannheim, then, both ideological and utopian ideas are incongruent with, or transcend, reality, but ideologies are 'harmoniously integrated into the world-view of the period'. Utopias tend to transform reality to accord with their own intentions. The first problem with the definition is that it is made to depend on the *effect* of the doctrine rather than on its content or theoretical structure; only time will tell whether a doctrine did or did not tend to transform reality or become harmoniously integrated, though presumably the class of self-proclaimedly revolutionary doctrines can *a priori* be classified as utopian. This also implies that a theory can only be utopian with respect to the period in which it was not yet realized: note how far the meaning of the term is now removed from the normal meaning of 'an ideal society', possibly because the relativist sees no grounds for the judgement 'ideal', only for the judgement 'different'. Mannheim calls his distinction between ideology and utopia 'completely formal'[25] but admits to problems in its concrete application, problems which we shall deal with in some detail in Part Two of this book.

The upshot of Mannheim's analysis, by contrast with his intentions, is not to show a polarity between ideology and utopia, but to show them to be epistemologically similar, on a continuum of incongruence with reality. They can be distinguished sociologically, depending on whether they represent the interests of an established or aspiring class, but not philosophically. Or again, they can be judged different historically, according to their effect on society – but only retrospectively. This analysis of utopianism thus differs substantially from that of Marx, who delineated its epistemological characteristics as being idealist, rooted in abstract reason, *not* growing directly from experience of material social conditions, and hence less congruent with reality and less capable of exposing and opposing ideology than revolutionary class consciousness which Mannheim, of course, considers utopian.

Mannheim goes on to discuss the social conditions for the production of utopianism, emphasizing that the achievement of the 'charismatic' individual utopian can only be utilized in collective life when it deals with current problems and 'its meanings are rooted genetically in collective purpose'. An effective utopia cannot in the long run be the creation of an individual; hence Mannheim's use of the term 'utopian mentality' to denote a climate of opinion, rather than referring to particular utopias.[26] Friedman also argues this necessary connection between individual and collective discontent, as will be shown later. Having analysed the various forms taken by the utopian mentality in 'modern' times – anabaptism, liberal-humanism, conservatism and socialist-communism – Mannheim discusses the apparent atrophy of this faculty in our own time, suggesting that it occurs because the aspirant classes have now attained political power through democracy: he deplores this loss. 'The complete elimination of reality-transcending elements from our world would lead us to a "matter-of-factness" which ultimately would mean the decay of the human will.'[27] Evidently Mannheim equates utopianism with voluntarism, the expression of pure will, and he concedes that the determinism of the sociology of knowledge might destroy this voluntaristic utopian impulse in whose 'spiritual elements' he strongly believes. Salvation lies with the intellectuals, he hopes, who are in a privileged position (or will be when all oppressed classes share political power, thus freeing them from particular social affiliations) to synthesize the best elements of all ideologies and utopias into a new utopianism: in other words, for Mannheim truth is attainable by intellectuals freed of sectional interests. There is already an evident contradiction in his thought here, in that the enfranchisement of the oppressed classes which he perceives has stifled utopianism (as he admits) rather than liberating the intellectual as he hoped. His optimism is also doomed to disappointment if one maintains that the 'aspirant classes' have not yet achieved *true* political power, so that intellectuals will be needed as spokesmen for particular interests for the foreseeable future. Either way, in practical terms the intellectual's role is problematic.

The contradiction between Mannheim's relativist and determinist exposition of the growth of ideas, and his invention of the free-floating intellectual, who would presumably revert to pure idealism, has been identified as a fundamental weakness of this last, speculative passage of his book, as has his eventual recourse to a non-relativist criterion to identify the nature of the utopian mentality. Mucchielli makes these criticisms and also notes the incongruity of classifying even regressive doctrines such as conservatism as utopian.[28] But Mannheim's real purpose is to find a definition which will comprehend what he considers the important social and spiritual movements since the Renaissance, rather than to deal with anything as precise and limited as the particular utopias which individuals have invented. It is therefore fruitless to consult his account for an exact analysis of the nature of utopian thought built on instances of the genre, although his *magnum opus* offers us an important account of the interaction of ideas and socio-historical conditions, which can illuminate the historical causes and effects of utopianism.

Neither according to Mannheim, nor to Marx, both of whom share a basically materialist approach to the creation of ideas, can utopia be described as ideology, it appears, although for Marx utopian socialism was the antithesis of his own scientific variety. Even if the utopia/science distinction is valid, it subsists on another plane from the ideology/science opposition, and utopianism cannot thus be equated with ideology. Before leaving this topic, some remarks on twentieth-century Marxist accounts of utopianism are necessary. Some orthodox Marxists still insist on a strict ideology/science dichotomy, so that utopianism necessarily falls into the former category, and even non-Marxists, using the word loosely, would also call utopianism ideological. But, defying this dichotomy, thinkers of the New Left have rescued a role for utopianism in Marxist theory. The voluntaristic approach of this movement is in the spirit of the utopian enterprise, which seeks to change society by *will*, and many of its concerns, such as alienation and the revolutionizing of work, also preoccupied utopians of the past.[29] The spiritual father of 'Marxist utopianism' is Ernst Bloch, whose *Geist der Utopie* (1918) and later massive work *Das Prinzip Hoffnung*

(1959) consider the roots and possible current applications of utopianism. He sees utopianism as arising psycho-sociologically from alienation and dispossession, and from 'the ineradicable tendency to create a better world'.[30] Utopias are abstract, ideological constructions which broach the 'inconstructible question'. But in Marxism Bloch sees 'hot and cold streams', the hot stream being utopian enthusiasm and the cold being materialist analysis, which has usually blocked the way of the utopian current. The adoption of a certain model of science seems to condemn utopia to abstraction and impotence – yet at the heart of Marxism lies that paradox, 'a concrete utopia', which is itself a novel science of 'exact anticipation', superseding empiricism because not confined to the description and analysis of reality. By contrast with Marx, Bloch relates utopianism to the question of practice: 'the future can only be done and anticipated in a utopian manner'.[31] In general, Bloch argues, utopia installs a dialectical movement in the heart of the ideology of the established order: it transcends reality through the principle of hope and by projecting the alternative, suppressed contents of history.[32] This speculative analysis opens the way to less rigorously orthodox re-formulations of Marxism for the twentieth century and to Bloch's own considerations of the political role of art, music and religion, all of which contain substantial utopian elements, in his view. Bloch was subject to the same criticisms as the New Left from orthodox Marxists; his introduction of such subjective elements as desire and the 'utopian propensity of man' into the analysis led to an innately individualistic theory, which was condemned. But his approach also inspired a number of disciples because, although categorizing utopianism firmly as ideology, it defined a respectable role for utopia within the dialectical movement and relieved the sterility of 'scientific' Marxism.

The scientist's critique

Contemporary social thought outside the Marxist school, while making less play of the concept of ideology, sets up stringent criteria for the definition of science, to which the social as well as the natural sciences are meant to conform, *mutatis mutandis*. How does utopia fare in these conditions? The dominant empiricist epistemology dictates an inductivist method or, following Popper,[33] a process of deductively testing the implications of theories, a criterion which utopian theory is in principle unable to satisfy, dealing as it does with the unknown and the possible rather than the observable and probable. Popper's famous *Open Society* in part constitutes an attack on the utopian effort to foist a coherent, rationalist, *a priori* scheme on the world, and a vindication of the essentially liberal tactic of piecemeal reform. But the utopian's approach is necessarily rationalist, giving an appearance of self-containment and being internally consistent and totalistic, for if he placed absolute weight on empirical reality or tried to assimilate his ideas to social 'facts', he could never construct an alternative society in his imagination. To achieve his end, the utopian has to privilege a theoretical structure (rather than empirical data), which is vulnerable to challenge, as are all theories.

Furthermore, the utopian sets out with an epistemological conviction of the possibility of achieving one final, exclusive truth concerning the best form of human relations and social organization, and this conflicts at least superficially with the open-mindedness of empiricist procedure and the tolerance of a variety of experiments and theories which that dictates. The political consequences of this difference of epistemology will be elucidated in Chapter 4. But utopian theory cannot entirely be written off as fantasy on account of its non-empirical nature, since it usually rests on a basis of observed human needs and desires, although this cannot be satisfactorily subjected to the empiricist's test of falsification. Of course, current developments in the philosophy and methods of science and social science have created an atmosphere more receptive to the utopian's rationalist and theoretical method, it being now admitted that even the most positivist social science incorporates strong, untestable theoretical and ideological elements, so that the exclusion of utopianism from the realm of social science is not a foregone conclusion.

In fact, utopians in the last two centuries have often claimed to be social scientists (a term which includes the political sphere) and even before that concept evolved they presented themselves as purveyors of unique social truths, or inventors of 'the one true system', a claim which was based on the view that historical reality had perverted the truth, and which referred back to some quasi-Platonic account of ideal human life. Admittedly, such claims to scientificity, as in the case of the utopian socialists, tended to rest on the systematization of selective perceptions and on introspection rather than on profound theoretical analysis, but much the same could be said of Comte, often acclaimed as the father of sociology. Certainly, the attempts to divine the principles of an ideal society, plus the peculiarity of the nature of perfection, which demands the best of everything, led most utopians to endow their societies with remarkably similar characteristics, which include stability, uniformity, self-regulation, self-sufficiency and a strong emphasis on community: this consensus might almost be mistaken for scientific agreement, based on social logic and induction.

It is no coincidence, according to Dahrendorf, that a good deal of modern sociology has projected these same characteristics on the structure of the societies which it purports to analyse:[34] utopian thought has in this way penetrated respectable social science, without itself necessarily being scientific. Functionalism, following in Parsons's footsteps, dwells on the self-maintaining and regulating system, and most orthodox sociologists start with the presumption that society's continuance unchanged is evidence for a harmonious consensus regarding values: disagreement is defined as *deviance* wherever possible, in order to leave the system theoretically intact. Dahrendorf deplores the 'loss of problem-consciousness' of this brand of sociology and its removal from everyday experience, and recommends the substitution of a conflict model. His attack is not aimed at utopianism *per se*, which he considers to have a useful critical function, but at the choice of a self-styled analytical procedure which virtually assumes that existing society *is* utopian. By and large, his criticisms stem from a single point of analogy between utopians and a functionalist model of society – the unchangingness of the system – and it can be shown that many utopias do comprehend change. If this is not a defining characteristic of utopia, the analogy and the argument fail. But Dahrendorf's criticisms usefully adumbrate the *rapprochement* between social science and traditional utopianism and indicate the influence of the latter – or rather, the ideological if not the factual accuracy of some of its discoveries.

While Dahrendorf makes the monotonous characteristics of the realized utopia the basis of his criticism, Nisbet takes a different definition of utopianism and arrives at a contrary conclusion concerning its usefulness: 'utopianism is compatible with everything but determinism, and it can as easily be the over-all context of social science as can *any other creative vision*'.[35] This casts utopianism in the same role as other alternative world-views and is reminiscent of Mannheim's 'utopian mentality'. But such attempts to detect a *rapprochement* between utopianism and modern social science are endangered by the multiplicity of meanings which can be given to utopia. With a term so widely and loosely used, a formulation such as that of Nisbet may be meaningless. Also, the definition of a proper method for social science is likewise so controversial that it is difficult to apply the criterion to utopianism; and recently Foucault has strongly denigrated the petty, inquisitorial methods of the social sciences and suggested that they will prove an ephemeral phenomenon in the history of knowledge.[36] So the assessment of utopianism *qua* social science is hedged about with difficulties. It was argued in Chapter 1 that social science is in part a modern surrogate for utopianism. If true, this would entail a shared content and a shared function: the analysis and improvement of society. But as Dahrendorf regretfully concludes, the ameliorating impulse seems to have vanished along with the overtly utopian elements. In any case, the 'surrogate' explanation does not suggest that utopianism ever *was* social science, measured by any yardstick.

There is, then, a gnawing problem for those who wish to contend that utopianism has a valid role in social thought: whether one adheres to a Marxist or a 'bourgeois' empiricist canon of scientificity, the rules are drawn so strictly as to exclude utopianism and devalue its importance. After all, what empirical status can be had by that which does not exist? And what are ideas without a supporting reality? These are the problems to be faced by anyone seeking to reinstate utopianism intellectually. Commentators in recent years have tried to confront them by postulating various *sui generis* criteria which utopianism, appropriately defined, satisfies. A major endeavour of this kind has been the delineation of a special role for utopia as a unique brand of speculative theory. As was stated before, much emphasis has been laid on utopia's capacity to create 'lateral possibilities', and this could indeed be seen as a respectable quasi-logical game in the world of social contingency. For instance, by observing the characteristics of a male-dominated society, one can perhaps deduce what qualities a feminist society would have; similarly, Saint-Simon noted the profligacy with which the 'drones' governed society and, by inversion, deduced that the 'bees' would institute an exemplarily thrifty form of government.[37] Again, Plato's survey of the characteristics of the non-ideal forms of government which would succeed the Republic has the same appearance of exploring systematically all the logical possibilities, even though it is presented as a temporal progression and decline. Of course, these are only games of contingency which aim to present their conclusions as necessary, but nevertheless they are controlled thought experiments, not haphazard fantasy. Indeed, they might be said to be following a respectable method: the enumeration and evaluation of lateral possibilities. And in fact the remarkable similarity of many of the institutions and characteristics of past utopias could be cited to support this account, showing that the 'method' produces results in agreement with each other.

Speculative thought of this kind receives a warmer welcome in France than in the English-speaking world, where mental exploration is not recognized as a special method. However, it continues to be a source of embarrassment, as Ruyer admits, that utopianism 'abandons the vehicle of experience',[38] running contrary to established empiricist requirements, and straying into a world where no intellectual holds are barred, it seems. In fairness, most utopians draw heavily on their observation of life and inner experiences for the bases of their theories: Fourier's psychological theory was clearly an account of his own 'passions', and in general a utopia, like our dreams (according to Locke), is composed of elements that its author and readers have experienced, however oddly they are pieced together.

But it is still difficult to assert utopia's respectability in terms that appeal to empiricists, and the most successful accounts of the subject abandon this yardstick partly or wholly. Defending the utopian method, Bauman tries to give an account of utopia which shows that its powers rival and in some senses exceed those of science. If true, this would justify the abandonment of experience. Utopia, he claims, legitimizes the status of 'the possible' in valid knowledge, whereas science can only approach 'the probable' on the basis of what has already happened.[39] Characterized thus, utopia's special role seems plausible until one recalls astrology, magic and all the other discredited 'sciences' which might equally have claimed to explore the possible. A similar proposed justification is that utopias reflect the tension between *being* and *becoming*, and the idea of *will*, both of which are unique to the human condition and so, presumably, demand a special vehicle. This is linked to the suggestion that a class of possibilities are present 'ideally' which may eventually come into existence and are evoked in utopianism. The problem with this and all the other attractive hypotheses – and every commentator on utopia offers one, if not several – is that we cannot encash any of them in the normal currency in which ideas circulate, since they constitute radical departures from our major epistemological frameworks and are more akin methodologically to metaphysics, aesthetics or even magic.

A different form of validation of the utopian enterprise draws on the relation between the predictive elements and action; rather as Gramsci thought that organized action 'verifies' predictions, one might see utopia as a practical syllogism which proves itself by the enactment of its conclusions. This hypothesis makes utopia verifiable by action, in principle, but falls foul of another long-running controversy: does not utopia lose its identity and nature in the realization? Many would argue that utopias are by nature unrealizable, a proposition that will be discussed in Chapter 9. However, almost certainly any truth value that is to be found in utopia will be in terms of its effects rather than according to the validity or scientificity of its contents. The key may lie in Adorno's dictum that 'society only becomes problematic when you conceive of something different',[40] which could be used to justify utopia's critical function, but considerably diminishes its positive value.

Utopia as symptom and symbol

Evidently, the intentions and methods of utopian writers differ so widely that any generalizations on the nature of utopianism will rely to some degree on an imposition of an exogenous framework of analysis on this heterogeneous corpus of works. Some try to fit all utopias to a social science matrix, some advocate a symbolic reading of the text, some allocate them an expressive function, the expression of perpetual discontent at the human condition. Such analyses as the latter necessarily neglect the authors' intentions to some extent. Equally, it is necessary to disregard the declared aim of certain utopians to write social science, for their texts are to be judged by criteria other than their own, and often more exacting. A recent fashion in analysis has been to concentrate on the conditions which generate utopian thinking and largely to ignore the contents and idiosyncrasies of particular utopias. Friedman offers an 'axiomatic theory' as follows:

1 utopias are born of collective dissatisfaction;
2 they are only born if there is a *known* remedy (which one or more people perceive); and
3 they only become realizable if they can achieve collective consent.[41]

This account would eliminate most of the famous one-man utopias from the category of 'realizable utopias' (the title of Friedman's book) since condition 3 is almost invariably absent. But, as Part Two of this book shows, many of Friedman's points are relevant to an analysis of utopian movements.

Working on similar lines, Mucchielli sees the process as one where the utopian 'assumes the mantle of humanity', and offers the following description of his act of creation:

1 an individual, *non-egoistic* revolt, containing a philosophical element of the myth of the ideal city;
2 lucid observation of society;
3 pessimism about intervening, solitude, despair;
4 'tragic contradiction' between revolt and pessimism;

5 a flight to the unreal by the invention of an ideal city; and
6 the construction, aided by earlier observations, of a utopia.[42]

The utopian expresses a reality which is in fact known to all men
(though often unconsciously) and he has a *volonté de délivrance* for
all mankind. Mucchielli distinguishes utopianism from reform and
revolution in such a way that it is not realizable, and is typically a one-
man dream, in contrast with Mannheim's account where individual
inspiration is absorbed into the collective consciousness, creating the
utopian mentality, and may even proceed to transform reality. Dwelling
more generally on socio-historical causes, Servier argues that they are
symptomatic of turning-points or crises in society, even if these are
only fully recognized retrospectively. Several general problems arise
with these forms of explanation. The genetic account sets the conditions
but does not explain the characteristic nature of utopian thought. Then
there is the paradox of how and why individual critical creativity
manages to spring from a collective unawareness of these crucial
moments. This interpretation also risks reducing utopia to something
that is merely symptomatic and expressive, not valuable for its
particular content or individual insight but only as the bearer of human
aspiration, the symptomatic tip of an iceberg submerged in collective
consciousness. Seen thus, utopia becomes an empty form, a signpost to
the existence of social problems, rather than a *social theory*.

  This form of analysis, which might be entitled 'explaining away
utopia', reaches its culmination in the so-called psychological explanations of utopia. Duveau, discussing the varieties of such explanation,
reminds us that for the psychologist the 'man who dreams of islands'
is an inadequate, feminine type, seeking compensation; he notes that
famous sensualists such as Rousseau or Restif tend to devise ascetic,
compensating utopias. Answering the charge made by Ruyer that the
utopian 'lacks vital heat', he also shows that a grouping of utopians by
characterological categories produces anomalous results, putting unlikely
bedfellows in the same class: for example, More and Robespierre might
both be said to have been paralysed by fidelity to an ideal.[43] His
categorization of authors on the antique 'choleric . . . sanguine' axis is
equally inconclusive, and the lesson to be drawn from Duveau's survey
is the pointlessness of pursuing this line of inquiry, since typical
utopians change over time as well as differing individually. This kind
of approach is fundamentally unsatisfactory, if not counter-productive,
for those interested in the contents of utopias and their significance:
the texts must be treated as if they had some objective validity (as
with all texts) and cannot be explained away by the quirks of their

authors. And if utopia is seen first and foremost as the product of an abnormal mind, the value or ideality of its contents is severely impaired, which is doubtless the intention of some critics.

A textual approach to utopia which is far more sympathetic is advocated and practised by Roland Barthes, who argues that for a text to be properly interpreted, it must live and 'play' through its reader; he also dwells on the idea of a 'utopia of language'.[44] In *Sade Fourier Loyola* (1971) it is with the language of *utopia* that he is dealing, for many French thinkers treat Sade as utopian as well as Fourier – if not Loyola! Barthes describes all three as creators of new languages, 'logothetes', and lists the operations necessary for this act of creation, which are:

1 self-isolation, for the new language must be in a 'material vacuum' from other languages;
2 articulation, the composition or reconstitution of individual signs;
3 ordering the sequences of signs according to a higher order; and
4 theatricalization, the production of the text.[45]

For our present argument, the point of interest is that these operations are precisely those which occur in the creation of any utopia, where in convenient geographical isolation a society is constituted by the ordering of a number of new 'signs' or social units, and the whole is theatricalized in the utopian text. Barthes would argue that a utopia *is* a new language, not linguistic but 'open only to the semiological definition of the Text'.[46] The close parallels between the invention of a new language and that of a utopian society, which takes place in Fourier's text, for example, are explicable in terms of the Wittgensteinian view that language games are underpinned by a common form of life – if this axiom can be said to hold in reverse. Barthes proceeds to read the 'language of pleasure' through Fourier's utopian texts, providing an idiosyncratic, even capricious, but stimulating interpretation – likewise with Sade.

The purpose of Barthes's approach is not to legitimize the utopian enterprise *per se*, but to show what enlightenment and pleasure can be derived from a semiological reading of an individual text, particularly in the case of utopianism. The text ceases to be an intellectual object for analysis and becomes an object of pleasure. 'The pleasure of a reading guarantees its truth . . . . *I unglue the text from its purpose* . . . . *I force the displacement of the text's social responsibility'.*[47] So Barthes, at a stroke, solves the epistemological problems, and the problems of relevance and realizability which have nonplussed those analysts of utopia discussed earlier – but at what cost in violence to the authors' intentions and the texts' political status? However, there is a good deal to be said for the validation of texts according to what we can extract from them, and this need not be confined to personal pleasure, as Marin's 'decoding' of More's *Utopia* shows.

In *Utopiques: Jeux d'Espaces* (1973) Marin offers a semiological analysis of utopianism at several levels. He contends that utopia is the empty space where historical resolutions of contradictions can occur, a space created by its quality of being always elsewhere, nowhere. Utopia constitutes a 'neuter', a space between two opposites - although Marin does not say so, it must be where the excluded middle ought to be. This characterization leads Marin to designate utopia as an 'ideological critique of the dominant ideology',[48] whose remarkable critical force lies in its distancing process. Utopian practice, he argues, poses as a *form* what theory discovers as a *concept*.[49] Marin at least makes clear what the epistemological status of utopia is *not*, by arguing that it is not, cannot be, conceptual, but *is* figurative. Utopia is 'polysemic' and unrelated to truth and being, our conventional categories of judgement.[50] Marin's deconstruction of utopia in terms of various semiological structures and on the conceptual, schematic and aesthetic levels, is full of illuminating insights, but wayward. However, there are conclusions. He asserts that the utopian form appeared at the breakdown of feudalism, is integral to capitalism, opposes the latter's regressive ideology and is *necessarily socialist*. From his characterization of utopia as a form of discourse with 'blind' anticipatory value follows his conclusion that utopia could only realize itself by destroying itself: essentially it is unrealizable.[51]

The sign-reader is no more innocent of imposing his own interests on a text than is the critic who wishes to demonstrate irrefutably that utopia is ideology, for the signs which are identified in the text are *a priori* related to the reader's own framework of significance, as when Marin anachronistically tries to relate More's defence of thieves to the position of the exploited proletariat.[52] But undeniably the semiological approach offers a fruitful reading of texts which are often barren of literary merit and somewhat stereotyped in their overt social content, as the bearers of hidden messages. Indeed, anyone familiar with these analyses and the various Freudian accounts of utopianism may find the plain-spoken Anglo-Saxon approach to the subject comparatively dull. The Barthes–Marin method is obviously challengeable on the now familiar empiricist grounds, but also because it makes nonsense of the intentions and free will of utopian authors. Yet sign-reading is a seductive occupation, and it is also tempting to think that utopias, like poetry, express symbolically or through signs truths which cannot be brought within the canon of reasoned argument but which are never-theless valid and forceful. However, this approach provides no general theory of the political significance and role of utopianism – or rather, it suggests that this may be minimal, confined to individual interpretation and reaction to given texts, and therefore unpredictable.

This chapter has discussed various accounts of utopianism which might broadly be categorized as philosophical, methodological and sub-jectivist. For Marx, the philosophical basis of utopian socialism was erroneous, being idealistic, ahistorical and non-dialectical: this led to certain errors of content and conclusion such as the omission of the role of the proletariat and the need for practice, and the preference for gradualist methods. According to Marx, an ill-conceived theory cannot abet revolutionary change, whereas a well-formed philosophical founda-tion would produce a social theory that was scientific in form, whose contents would be valid and capable of acting as a catalyst. The metho-dological criterion applied by empiricists to test the scientificity of utopia takes for granted an empirical account of science, which utopias in general cannot satisfy because of their predictive and speculative elements. Philosophical criticism is largely absent from this account (although ultimately the objection is philosophical) and the utopian method and resulting contents are subject to criticism: utopianism is ruled out *ab initio* because it is non-empirical in its procedure. By contrast, the third approach, which has been espoused by a variety of thinkers, eschews the 'utopia or science' debate and the attempt to discover whether utopia is objectively well founded, and embraces and emphasizes subjective factors. From Mannheim's and Bloch's acknow-ledgements of the inspirational quality of utopian theory to Barthes's recommendations of the pleasure of the utopian text, all such approaches characterize utopianism chiefly by the unique reaction which it can provoke in individuals. They suggest, but do not systematically account for, the action-producing effect of such texts, and their virtue is that they formally recognize the emotional and spiritual appeal of utopianism. But such accounts still appear inadequate to a Marxist wanting to find a systematic link between theory and practice, or to a political analyst hoping for generalizable correlations between the truth of the political text and the readers' political behaviour.

This chapter has inevitably had to content itself with stating rather than solving the problem of the epistemological and ideological status of utopia, but it has tried to challenge the tyranny of the science/ utopia and ideology/science opposition. In the context of utopian theory, 'scientific' is sometimes used as a synonym for 'realistic' (and so, good) but *soi-disant* scientific theories may turn out to be unrealistic and unrealizable, while apparently non-scientific theories may for some reason be espoused and put into practice. Even if the ideology/ science polarity could be conclusively established, we would not cease to study the role of ideology: likewise, the effects of utopianism, however unscientific, are of abiding interest. As for conclusions, clearly we should respect the polysemic nature of utopianism and should not shun a certain eclecticism in reading and treating the texts. The philosophical status of a doctrine is rarely the key to its success in politics, and attempts at logical castration or rational refutation are often inappropriate and impoverishing: utopian texts are a rich resource. And since the epistemological rightness of a utopian theory is far from guaranteeing its enactment, the question of what produces a utopian movement is better approached via studies of utopian activities and experiments, and this we attempt in Part Two.

Suggested reading

The most important account of the Marxist critique of utopianism is given by F. Engels in *Socialism: Utopian and Scientific*, but similar attacks appear in several other works by Marx and Engels, including *The Holy Family, The German Ideology* and *The Communist Manifesto*. Marxists who insist on the possible reconciliation of the Marxist and utopian traditions are M. Abensour, 'L'histoire de l'utopie et le destin de sa critique', *Textures*, nos. 6-7, 8-9 (1973-4); and E. Bloch, *Geist der Utopie*. This hope is also implicit in H. Marcuse's *Eros and Civilisation* and *Essay on Liberation*, an influential book in the radical tradition which grew out of the 1968 'events' in France. The debate on utopianism in English Marxism is considered by P. Anderson in Chapter 6 of his *Arguments within English Marxism*. K. Mannheim's analysis in *Ideology and Utopia* categorizes Marxism firmly as part of the utopian mode. The interconnections between utopian thought and social science are discussed by R. Dahrendorf, 'Out of utopia', in *Essays in the Theory of Society*; and by B. Goodwin, *Social Science and Utopia*. A selection of the suggestive semiological readings of utopian texts favoured by the French is given in the symposium published as Colloque de Cerisy, *Le Discours Utopique*. For an entertaining and influential example of this approach, see L. Marin, *Utopiques: Jeux d'Espaces*, which includes an analysis of Disneyland as a modern utopian fantasy.

4 Utopia's enemies[1]

Utopia – the Gulag.[2]

Even with the best intentions of making heaven on earth [utopianism] only succeeds in making it a hell – that hell which man alone prepares for his fellow-men.[3]

Why have liberal democrats so strongly denigrated the idea of utopia? The answer lies in an opposition between utopianism and liberal-democratic theory (LDT hereafter) which is fundamental and structural, rooted in incompatible and rival views of the nature of knowledge, science and social existence. From these antithetical epistemologies spring conflicting value systems and contradictory theories. In order to examine the antithesis, the utopian will be considered here as a social critic who argues from a perfectionist vision of the Good Life and tries to promote social change through the device of an alternative construction of society. Integral to this process is the implicit or explicit propagation of an alternative world-view. The relationship between the utopian's beliefs and his actions is problematic and will be discussed later, but by definition the utopian must at least prefer his utopia to other conceivable and existing forms of society.

In contrasting utopianism with LDT and the anti-utopian criticisms advanced by liberals, one is frequently discussing the characteristics imputed to utopian thought by its critics, which differ significantly from those described in earlier chapters. The argument which follows will often dwell on the antagonism between an archetypal utopian and an archetypal liberal democrat, with an evident risk of caricature. The archetypal utopian is the creation of many liberal theorists, but the archetypal liberal democrat represents a cluster of ideas and attitudes related to the liberal–democratic outlook as perceived by the present authors.

The polarities between utopianism and LDT are most manifest when utopianism is treated, as so often, as a species of totalitarian thought, and so we shall first consider the onslaught of the anti-totalitarian school of thinkers. The concept of totalitarianism has insinuated itself thoroughly into political theory since its genesis in the 1930s, and a number of books written in the 1950s and 1960s sought to determine whether the concept was defined by appearance - the various political phenomena which go to make up Friedrich's 'six-point syndrome'[4] - or whether it referred to an essence - the ultimate essence being the subordination of the individual to an omnipotent state. The resolution of this methodological debate was not, however, important in the treatment of utopians as totalitarians, since their critics tended to make comparisons of essence, appearance or both, according to which best suited their case. Popper's treatment of Plato exemplifies this no-theoretical-holds-barred approach.

The fashion of likening past political theorists to modern so-called totalitarians began in the 1930s when Richard Crossman enlivened Oxford tutorials by inventing mutually congratulatory dialogues between Plato, Stalin and Hitler.[5] The theoretical elaboration of the concept of totalitarianism led to its being applied to Enlightenment philosophers, French Revolutionaries, Hegel, utopian socialists, anarchists, Marx and Marxists of all hues. Popper and Talmon pioneered this retroactive style of criticism and others echoed their conclusions; in 1957 they and others developed their theme at a conference on 'Utopia and politics'. The fundamental charge was that all utopian thought depends on an exclusivist and authoritarian political outlook, antithetical to and destructive of the 'open society', a society marked out by liberty and tolerance. While some theorists espousing this approach had been visibly scarred by the experience of Nazism and were prone tendentiously to exaggerate the virtues of liberal democracy, similar criticisms are also made by those with other axes to grind: one such appears in a book by the anarchist Berneri, *Journey through Utopia* (1950), who takes issue with utopianism because of the loss of individual freedom it would entail. There are also conservative critics who are equally sceptical about liberal democracy, such as Cioran.

Who's afraid of utopia?

As a preliminary to discussion, some of the arguments of the enemies of utopianism must be recounted. In a classic critique, Popper contrasts *utopian engineering*, based on an *a priori* idea of rationality and a Platonic notion of ideal ends and means, with *piecemeal engineering*, which proceeds from the perception to the eradication of social evils.[6] He condemns the utopian for playing God, reconstructing society on the basis of human knowledge which is incomplete and fallible. Plato and Marx are singled out and condemned for trying to impose their personal visions on society, and Popper reinterprets Plato's *Republic* as a totalitarian nightmare – an interpretation based largely on misquotation and misrepresentation, as Levinson reveals.[7] Popper argues that the need for a 'clean canvas' dictates that the utopian should 'purge, expel, banish, kill', and that dictatorship is inevitable, since utopia is necessarily ruled by the Few. However, Popper's fundamental criticism is, in our view, methodological: the piecemeal, democratic method of change, operating by trial and error, is more scientific by Popper's empiricist standard than the utopian method which, he claims, seeks to impose *in toto* a rational, unchanging, aprioristic blueprint. This lack of susceptibility to change and experiment makes utopia the antithesis of the open society. Popper's critique therefore locates the fundamental error of utopianism (and totalitarianism) in a misapprehension of method and a false epistemology – that is, one based on unfalsifiable postulates about the nature of man.

Talmon likewise upholds the liberal's trial-and-error political empiricism against the doctrinaire approach of 'political messianists' and 'totalitarian democrats', terms by which he denotes thinkers, many of them utopian, of the late eighteenth and early nineteenth centuries. He asserts that they had too perfectionist an attitude towards the values of liberal individualism and so, paradoxically, were led to remove all the intermediaries between man and state, and all pluralist institutions, producing a political monolith. Consequently, collective conformity was to be achieved by direct coercion and the whole of life would be 'politicized'.[8] For Talmon, the idea of the 'reign of virtue' entails the persecution of opponents, who are defined by the would-be perfectionist as evil. Furthermore, the notion of an ideal man removes the 'life-enhancing' conflict between spontaneity and duty, in Talmon's view. He argues the incompatibility of an 'all-embracing, all-solving creed' with liberty: likewise, liberty cannot coexist with maximum social justice and security. Totalitarian states are also notorious for their abolition of law, on which liberty, for the liberal, depends. Liberty and spontaneous choice are thus the starting-points for Talmon's critique, which is founded on a deep suspicion of all perfectibilism and rationalism.

Spontaneity is also the pivotal value in many of Hayek's political writings which, while not directly rejecting utopianism, condemn the 'constructivist rationalism' which is certainly constitutive of the utopian mode. Hayek's 'catallaxy', a free-market society, is contrasted with planned or organized societies; a self-generating 'spontaneous order' is more subtle, complex and beneficial than any 'planned arrangement', he maintains.[9] Hayek's admiration for the catallaxy suggests an almost *aesthetic* approval of the empiricist method and its outcome, and seems to be linked to a fundamentally sentimental conception of nature and spontaneity, rather than resting on a real refutation of rationalism. At the heart of Hayek's analysis of the free market there can be detected a hint of a Higher Purpose, or at least a conviction that whatever is, is good. Hayek's view incidentally carries a strongly derogatory import for human rationality, in that it implies condemnation of any attempt to change society rationally. Thus the defence of spontaneity militates against rationality *qua* considered action, against voluntarism and, *a fortiori*, against utopia. Hayek exhibits a naturalism and an anti-rationalism more developed than Talmon's or Popper's, though it is true that most opponents of utopianism and totalitarianism, and even of planning, are also champions of 'natural', fallen man and the rich variety of his blemishes. They distrust his rationality when it goes beyond his own interests to theoretical matters or to planning for others. As a corollary, society is viewed as a growth rather than an artefact, which implies that pruning, not radical reconstruction, is the appropriate treatment.

Whether Hayek is to be labelled as a liberal or a conservative seems debatable, but there are also a number of straightforwardly conservative thinkers who take issue with the utopian tradition and whose views merit consideration. In his condemnation of rationalism in politics, Oakeshott argues that the rationalist stands for independence of mind and for 'thought free from obligation to any authority save the authority of reason'.[10] The rationalist's personal experience is elevated to principles, self-formulated rules which make no acknowledgement of the cumulation of principles through tradition and history. He is disposed to destroy and create, not to reform. Oakeshott also distinguishes technical and practical knowledge, arguing that the rationalist ignores the latter and seeks to provide a rule-book of the former. His definition of the rationalist is equally and explicitly a definition of the utopian: 'the "rational" solution of any problem is, in its nature, the perfect solution. There is no place in his scheme for a "best in the circumstances", only a place for "the best" '.[11] Oakeshott cites Godwin and Owen as rationalists *par excellence*, but ultimately he is attempting to discredit a whole mode of thinking rather than particular thinkers.

A traditionally conservative, though idiosyncratic, critique is offered by Cioran, resting on an ultra-Hobbesian view of human nature: he says that he cannot conceive of man without his propensity to harm![12]

Men are steeped in original sin, and they vainly seek the lost Paradise through utopian schemes. Yet if men already torment each other in existing society, would not the torture be far greater in utopia? He finds utopian texts 'exasperating' and recommends Fourier's description of the phalanstery as 'the most efficacious of vomitories'.[13] The Christian doctrine of the Kingdom of Heaven condemns in advance the hope of utopia on earth and, although viewed as the new apocalypse, utopia is really a new hell. Cioran also deplores the abdication of liberty which utopia entails, but *en passant*.[14] As this suggests, conservative hostility to utopianism assumes, but does not specially focus on, the anti-totalitarian arguments which sway liberals, preferring to invoke emotional, aesthetic and religious considerations.

Another French conservative, Lapouge, castigates utopia as machine-like, the self-styled enemy of nature; his book, *Utopie et Civilisations* (1973), documents the development of the utopian idea concurrently with social artifices and mechanical inventions. He perceives utopia as too algebraic and geometric, a closed system, a 'chained world' and an attempt to petrify history. Utopia is a world of mathematicians, based on necessity, rejecting chance: no wonder that it 'strangles liberty'. Lapouge finds the distasteful marks of utopianism in Napoleonic planning, in Nazism, in Soviet five-year plans which 'convert a succession of years into a simultaneity' and in the Manson sect.[15] He also finds religious authority on his side: 'God does not like the utopian genre at all, as he signified for the first time at Babel'.[16] Thinkers who may be styled conservative, then, approach utopianism at a rather different tangent from the liberals, seeing human nature as irretrievably sinful, and rejecting as artifice or as 'against nature' any blueprint for a better society. It is presumably these heartfelt convictions which have prevented conservatives from showing the interest in utopianism which some liberals, such as J. S. Mill, genuinely felt. It should not be overlooked, however, that some utopias contain conservative elements, such as Comte's positivist utopia, so that the antipathy is not mutual. The present chapter will be directed towards the criticisms of liberals rather than conservatives, since the former can be treated within political theory while the latter embrace wider considerations which cannot always be debated logically.

In this context, it has only been possible to survey the more prominent contemporary opponents of utopianism, but an excellent account of the long enmity is given in Kateb's *Utopia and its Enemies* (1963). By way of summary, we can cite the succinct account of the liberal critique of utopianism as a species of totalitarianism offered by Schapiro who lists the utopian's failings as follows:

1 he is preoccupied with ends and indifferent to means;
2 he views man and society as a totality;
3 he makes firm and dogmatic assumptions;
4 he is preoccupied with management; and
5 he neglects human variety.[17]

Note that only 1 is overtly reprehensible, but the world-view of the committed liberal makes the other four equally dangerous and culpable. Schapiro exculpates utopians of one charge only: unlike totalitarians, they do not falsely pretend to a sham of democracy since their authority is explicitly based directly on 'moral rectitude'.

How can the defenders of utopia set about repulsing such attacks? An obvious first line of defence is to point out the plurality of the utopian tradition, as does Abensour, who accuses the attackers of failing to distinguish between utopias of abundance and those of scarcity and between statist and non-state utopias.[18] But in fact a stronger defence is needed because what is being impugned is not simply a heterogeneous corpus of works branded as utopian, but the very project of exploring social alternatives theoretically. However disparate particular utopias may seem, they are said to derive from the same approach to politics, and it is that which is called into question, theoretically and methodologically. Therefore in a discussion of utopianism and political thought we must examine point by point the substance of the liberal democrats' criticisms.

The anti-totalitarian writings highlight the contrast between political phenomena in a liberal democracy and those said to characterize utopia: the exclusion of freedom of choice (anti-liberal) from utopia and the necessity of elite or dictatorial government (anti-democratic) are two primary contrasts, supplemented by the assertion that the utopian would have to use violence or coercion (inhumane) to attain his ends, ends to which opposition is aprioristically assumed by liberals. But such phenomena characterize authoritarianism in general rather than totalitarianism in particular.

Further scrutiny of the concept of totalitarianism suggests that in the debate about utopia it is in fact a red herring which we should exclude. Totalitarianism is an anti-ideal which so neatly negates the values and institutions of liberal democracy that the creation of a scapegoat must be suspected. The fact that its inventors cannot agree on a definition makes it even more suspect. As was said, analysts of totalitarianism adopt either a 'methods' or an 'essence' approach; the former identifies a cluster of characteristics common to all 'totalitarian' states, while the latter posits a more abstract 'statist' essence. Both assume what they attempt to prove, the existence of a distinctive political form which could be called totalitarian, and so both generate anomalies. Consequently many theorists now stigmatize the notion as vacuous or inoperable. Barber conceptually dismantles the concept without any difficulty, but rescues a residual doctrine which he calls 'totalism' (the expansion of the public sphere at the expense of the private) which is less culture-specific, and which he treats non-pejoratively.[19] It follows from his account that utopians are usually totalist, but not by definition totalitarian. If Barber's analysis is accepted, the concept of totalitarianism can be eliminated from our discussion of the confrontation between LDT and utopianism, which can better be analysed without the intervention of such an emotive intermediary. We shall also be spared the embarrassment of taking seriously the anachronistic application of a concept which clearly belongs to high-technology culture to pre- and non-industrial utopias.

The monopoly of truth

But the essence of the charges made by Popper *et al.* remains when the abusive label 'totalitarian' is removed, foremost among them the accusation of absolutism in outlook and intent. Typically, utopias rest on an absolutist epistemology such as Plato makes explicit in his theory of transcendental Forms or Ideas. Many less metaphysically sophisticated utopians make an appeal to the 'human essence' as the ultimate source of truth and value. In the Enlightenment, secular theorists posited that moral truths were established by reference to human nature, just as scientific truths were by reference to nature. Descriptive truths were thought to entail prescriptive truths and, at the level of the individual, knowledge entailed virtue. From human nature the utopian deduces truths about the right form of social organization and the proper disposition of power and material goods. This arrival at a unique solution is seen as absolutist and arbitrary by liberal critics – although the charge of arbitrariness can hardly hold if the utopian's premises and reasoning processes are revealed, as is usually the case. Most utopians do in fact seek to make their methods public, being proud of them, and to prove their conclusions to a disbelieving world, especially the *soi-disant* social-scientific socialists of the nineteenth century: very few try to mystify their thought processes or claim direct revelation.

But it is the exclusivism of utopia's truths that most worries liberal democrats. The utopian's notion of an ideal, and therefore uniquely good, society seems to imply a desire or intent to exclude all other social possibilities, which presents a challenge to three crucial liberal-democratic convictions.

1 The idea that political truth is variable and can best be approximately established by the regular counting of preferences by democratic means.
2 The consequent conviction of the need for *tolerance* of all shades of opinion, even the erroneous, and all competing truths (the open society ideal).
3 The conviction that a heterogeneous, pluralist society best fosters the variety of ideas which is an indicator of social good health.

At the heart of liberal political ideals such as tolerance, *laissez-faire* and pluralism lies an empiricist epistemology which dictates scepticism of any claim to exclusive and final truth. The incompatibility of the utopian method of theorizing with empiricism has already been discussed in Chapter 3. The utopian's approach cannot be other than theoretical and totalist, since if he were to admit the paramountcy of data gathered empirically in existing society, as the empiricist demands, he could never conceive of an alternative paradigm or rationally construct a different social form. In addition, human behaviour is so diverse that the empirical method would lead to no clear-cut conclusions about human needs, and no definitive human values such as the social critic must work with.

Man has the faculty of fantasy; he can imagine that which is not. The empiricist chooses not to use this faculty, confining himself to observations of what *is* (which all too often turn into justifications of the *status quo*), while the utopian employs it in constructing alternative possibilities: in so doing he inevitably selects a theory-based method, since empiricism can carry him no further than the existent. In addition, the only rational approach for the utopian is to aim at complete realization of his ideal which necessarily excludes all other possibilities, since utopia is conceived as a coherent society in which each element supports or depends on the others: the Guardians without Plato's education system would be mere despots, and a half-realized utopia would be no utopia at all. Utopian society is an integrated whole, obliterating liberal distinctions between public and private, and between economic, social and political – so it is called 'totalistic' and exclusivist by its enemies. The basis of the confrontation between utopianism and LDT is thus to be found in differences of epistemology and method which make utopianism appear to liberals as a *sui generis* mode of thought inimical to LDT *whatever its content*. But the more explicitly political aspects of this opposition must now be elaborated.

Liberal-democratic critics, believing in a multiplicity of truths, contend that the doctrinaire utopian will impose 'real' interests on men in contradiction to their felt, expressed or apparent interests, interests which under a democratic system are empirically verifiable by voting. Thus the utopian's own rationalism will deprive other individuals of rational choice. Liberal economists take revealed preferences to represent real choices, no matter how strong an element of determination, ignorance or *faute de mieux* may have existed in the formulation of such choices. Likewise, liberal-democratic theorists treat preferences manifested through the political process as acts of free choice and indicators of political rightness. Expressed preferences therefore conveniently embody both subjective and objective elements. Most liberals do not deny the possibility of objective truths in politics, but argue that there is no political method which firmly guarantees the selection of correct policies (*vide* the problems surrounding social welfare functions)[20] so that the pursuit of univocal, objective political truths would require dictatorship. Again, some pluralists hold that there is actually a plurality of incompatible political interests which generate conflicting sectional 'truths' and must be reconciled through democratic procedure. A search for 'real' interests threatens to ignore this heterogeneity and to impose a uniform solution autocratically, denying men the free choice and opportunities for self-differentiation which are vital to self-fulfilment. Another reason for distrusting 'real' interests is that the departure from expressed preferences leaves no safeguards to ensure that the state does not exploit and oppress men in the interests of rulers who invent 'real' interests which suit their purposes (as Soviet Russia officially reinstated the joys and heroism of motherhood when under-population seemed a danger). The liberal therefore fears tyranny and exploitation in utopia. He also upholds the sanctity of revealed preferences as expressions of rational choice, that is, as manifestations of the freedom which liberal society strives to foster. Even wrong choices embody this virtue to some extent. The imposition of 'real' interests, however objectively right, is tantamount to depriving men of their liberty and destroying their selfhood.

But the association of choice with interests and political freedom must be called into question. The objective constraints are well known: distortions are caused by the electoral and representative systems, pre-selection of issues occurs in party manifestos, and so on. Subjective factors equally serve to diminish the individual voter's rationality: his ignorance, lack of time, the possible intransitivity of his preferences. As Downs suggests, there are cases where it is clearly rational *not* to vote,[21] though it appears that people may continue to do so because it serves an *expressive* function: such voting is *affective* rather than *rational* action. The myths of rationality and freedom which have been constructed around the act of voting can so easily be undermined that perhaps the utopian's substitution of his own rationality and choice matters less than critics claim. In particular, if the main function of political choice is now expressive, this is a satisfaction which the contented citizens of utopia will hardly miss, since expressive voting usually voices discontent. In any case the desire for political self-expression might be more culture-specific than we care to admit, the merely temporary creation of our own democratic politics.

Crucial to the debate about interests is the notion of ideology and its forerunner, Rousseau's account of the corruption of human desires and motives by society. Once interests are admitted to be environmentally determined and manipulable, the utopian's contention that men can be mistaken about their ultimate interests as human beings through ignorance, delusion or corruption can be defended. Even pre-Marxian utopians manifestly thought in these terms: Owen used the metaphor of 'withdrawing the mental bandage by which, hitherto, the human race has been kept in darkness and misery'.[22] It then becomes permissible to educate men into the knowledge of their 'real' interests, or even at first to impose such interests. But liberal orthodoxy insists on currently expressed preferences as signposts to permanent human desires, identifying the notion of false consciousness as part of Marxist conspiracy theory, and so discrediting it. Thus, the liberal attacks utopianism from the safety of a tautological stronghold: society is, and must be, like *this* (e.g. based on merit and competition) because men are like *that* (e.g. acquisitive and competitive).

The notion of ideology opens up two paths for the utopian. He may discount expressed preferences because social institutions have debased men and distorted their needs, in which case the remedy is to create utopian institutions which will allow men to be 'natural' or which will eventually perfect human nature. Alternatively, he may dispense with the embarrassment of perfectibilism and argue that interests are always a result of conditioning, but that our present interests are created by a *false* consciousness, caused by misdirected conditioning; his utopia will generate authentic interests which express man's true humanity, and then align men's subjective desires with these by persuasion. The former project provides a standard in the idea of innocent or perfect human nature and may offend the liberal less than the latter, which allows that human values are formulated through social structures. Rousseau and Marx respectively are identified with these two archetypal radical strategies, but utopians before and since have always adopted one or the other. Either way, the utopian is at odds with liberal democrats, who tend to equate the *desired* with the *desirable* – a piece of moral algebra as philosophically vulnerable as any utopian's conjuring with real interests.[23]

Tolerance and violence

The gravest political charge that liberals make against utopians is that they would implement their ideals by coercion if necessary. This is supported by the liberal's conviction that nobody would willingly live in, or accept the change to, utopia – and also by the quasi-epistemological assertion that single-minded belief signifies a proclivity to intolerance and coercion.[24] To evaluate these charges, we must re-examine the ideas which underpin the liberal ideal of tolerance. Particularly revealing is the liberal attitude to values – *de gustibus non disputandum* – that found additional philosophical support in the logical positivism of this century, which maintains that values are outside the realm of verification, reducing them in effect to matters of taste. In political philosophy, the positivist approach dissevered truth from value, departing from a long tradition in which truth was endowed with a moral quality and knowledge of the ideal was said to compel action. How would Socrates have viewed Weldon's assertion that values can only act as 'conversation stoppers' in political argument?[25] Liberal democracy has affinities with the logical positivist position in that it considers that political debate should aim to expose the truth (*qua* 'facts'); the combatants may as a result volunteer to change their values. The utopian's assertion of a single set of values as the right one runs contrary to this recommended procedure.

Furthermore, the utopian's treatment of facts also makes him suspect since he claims, explicitly or implicitly, conclusive knowledge about the human predicament, which is impermissible on the falsificationist principle recommended by Popper and others. Today, empiricist and positivist assumptions are under siege as the value-laden nature of all theorizing is increasingly conceded, and these developments seem to some extent to sanction the utopian's position.[26] But the move away from positivism appears not to have modified the democratic conviction that in politics the only way that I may 'impose' my values on you is to convince you by rational argument, turning on indisputable *facts*: a procedure which for various reasons the utopian is unlikely to be able to adopt successfully. The utopian's enterprise is thus discredited by the dominant philosophical outlook because, first, his hypotheses cannot be established beyond doubt, and second, his ideals are unverifiable. His wish to impose his hypotheses and ideals by realizing his utopia is thus both misguided and contrary to the spirit of tolerance.

Because the utopian wishes to supplant existing values and to implant his own, he is stigmatized as doctrinaire. (As the 'end of ideology' debate of the 1950s suggested, liberal doctrines are perceived as ideologically neutral, a near-anagram of 'natural', and so not doctrinaire.) In principle, the ethos of tolerance requires the liberal to refrain from criticizing the *content* of a doctrine (unless it violates a primary value such as the sanctity of human life) but allows him to object to its *form* – its exclusiveness, unscientific origin, or contrived imperviousness to criticism. Such objections, when advanced, reflect the liberal's fear that a dogmatically held or absolutist political goal will justify the use of illiberal, undemocratic or inhumane means. The utopian is characterized as someone so enamoured of his final goal that he will employ *any* means to realize it, or would if he could.

The axiom 'the ends do not justify the means' clearly expresses an important procedural value whose contravention is *prima facie* undesirable, though its moral status is so controversial that it cannot be discussed satisfactorily here. But do utopians in fact justify coercion, force or violence in pursuit of their ends? Since the French Revolution a number of thinkers called utopian have explicitly advocated violent revolution as the *necessary* route to a better society: among them, Babeuf, Blanqui, Weitling, Marx (usually) and modern Marxists of many persuasions. Such advocacy generally rests on the 'economy of violence' principle, not on revenge, and the conviction that no dominant class will resign its position without being forced to do so. A number of utopians, among them Fénélon, proposed benevolent dictators who would initially be authoritarian, but not violent. But the vast majority of thinkers conventionally regarded as utopian have chosen other means: change by the example of experimental communities, by enlightened lawgivers or constitutional governments, by education, via a cataclysmic event, by evolution, by the setting up of colonies away from the corrupt Old World, or simply through the force of the utopian's revelations on rational men. Pre-modern utopias were conveniently situated in an Elsewhere or No-Place so that the question of how they had come about did not arise, or was relegated to ancient history. So, although a minority of utopians have seen coercion or even violence as a lamentable but necessary means to change, a survey of utopian literature provides no evidence for those who wish to establish a universal and necessary association of utopianism with coercive means.

Whether utopia is to be convicted or exonerated on this score evidently depends on how it is characterized. In *Utopie et Violence* (1978) another anti-utopian, Freund, finds utopian elements in modern theories of protest and associates utopianism with terrorism on the ground that they are both linked to the desire to create a new man. He distinguishes the 'classical' utopia, the harmonious city, from the 'vulgarized' utopianism which is typical of today's ideological and violent political movements.[27] Clearly Freund is using 'utopianism' in a wide sense to connote any doctrine with strong idealistic content. He attributes to utopianism a 'metaphorical reason' for violence, its desire to change human nature, which men will inevitably resist - and this charge is a common one. As so often, the issue turns on how the utopian operation is defined: most utopians claimed to be providing the conditions in which man's real nature could develop and flourish, by the removal of corrupting institutions. Some, like Owen or B. F. Skinner, who believe man to be infinitely educable or conditionable, claim to give man 'the best possible constitution', in Owen's words. *All* deny that what the critic takes necessarily to be 'human nature' from his particular standpoint and observation of present society is in fact necessarily so. But if, on the other hand, the critic is right, then most utopian schemes indeed 'do violence' to human nature and are likely to entail violence in their realization. We shall revert to the question of human nature again during this argument.

Does a utopian scheme, by its very nature, entail coercion in its realization? A formal answer 'Yes' must be given here if we are considering utopias intended to restructure a whole society - although coercion would clearly be unnecessary in the case of separatist communities which people joined voluntarily. 'Yes' is the answer because it is empirically very likely, although not logically necessary, that in a total rearrangement of society the Pareto principle (or rather, its implicit prohibition that anyone should be made worse off) would be violated. Any social change, and especially the radical changes which utopia entails, will necessarily make someone worse off compared with his previous position: such changes will be unwelcome. This would still be the case even if abundant resources could be created so that everyone had as much as or more than before, for some people would still lose *relatively*, in terms of status and privilege. It follows that the loser will be unwilling and must in the last resort be coerced into accepting utopia. But this is not the end of the story. Whether this coercion will *be* violent depends on the historical conditions; whether it is *called* violent depends on one's viewpoint. For some, expropriating the expropriators is a morally justifiable act, for others it is the violation of a basic human right. While utopia would necessarily involve the initial coercion of some individuals (notably the relatively privileged of the previous society, which can be seen to raise many interesting questions about positive discrimination), that coercion is not necessarily to be defined as violence and could probably be justified on some 'greatest happiness' principle. But violence against the individual, and revenge, the tragic accompaniment of most revolutions, are not advocated by utopians or entailed by the nature of utopia, and need not be discussed in this context, although in real life the question of historical revenge is a real and perplexing one.

The other question which merits an answer here is whether the special nature of utopian theorizing makes it prone to produce violence. What seems to be a spurious association of utopianism with violence has arisen because of the imputation of 'necessary' consequences to the utopian mode of thinking. When Popper and others decry utopianism for inherent violence, they are informed by a false theory of the connection between belief and action. Liberals assume that doctrinaire or absolute beliefs necessarily *entail* action, while tolerant convictions do not. If belief entailed action, no liberal could properly hold beliefs, since these would potentially constitute an 'imposition' on others, which tolerance forbids. But liberal doctrine is saved from such enfeeblement by an idea of extensive individual independence (*privacy*, an area of autonomy where we can believe what we like) and a restrictive definition of what counts as an imposition (such as J. S. Mill's 'material harm to others').[28] However, utopianism is often regarded as if it alone entailed all the means necessary to fulfil its end: the idealist is supposedly a fanatic at heart. But a philosophical analysis of belief suggests that the true believer is not logically obliged to impose his views on others, although he *is* required not to contravene them by his own actions. At most, the notion of belief implies that a believer should promote his views with some authority, rather than considering them a matter of opinion only, or 'as good as the next man's'. The utopian Déjacque offers an exemplary statement of committed yet open-minded utopian belief: 'I am not exclusive, and I would willingly abandon my (ideal) for yours, if yours seemed more perfect'.[29] But even if the utopian believes his truth to be absolute, 'absolutes do not imply their imposition', as Stankiewicz remarks in defence of Rousseau.[30] This recalls us to the contrasts and confusions between 'authoritative', 'authoritarian' and 'totalitarian' and suggests that the utopian genre is authoritative by nature, but no more.

One other form of argument employed by liberal democrats and others who have studied utopianism is that no man would voluntarily live in a so-called utopia, so that coercion would be necessary, an argument neatly summarized by Nozick.[31] The critic reasons that since he, and like-minded men, would not countenance life in a certain utopia, it would have to be set up and maintained by force. But he is not putting himself in the place of others, as the principle of solidarity recommends, but putting them all in *his* place! Such reasoning falsely elevates the inclinations and character of the critic into universal principles, and his covert assumption of human homogeneity ('like-minded men') ignores the fact that tastes differ. It also disregards the necessary truth that men differently located in current society would view the transition to utopia differently: some would lose, some gain, while others have nothing to lose anyway. As was said above, utopia, like all social reforms, displeases some vested interests, but the utopian need be no more coercive at the outset than were the liberal founders of the Welfare State. And it is unreasonable to use the criterion of Pareto optimality against the utopian if it is not invoked against other reformers.

Freedom and utopia

The fear that coercion would be needed to achieve utopia is reinforced by the supposition that life in utopia would be unfree. In a trivial sense, every utopia excludes all other possible forms of society and so restricts freedom of choice; however, the exclusion of non-preferred choices does not constitute a restriction on freedom. More substantial is the criticism that *any* utopia, compared with liberal democracy, would relatively restrict the freedom of some individuals. But surely the desirability of such changes is to be judged according to a broader idea of what is a good and just society. The Pareto principle in effect enjoins that all existing freedoms are sacrosanct, for nobody's freedom should be increased at the expense of another, but reverence for this axiom is synonymous with support for any *status quo*, however bad, and begs the question of how just the present distribution of freedom is, which the utopian insists on asking.

Freund raises many old fears about freedom in utopia, and points to the irony that utopians 'promote' freedom by the minute regulation of life and the suppression of spontaneity. But, as was argued in Chapter 2, such regulations supposedly reflect, rather than thwart, man's natural desires. When this favourite dichotomy between utopianism-*qua*-rationalism and freedom-*qua*-spontaneity is examined closely (and the terms themselves are a later outgrowth of the reason versus passion debate) the polarity breaks down and Hayek's praise for the catallaxy, with all its spontaneous injustices and unfreedoms, appears ungrounded. Civilized man is, after all, a highly conditioned creature and any generalizations about his 'spontaneous' inclinations or free will are bound to be largely tendentious. We take an over-indulgent view of our own society if we single out and blame utopias for suppressing spontaneity. Indeed, many liberals are deluded about the nature and importance of liberty in contemporary society. With respect to Hayek's characterization and condemnation of utopia as the totally planned society, we must question his assertion that a catallaxy would promote freedom. If my freedom is accidentally diminished by others' self-interested acts I am, objectively speaking, no more free than if a utopian rationally plans to restrict my freedom for the general good. The element of intentionality, the fact that the utopian knowingly limits my actions, does not further diminish my freedom in real terms. Hayek's preference for *laissez-faire* rests on his dislike of planners, but many find the blind rule of market forces equally repugnant, and no more natural! One might add that some utopians, such as Fourier, go to great lengths to demonstrate that the principle of organization of their utopias is that of spontaneity and that the actions of individuals will be harmonized instinctually and/or voluntarily.

Again, it can be argued that the liberal view of freedom has already served its turn. Historically, doctrines of individualism and freedom of choice were important in facilitating the breakdown of traditional, closed societies and vindicating the product differentiation so crucial to capitalism. But the doctrine is now ossified as a belief that property, possessions and free choice allow us to differentiate, express and realize ourselves as human beings. The freedom to consume thus becomes paramount – and most utopias are not the consumer paradise. The prospect of the disappearance of product differentiation and freedom of choice in utopia generates a horror of uniformity which is not solely aesthetic, for liberals also fear the imposition of a uniformity of products and opportunities on immitigably different men and a consequent suffering among minority groups. But variety and freedom of choice in society *qua* the market are not *a priori* essential to human happiness, and have not been so historically, and this objection to utopianism must be regarded as sceptically as the claim that 'like-minded men' would refuse to inhabit utopia.

More abstractly, utopia has been seen as structurally unfree because its unique prescription for the good life admits neither opposition nor change – hence, the 'closed society'. Unfreedom in this sense is a direct consequence of epistemological exclusiveness. But although the utopian depicts a perfectly working model requiring no change, he may not wish his society to be *static*. What the reader gets is necessarily a snapshot of utopia. Utopian theory is not an architect's blueprint but a suggestive model, and utopian practice would doubtless allow the freedom to change; indeed, utopias based on a theory of history such as those of Marx, Saint-Simon and Fourier, predict change and improvement even in utopia.

Many utopias dispense with a legal system or rely on individual virtue, collective morality, education, conditioning, or on a manufactured or spontaneous coincidence of the individual and general will, and it can be argued that the law, a necessary instrument in a conflict-based society, would prove unnecessary in a harmonious utopia where consensus reigned. But this absence of law appears dangerous to liberals, according to whom the alternative forms of social control circumvent rational choice, whereas the legal system allows the choice of obedience or punishment.[32] Again, it must be remembered that utopias rely on their citizens conforming voluntarily to whatever rules exist because happiness self-evidently lies that way – which leaves the rational process intact. Also, their laws are supposedly the laws of nature and cannot, as such, infringe men's freedom. Objection in principle to the other, non-legal forms of control is hypocritical – who could argue that even a liberal-democratic state does not use such devices in the effort to produce order in society? – although an extensive use of, say, conditioning in a particular utopia might rightly be criticized.

Objections to the abolition of law are also based on a profound distrust of the rule of men, and they raise again the pivotal question, 'Quis custodiet custodes ipsos?' The classic liberal-democratic answer to this is that democratic politics acts as a brake on the whims of rulers, a brake which is lacking in most utopias. The charge that utopia would inevitably become authoritarian and oppressive without adversary democratic politics can be countered in various ways: the shortcomings of democratic politics in reality can easily be illustrated,[33] and it can also be argued that the adversary process does not guarantee the truth or rightness of policies – but this again relates to whether politics is seen as a search for truth or a reconciliation of opposing interests. While *we* are in a state of prolonged imperfection needing special remedies, utopia starts from a position of established perfection, so perhaps it would be an adequate guarantee if citizens could express discontent when it arose, without the institutionalization of machinery for political debate. But to assert this requires an act of faith in the utopian's original vision.

As to the likelihood of the corruption of rulers, one can identify the safeguards set up by utopians – not least, Plato's rigorous education system and other constraints on the Guardians – but this will not persuade the critic with a conviction of the innate wickedness or corruptibility of human nature. The utopian's case rests on his optimistic faith in the goodwill and virtue of both rulers and ruled in ideal conditions. In abolishing possession and private property, as most utopians do, they touch on the supposed root of original sin and human evil and could thus be said to be addressing themselves to the problem defined by the pessimistic critic. But since no propositions about human nature, optimistic or otherwise, are conclusively demonstrable, room for scepticism remains. In the same connection, Freund advances a typical anti-utopian argument, contending that the achievement of utopian designs leads to despotism because utopianism plans to change men via institutions. To deny human nature is also to deny history, he argues.[34] In fact, much liberal-democratic criticism of utopian thinking can be reduced to certain tenets about human nature: that men will always be as competitive and avaricious as capitalism makes them, and as corruptible by power. Ultimately, the evaluation of utopianism depends on whether that belief can be suspended.

One further point which touches on freedom in utopia concerns the structural relationship of the individual with the state. The popular cliché, given vivid reality in such dystopias as Zamyatin's *We* and Karp's *One*, is that the individual is subordinated by coercion to the totalitarian state, which in fact represents an elite. The consequences are the loss of individual identity and enforced uniformity. Critics argue that the same would hold for utopia. This charge could be debated at great length, given that both the relation between the individual and the state and the concept of individuality are intangible, and open to many different conceptualizations, which are by and large unverifiable. Briefly, it can be said that, by contrast with reputedly totalitarian states, utopias strive to realize a voluntary mutual subordination of each individual to all other individuals, *qua* society. As Saint-Simon and Fourier insisted, remembering Rousseau's lectures against the humiliating dependence of man on man, the dependence of each on all is neither degrading nor debilitating. The concept of the state hardly existed for them: society was the supreme collective body. The purpose of a society so structured is, of course, co-operation for the common good – but the common good is defined as happiness for each. This characterization of utopia inevitably recalls the social contract theories, but departs from them in that it does not entail delegation to a government, nor, in the absence of a government, does it place the main emphasis on the maintenance of formal, 'natural' rights as did Locke, for example. The guarantee for the individual is the promise of happiness, a more flexible concept than that of particular rights, and some would say more dangerous on that account. So it appears that critics choose to conceptualize the role of the individual in utopia in an unflattering way when other descriptions are more suitable and more expressive of the utopian goal.

To recapitulate, the essence of the liberal-democratic opposition to utopianism lies in the fear that the postulate of a *summum bonum* places ends above means, overlooks human differentiation and the need for variety, and imposes an unchanging harmony and uniformity on a heterogeneous and historically developing humanity. This approach would necessarily suppress individuals and minorities, who need democratic protection. Further, the vision of the Good may be mistaken, or tailored to the advantage of the utopian. Since utopian citizens cannot take a decision to abandon the stipulated goal, the people are excluded from political power and utopia is, in effect, authoritarian. By contrast, ideal liberal democracy is fully participatory, and open-ended with respect to the ultimate good. Many of these accusations are grounded in the difference between empirical thinking and the theoretical mode which utopianism requires. While the liberal appears to be criticizing the phenomenal content of particular utopias, his real butt is the epistemology which engenders conviction and utopianism. Utopia can be defended against liberal criticism in a piecemeal fashion – for example, by showing that particular utopias are open or democratic – or, more effectively, by a defence of the underlying world-view. It can also be defended via an exposure of some of the weaknesses of the liberal's own beliefs, which are legion.

However, some utopians have provided a self-defence, in terms of an intentional rejection of liberal-democratic ideals. Democracy in practice has often been neither efficient nor harmonious and therefore was rejected by some nineteenth- and twentieth-century utopians as part of the irretrievable *status quo*. Post-Enlightenment utopians were

unenthusiastic about democracy at a time when reformers and revolutionaries looked to this political ideal for salvation. The complete
repudiation of politics and government by anarchists was not only an
indictment of democratic practice but also a theoretical statement,
reflecting the prevalent utopian conviction, most famously expounded
in Rousseau's *Social Contract* and echoed in Marx's vision of the classless society, that the ideal society would be a homogeneous community
in which rival interests would not need to be promoted, so that democratic politics would be unnecessary. This is the fundamental reason
for the omission of democracy from many utopias, but the issue here
is clouded since utopians have not universally rejected democratic
politics, but have often redefined it as 'administration' so as to
exclude the adversary element which we consider essential. (It is also
true that some liberals have wanted a minimal state not much different
from that of the anarchists - does this make them utopian?) It is the
advocacy of democracy for its own sake, with the implication of a
political apparatus and adversary politics, which conflicts with the
apolitical utopian ideal and, potentially, with the liberal ideal. Certainly,
the nature of utopia prevents a special value being placed on the expression of opinion, which democrats cherish, since an anticipatory
solution to utopia's dilemmas has been prepared by the utopian writer,
and debate would be superfluous. This, then, is why many utopians
prefer administration to government, a preference which further
scandalizes the critics of utopia, who associate administration with
bureaucracy, and bureaucracy with totalitarianism.

A separate, powerful reason for rejecting democracy is the espousal
of various forms of elite government, discussed in Chapter 2, which
puts expertise at a premium. Given that not all are capable of possessing
the same degree of specialist knowledge, specialists should have the
power, runs this argument. Such assertions directly contradict the
idealistic democrat's attribution of a modicum of wisdom and good
sense to every voter, but even critics of elitism have to concede that
the utopian's assumption corresponds more closely to reality. Clearly,
the 'intellectual elite' conception is not conducive to democratic
politics, even if modern elitist theories of democracy suggest that the
two forms can be reconciled in practice - at some cost to democracy.[35]
Equally, the organicist approach typical of many utopians from Plato
onwards is also theoretically opposed to the levelling assumptions of
democratic theory - and residual versions of the organic metaphor
persist, even in as 'scientific' a doctrine as modern Marxism. The
absence of democracy from utopia can thus be attributed to positive

convictions in many instances, and to arguments which must be taken seriously and not merely dismissed as crypto-totalitarian.

Modern convergences

While the polarities between LDT and utopianism are marked, the latter appears to be largely compatible with *radical* democratic theory (RDT) of the Rousseauesque or Marxian variety. The idea of the General Will combines well with the utopian concepts of a determinable common good and social harmony. The concepts of true knowledge and real interests subtend the General Will as well as the utopian ideal. True, utopians often choose to dispense with the apparatus of popular sovereignty – but then, so could Rousseau and Marx at a pinch, and indeed critics maintain that Rousseau's Legislator would displace his popular assembly, although he denied it. Many utopians would not follow Rousseau in arguing that political debate is intrinsically good, but such discussion was in fact intended to have a therapeutic effect, to constitute an airing of interests and grievances: it could not alter the political truth which the General Will embodied. The argument of RDT is that politics is co-extensive with life, and is not the specialized function which LDT makes of it. Talmon brands this view as a menacing 'politicization' of life, but rather it signifies that no distinction is made between private life and membership of society, a view shared by utopians. Since the separation of the public and private dimensions is crucial to LDT, their fusion in utopianism and RDT appears highly suspect and both forms of thought are condemned by the liberal school for the same reason.

Curiously, despite all the foregoing arguments, changes have taken place in LDT itself in the last thirty years which diminish the polarity between it and utopianism, at least in structural terms. Pluralist democratic theory (PDT) is implicitly concerned with system maintenance and stability and also countenances the acceptance of planning and the rejection of the orthodox liberal ideal of non-interventionist government: characteristics which, when found in utopianism, gave rise to the deepest disquiet. The all-pervasive idea of consensus recalls the notion of social harmony, and although pluralist democrats hesitate to define the *summum bonum*, they define the best *means* to it as being a pluralist democracy. It might be argued that PDT restricts its quasi-utopianism to the political system, leaving 'private' life untrammelled by the requirements of consensus and stability. Such a distinction is deceptive: commitment to the American way of life is certainly expected of the American citizen and orthodoxy within the consensus includes cultural, social and economic values. Modern democracy in operation has some of the features one would expect to find in utopia: many policies become bipartisan ('non-doctrinaire' or 'non-ideological') and so unchallengeable, and the effect of the consensual approach is to remove whole policy areas from the sphere of politics so that they become part of the 'natural' environment, not a matter for debate or choice - the most notorious example being defence.

But revised democratic theory diverges from utopianism in that it extols the virtues of an almost contentless system, transforming procedures into ideals. It cannot define and commit itself to a substantial, determinate Good because, by liberal logic, such a Good would entail its own imposition. 'What the people wills' or 'what interest groups want' are suitably insubstantial variables. But behind this democratic façade momentous decisions are taken by experts operating on long-term plans and promoting a *summum bonum* (which never reaches the debating chamber) best described as the survival of the cultural system[36] alias 'the good society itself in operation', as Lipset describes American democracy.[37] Posed in these terms, the gap between the utopian mode of thought and that which lies behind the operation of democracy in advanced industrial society seems smaller. While Popper and Hayek are still revered, 'constructivist rationalism' in the guise of expert planning has largely superseded politics, whether covertly or explicitly, and society no longer remotely resembles the catallaxy - if it ever did. The main divergence is that modern democracy disguises its aims, which therefore cannot be questioned, while utopianism makes public its Good. It appears, then, that the epistemological exclusiveness and many of the procedures of the archetypal utopia are well established in our own reality: such developments show that worldviews are in fact porous, and can interpenetrate. The antitheses on which liberal hostility to utopianism rests appear somewhat artificial in the light of reality. However, the 'utopia versus democracy' debate has been and is important in present political argument because anti-utopian attitudes are still invoked to discredit political doctrines smacking of utopianism, as in Bauman's critique of socialism.[38]

A final question which might be put to the liberal-democratic critic of utopianism is whether his own theory is not grounded equally in utopian assumptions. As Marx himself admitted, liberal doctrines had a revolutionary heyday, liberating man from feudal doctrines and hierarchies. Likewise, democracy was seen at one time as the unique solution for political despotism and oppression, the ideal form of government. The arguments presented in this chapter make manifest many liberal assumptions: the presumption that men's permanent interests are those felt in a liberal market society (egoistic, utility-maximizing, competitive), that men come to know these interests through free and rational choice, that such choice is indeed possible, and that it is the *summum bonum*. From the political writings of the last three centuries we could construct a model of liberal democracy which emphasizes the free will and equality of the individual and provides ideal conditions for him to pursue his self-interest which will automatically produce a fair and prosperous society. Adam Smith's Invisible Hand argument is the famous prototype of the *laissez-faire* utopia, and Hayek's catallaxy takes on a similarly utopian appearance. Both theories have the incidental virtue of elevating the existent into the realm of the Good, without even the rigmarole of proving that the existent is *desired*. The addition of regulative democratic institutions to the liberal model, although producing certain tensions, gives the liberal utopia a spiritual and expressive dimension, developing man's potential, as J. S. Mill argued in his advocacy of representative government.[39] In terms of providing the Good Life, liberal democracy decrees that everyone shall have what he/she wants – and works for. What could be more utopian?

The dystopian reality of liberal democracy arises, evidently, because of the constraint of scarce resources and because the premiss of human equality and equal opportunity is not fulfilled. Liberal democracy is thus a living example of the defects of a realized utopia. As the dominant ideology, it is forced to reject utopian assaults on its own position and, as this chapter has shown, in self-defence it attacks not only the content of utopian schemes but the presumptuousness of the utopian form of thinking. But many critics today would argue that liberal-democratic advanced capitalism is more rigid and closed and intolerant than the utopias which it condemns: Marcuse's critique of our one-dimensionality and repressive tolerance is a prime example of the genre.[40] The moral is therefore that reality bears out Mannheim's account of the historical transformation of utopia into ideology, and his assertion of the need for a constant supply of new utopias.

Suggested reading

The classic attacks on utopianism are to be found in K. Popper, *The Open Society and its Enemies*, and J. L. Talmon, *The Origins of Totalitarian Democracy* and *Political Messianism: The Romantic Phase*.

However, their views have been taken up and elaborated less emotionally and more analytically in such works as C. Brinton, 'Utopia and democracy', in F. E. Manuel (ed.), *Utopias and Utopian Thought*; J. W. Krutch, *The Measure of Man*; and J. Shklar, *After Utopia*. G. Kateb gives an account of the debate in *Utopia and its Enemies*. The stigma attached to utopianism as a disciplinarian or dictatorial form of thinking persists despite general scepticism about the concept of totalitarianism. J. C. Davis criticizes early utopias on precisely these grounds in his recent *Utopia and the Ideal Society*.

Part Two

Utopia and political practice

5 The social origins of the utopian impulse

The main aims of the first part of this book were to clarify the concepts of utopia and utopianism, and to establish some measure of the importance of utopian thinking in the development of Western political ideas. In order to appreciate the significance of utopianism as a theoretical device there can be no doubt that a great deal of attention must be paid to the analysis of utopias as literature; that is, one must consider in some depth the form and content of utopian writings, and come to some judgement concerning such matters as the author's logic and consistency, his ethical assumptions, the relationship between statements of fact and value, justifications given for major political recommendations, and so on. This line of questioning is clearly a key ingredient of the study of political theory. Indeed, some people would wish to go even further, and would argue that textual analysis is the heart and soul of political theory. From such a perspective the chief priorities are seen to be, first, the extraction of the essential meaning of the author's main concepts and theories, and second, the step-by-step investigation of the author's ability to persuade the reader that he (the author) has reached valid conclusions by way of sound argument. Accordingly, the issues of, first, interpreting the meaning of a particular thinker's work, and second, deciding whether that thinker is actually *right*, become the focus of attention in this kind of approach.

In order to perform these tasks some students may feel that all the information they need is to be found in the words of the text itself. Yet there may be others who consider it necessary to go beyond the text and gather additional information concerning the author's life, his background and experience, and the general socio-economic and political setting in which he produced his literary output. Such information may be required, for instance, to illuminate the meaning of certain technical terms and uncommon vocabulary, or to clarify obscure references to persons or facts with which the reader may not be familiar. A text which is fairly old, or which has been translated from a foreign language, or which is highly technical and specialized is perhaps most likely to give rise to these difficulties, but there are few writings in political theory which will not involve some problems of comprehension. It is most unlikely that the modern student of, say, Plato's *Republic* or More's *Utopia* could properly extract the full meaning of the text without relying on the help of a perceptive editor or commentator, or without doing some of his own further research.

From utopian theory to utopian practice

Once we are able to define, through textual analysis, the values, attitudes and beliefs which find expression in the works of a particular political theorist, how should we then proceed in order to actually assess the worth of that theorist's ideas? The answer to this question must depend partly on the purpose or purposes which the theorist concerned sets out to achieve. As far as utopias are concerned, it was seen in Chapter 1 that there are a number of quite distinct purposes which they may be intended to serve, and it would hardly seem reasonable, therefore, to judge all utopias according to precisely the same criteria. A utopia whose main aim is to highlight the defects of an existing society (the essentially critical utopia) demands different treatment from one which is offered as a supposedly practical manifesto for establishing a new, alternative society (the constructive utopia). In the first case, the utopia is not necessarily intended to be taken too seriously as a programme of action; in the second case it obviously is. It is always possible, of course, that some readers may find the first utopia so compelling that, even though its author did not intend it to be taken too seriously as a blueprint for the future, a movement may emerge urging the achievement of this utopia in practice, or at least inspired directly in its ambitions by this particular utopian vision. A good example of this is provided by the reception of More's *Utopia*. The main purpose of this work seems to have been satirical and critical, that is, it attempted to reveal the evils and inadequacies of English social organization in the early sixteenth century. Yet many later thinkers were sufficiently impressed by More's description of an alternative society to take it quite seriously as a basis for their own theories of social construction. Three hundred years after More's book first appeared, Etienne Cabet, exiled in England by the French Government (1834-9), read *Utopia* for the first time, and by his own admission the experience was instrumental in his subsequent conversion to communism. Many of More's ideas found their way into Cabet's own utopia, *Voyage en Icarie* (1840), and within a relatively short time Icarianism formed a spectacular mass movement of between 100,000 and 200,000 adherents. A text intended originally as a satirical essay, a work of social criticism, had been reinterpreted by Cabet as a guide to political action, and with staggering, although short-lived, success.[1]

Anyone wishing to judge the importance of a particular utopia such as that by More is thus faced with three quite distinct issues. First, there is the question of the text's validity as an exercise in political argument (offered in the case of More as a striking criticism of sixteenth-century English society). Second, there may be some constructive dimension to the text, some vision of a possible alternative society (even if this was not stressed by the author himself). Third, there is the work's historical influence and its capacity to arouse enthusiasm and support, and to stimulate the active efforts of individuals or groups of people who may wish to achieve certain goals represented by this picture of an ideal society (goals possibly reinterpreted and restated in modified form by a later thinker, as was the case with Cabet's use of More's book).

Traditionally, particularly in the English-speaking world, the study of political theory has tended to concentrate on the first two areas of concern, while the third has generally developed within the framework of other disciplines more firmly rooted in some kind of sociological perspective. This is an emphasis which has been particularly conspicuous in the study of utopianism. In recent years, however, there has arisen a new interest in the processes by which political ideas enter into the world of political practice, an interest which involves not only the attempt to give a descriptive account of the way in which ideas have had a practical influence, but also the realization that some explanation is necessary as to why some ideas are politically more influential than others, and why the impact of a particular set of ideas often seems to vary from one set of social circumstances to another. In the second part of this book we set out to deal with these issues as they relate to the specific case of utopian thought. One of the reasons why utopianism deserves to be taken seriously (complementing the reasons already outlined in Chapter 1) is that it has so often been a stimulus to political activity, and has formed the basis for many kinds of movements and organizations. Even the student who finally comes to the conclusion that all utopias must be condemned because of what he considers to be their lack of realism or their illogicality must acknowledge that utopias have frequently had an impressive practical, as well as intellectual, influence.

In order to understand this practical dimension of utopianism we certainly cannot afford to rely solely on our reading of utopian texts, as some people who adopt a more traditional and analytical approach to the language of political argument may be inclined to do. The kind of additional information referred to earlier, concerning an author's life, his background and experience, and the general socio-economic and political setting in which he produced his literary output, furnishes us with vital clues as to the power of a particular utopia to stir the imagination and sentiments of readers (and indeed of non-readers who may nevertheless be impressed by what they learn about this utopia at second hand), and to mobilize them into political activity. Without these clues the search for an adequate explanation of utopianism's influence is likely to lead to poor and unconvincing results.

To begin with, we need to consider the question of how and why particular concepts of utopia arise, for it seems evident that utopian theories do not fall from the sky according to the dictates of pure chance, or through some divine intervention, but must surely be the products of particular social conditions and the circumstances to be found in particular societies at particular stages in their development. The utopian impulse finds expression in particular theories of utopia, such as those associated with Enlightenment rationalism, early socialism, Comtean positivism or modern psychological behaviourism. These theories could not have emerged at *any* stage of history (although one can obviously point to earlier anticipation of all of these cases), but came to flourish in specific circumstances favourable to their growth. Utopias are the response of particular individuals and groups to quite specific problems and difficulties which they have encountered either directly through personal experience, or more indirectly through scholarly investigation. While it may be possible to define these problems and difficulties in very general, universal, terms (e.g. the problem of individual freedom versus the authority of the state), they are usually posed in the form of more concrete manifestations (e.g. the growth of hostility towards the teachings of an established church, the rise of a new political elite, the development of new forms of economic production) to which the author in question is seeking to respond. Utopias are the work of particular minds attempting to solve a particular problem or series of problems (often of a very practical nature) which have arisen due to a certain, quite specific, configuration of social, economic and political conditions.

Early socialism as a response to capitalist industrialism

The point being made here can perhaps best be clarified through the use of one particular, and very important, illustrative case study: that of the socialist utopianism of the first half of the nineteenth century, especially the schools of thought which flourished between about 1830 and 1848.[2] Why did utopian socialism flourish during this period? Such a question has usually been dismissed as irrelevant to the study of political theory, but it is our contention that the question must be answered if the nature of utopian socialism and its influence (both intellectual and practical) is to be fully understood. Whereas an ortho-dox attempt to answer the question might involve looking at utopian socialism as the expression of rather abstract conceptions such as romanticism, rationalism and the spirit of progress, we wish to argue that a more reliable and more informative approach must take as its basis methods of investigation grounded in a more sociological frame-work of analysis. The central aim must be to locate the social origins of the key, constitutive values, attitudes and beliefs associated with utopian socialism at this time. It must be admitted that this is a difficult enterprise, since there are still many gaps in our basic knowledge of the social factors which were at work. We simply do not have all the background information which we require in order to develop a com-prehensive explanatory theory. But what evidence does exist suggests that the starting-point for an explanation is an appreciation of the broad socio-economic changes which were occurring in Western societies during this period, and to which utopian socialism seems to have been a direct response.

The period in which the early socialists were formulating their theories was one of widespread socio-economic upheaval, a period in which the development of capitalist industrialism was causing in all Western societies (although at different rates of change) a severe dislo-cation to the situation of many social groups. Most importantly, it was a period in which a new working class was being created. This class was not an integrated whole, however, but was very clearly divided between different occupations: between the agricultural and manu-facturing sectors, and, within manufacturing, between artisans and handicraft workers on the one hand, whose status and livelihood were threatened by new forms of mechanized production, and, on the other hand, the labour force employed in the factories. As a consequence of this process of dislocation, traditional social values associated with an essentially pre-capitalist (perhaps even pre-industrial) society lost much of their relevance, and new norms were called for which were more appropriate to the stage of socio-economic development attained in the Western countries. The essential constitutive values of utopian socialism may be seen as a response to this problem. They represent various attempts to formulate new normative systems in a period of upheaval. Inevitably, however, these normative systems retained links with the older, more traditional values which were being displaced. This contradiction, if one may call it that, is to be seen first of all in the idea of social harmony, which was undoubtedly the key goal towards which all the utopian socialists directed their efforts.

The actual word 'harmony' is encountered in much of the utopian literature and in many utopian schemes during the early nineteenth century, from George Rapp's Harmony Society (a community of German separatists who settled in America in 1803) to the systems of Fourier ('harmonism' was the supreme human passion, and the future social order would be known as Harmony), Weitling (see, for example, his *Garantien der Harmonie und Freiheit*) and Owen (whose two major experimental communities were at New Harmony and Harmony Hall, Queenwood). Other thinkers (for example, Saint-Simon, the Saint-Simonian disciples, Cabet) may not have placed quite so much emphasis on the word itself, but the idea for which it stood was clearly implicit in their thought. One might argue that all utopian thinkers throughout history have put forward a vision of social harmony. In the early nineteenth century, however, the concept assumed a new significance with a number of very specific connotations. It derived in part from a Newtonian view of the universe as an orderly, perfectly integrated, system; and there can be little doubt that Saint-Simon and Fourier, both of whom drew analogies between laws of social attraction (which each believed he had discovered) and Newton's laws of universal gravitation, were impressed by this scientific argument. Saint-Simon also admired the physiological harmony of the human body, and saw no reason why such an arrangement could not be reproduced in society. (This is an outlook which reappears in the writings of Cabet.) The idea of harmony suggested certain artistic principles, too, especially in music (Fourier, once again, was fond of this analogy); and it even linked up with the theories of the liberal political economists, particularly Adam Smith and Jean-Baptiste Say, who claimed to have discovered a natural harmony of economic interests in society. But perhaps even more important than all these suggestions is the fact that the notion of harmony implied a distinctive view of social relations according to which a great premium was placed on the capacity of members of society to live together without conflict and with common interests, united by ties of true love and affection. One of the most usual ways of presenting future society was in the image of a large, happy family, and in the case of some utopian socialists, notably Owen, Fourier and the Saint-Simonians, this actually implied superseding the traditional, more limited nuclear family (regarded as a bastion of self-interest, antiquated religious doctrine and social divisions), and allowing sentiments of love (including, perhaps, feelings of sexual desire) to find expression much more spontaneously and with the minimum of restriction.

The social origins of these ideas are not difficult to discern. The vision of a future state of harmony was born amid conditions which were quite obviously lacking in harmony. Revolutionary upheaval, socio-economic dislocation caused by new mechanized methods of capitalist production, the decline of traditional sources of legitimacy and authority – these were painful facts of life during the period in question, especially painful for those groups, such as the artisans and handicraft workers, whose life-style and mode of work were threatened most directly by the pressures of change. Any vision of the future, if it was to appeal to those groups suffering most under these conditions of social transformation, had to promise salvation from the worst evils, and salvation was bound to be seen in terms of the opposite of upheaval and instability, in other words as harmony.

In this respect the utopian socialists put forward a radically new view of politics. The idea of politics, traditionally associated with competing interests and the resolution of conflict, was now seen to be in need of reformulation. Politics would be transformed into an activity concerned with rational-scientific questions, especially in the sphere of economics. Harmony would require administration rather than government, a notion emphasized particularly by Saint-Simon and Weitling.[3] It would also involve the rejection of individualism (equated with a conflict of interests) and its replacement by some more collective form of organization.

This idea of an alternative to individualism can be clarified more precisely by examining three further concepts which were essential ingredients of the theories of the early socialists, and which served as components of the broader notion of harmony: association, community, co-operation. Association was a particularly important idea. As one commentator has put it, it had the force of a kind of messianic vision during this period.[4] Its power stemmed from the widespread demand voiced by workers in the early nineteenth century to be granted the right to associate for various social and economic purposes. At a time when workers were frequently deprived of this right, the call for association represented very positive, concrete aspirations. In

England, for example, the anti-combination laws of 1799 and 1800 were attacked by English utopians such as Owen. Their repeal in 1824 allowed certain kinds of association to be formed, and thus represented a partial realization of early socialist aims. In France, on the other hand, the 1791 Le Chapelier law (which abolished guilds) and subsequent additions to it made 'anything like the English trade-union movement impossible'.[5] Hence the continuing ferment caused by demands for association in France in the 1830s and 1840s, culminating in the efforts of the revolutionaries in 1848 to use producers' associations as the basis for a new 'democratic and social republic'. In Germany the situation was different again owing to the fact that the traditional guild system still existed. The distinction in status between masters and journeymen was widening, however, and this prompted many groups of journeymen to support demands for the creation of new workers' associations as an alternative to the guilds. Such demands gained much support among the émigré workers in London and Paris, where, for obvious reasons, German workers were influenced directly by the beliefs of their English and French counterparts.

Association promised a variety of future benefits: at least the achievement of better working conditions through increased bargaining power, and perhaps even the ownership of property by workers who could not afford to buy property individually. Buchez, who for a time supported the Saint-Simonian movement, believed that in this way one could eliminate the capitalists.[6] It was also argued that if workers stopped competing with one another on the labour market, and replaced competition by association, the downward trend in wages – a trend which was regarded as the inevitable consequence of competition between workers – would be reversed, and there would be greater security of employment. But as well as looking forward to the future, association also hearkened back to the past, to the actual experience of solidarity and combination among workers in guilds, trade and craft clubs, the French *compagnonnages*[7] and so on. Such experience was important, in particular, for workers with clearly definable skills: the artisans and handicraft workers, the journeymen and apprentices. The consciousness of association in a special trade or craft was here vitally significant, quite different from the position in which the workers employed in the new factories found themselves.

'Association' usually seems to have been used by the utopian socialists to denote a small-scale group organized in a particular occupation or place of work. The Saint-Simonians, however, took great exception to this vision of a society built upon numerous small associations, and they advocated instead 'universal association', a scheme intended to unite entire societies and, ultimately, whole continents and indeed the total population of the world.[8] This is certainly one very important reason why, in the 1830s, the Saint-Simonians came to be widely regarded as advocates of a conspicuously authoritarian, perhaps even the most authoritarian, version of socialism.

After association, another very crucial concept for the utopians was community. At first sight it is tempting to dismiss this as a somewhat vague goal, but the notion of community, as part of the total vision of a harmonious society, grew out of certain very real experiences of a sense of common living and common identity shared by persons living in distinct locations, belonging to, say, a friendly society or trade club, pursuing their occupations in the same workplace, or even attending the same church. Many social historians have revealed the importance of this community identity among workers during the industrial revolution. Thus, to take just one illustration:

Another interesting phenomenon observable in Lancashire was the perpetuation of semi-independent communities on the outskirts of industrial towns whose members felt a strongly particularistic rather than urban loyalty, and this doubtless inhibited class development in these areas. Similarly, many cotton operatives persisted in feelings of loyalty towards a mill-community and an individual mill-owner, accepting the latter's political tutelage rather than striking out politically on class lines.[9]

In time the idea of community assumed the specific connotation of actually going out to a new location and building a new village, town or workplace. Hence the mania for experimental communities and deliberate environmental planning associated with many utopian socialists and their followers throughout the nineteenth century.

In France the term *commune* had obvious implications as a unit of local government. There was no problem, therefore, about understanding the general meaning of *communauté*. A difficulty did arise, however, when *communauté* was used by Cabet and others to mean a system based on communal ownership of property, for this was a much more specific meaning than had previously been understood. In this way community became inextricably linked with communism. And this in turn gave rise to an ambiguity, because in France at least communism tended to be associated with insurrectionary methods (as advocated, for instance, by Blanqui), whereas Cabet recommended a strategy rooted firmly in pacifism.

Co-operation was a third crucial idea implicit in the utopian socialist's picture of social harmony. As with association and community, the concept of co-operation tended to suggest both something which had actually been experienced – for example, the co-operation among workers in various clubs and friendly societies, or even the co-operation between masters and apprentices in certain trades and skilled occupations – and also something yet to be attained in other spheres of working life. The small workshop typical of pre- and early capitalist society presented the utopian socialists with a ready-made image of true co-operation. The modern factory, although still in its infancy in the first half of the nineteenth century, threatened to destroy co-operation through its separation of employers and employees, and also its dehumanizing effects on the individual worker. Hence the meaning of co-operation became perfectly clear; and indeed the rise of, for example, the co-operative societies in Britain and the *sociétés de secours mutuel* in France[10] showed that co-operation was also a realistic goal.

The co-operative principle was further extended by Owen and Fourier, who believed that it could offer an alternative mode of social organization to capitalism. According to this more specific view, the co-operative philosophy demanded that a club or community should be controlled by those who made some direct contribution to the production of wealth, and the aim should be to distribute any resulting income among these producers, thus avoiding the employer's profit margin. This could perhaps be regarded as a new principle. Yet at the same time many advocates of co-operation saw the scheme's virtue in terms of its ability to permit workers collectively to acquire wealth. As was mentioned earlier in relation to the idea of association, the suggestion here was that workers might not be able to afford property individually, but they could when grouped together in co-operation. This would seem to be not so much an attack on ownership as a desire to spread the benefits of ownership to groups of people normally deprived of them. And the fact that Owen came to advocate communism, while Fourier always defended the institution of private property, emphasizes the ambiguity involved in these early co-operative schemes.

From the above comments it can be seen, we hope, that the emphasis on harmony, with its further suggestions of association, community and co-operation, was not a totally vague, abstract construction, as might be suspected from many accounts of early socialist thought. It was much more than a romantic vision of the future, for it was derived directly from the actual experiences of men in small-scale groups, and from certain quite specific social and cultural traditions. Thus, the sense of association, community and co-operation grew out of life in the village, town, commune and workshop, or among members of a particular religious sect. This key idea of attaining social harmony was not, therefore, entirely unrealistic (as the designation 'utopian' is frequently taken to mean), although one might argue that as the capitalist system developed, it became increasingly difficult to achieve in practice. In fact, when the utopians came to work out detailed strategies by which to achieve harmony, they often floundered, and disagreements, controversies and heated disputes became characteristic of the socialist movement in the 1830s and 1840s. Thus, although they might agree on the importance of striving for association, community and co-operation, socialist thinkers could not agree at all on the specific steps required in order to make these qualities operational. The consequence was a range of what may be called strategic value conflicts, the most important of which will now be considered in order to illustrate how different utopian thinkers, writing in response to the same problems, can actually be led to very different practical recommendations reflecting various interpretations of those problems, interpretations which are in turn rooted in a range of socially formed assumptions and attitudes.

Towards the socialist utopia: six strategic dilemmas

1 Industrialism versus anti-industrialism

Probably the most basic conflict of all concerned the whole question of the desirability of an industrialized society. To the utopians industrialism implied, first and foremost, the advent of mechanization and factory employment. From one point of view this promised remarkable levels of economic growth and productivity, welcomed unreservedly by Saint-Simon in his enthusiasm for *le système industriel* (an enthusiasm carried on after his death by his disciples), by Cabet, who described his Icarian doctrine as being totally opposed to agrarianism, and also by Owen. But on the other hand it threatened the livelihood and status of artisans and handicraft workers, who faced the prospect of being taken away from their homes and workshops and being either 'proletarianized' (i.e. pushed into factory employment) or made completely redundant as the machines took over. Agricultural workers, too, were likely to see industrialism as a threat to their way of life, although Saint-Simon urged them to regard agriculture as a part of industry (he adopted such an outlook because he viewed agriculture as a productive occupation and therefore no different from manufacturing in that specific sense); and Owen foresaw a need for more, not fewer, agricultural workers once the superiority of spade husbandry over the plough was recognized. The strongest defences of agrarianism and handicraft are to be found in the writings of Fourier and Weitling, who were particularly concerned to remove the threat which industrialism posed to more traditional – and in their view, more noble – occupations.[11]

There were economic arguments, also, to support hostility to industrialism. The spread of machinery was widely seen as a cause of overproduction, an idea associated particularly with the theories of Sismondi, who accordingly wanted to halt industrialization. In addition the policy of actually destroying machinery was adopted in practice by many workers' movements in the early nineteenth century, from the Luddites in Britain to the Silesian weavers who revolted in 1844. Even Chartism advocated workers' opposition to mechanization.

2 *Private property versus common ownership*

After the question of industrialism, the next most divisive issue concerned property ownership. Some utopian socialists, notably Saint-Simon and Fourier, saw no need at all to get rid of private property as long as owners were obliged to put their property to productive use. The Saint-Simonian disciples, also, did not seek to abolish private property, but thought it desirable to put an end to the transfer of property rights through inheritance. Instead the allocation of property was to be determined by the state authorities, acting in the general interests of society. Other thinkers, however, identified private property as the basis of capitalist exploitation and advocated schemes of communism (the later Owen, Cabet, Weitling). Such an identification is not surprising. Under modern working conditions there was a clear physical separation between those who owned property and those who did not. Property ownership brought many advantages apart from the obvious pecuniary ones. Voting rights, for example, were usually related to wealth in the form of property. Furthermore, as has already been mentioned, for workers who could not afford to purchase property as individuals, communism seemed a very realistic alternative. This particular idea motivated many of the founders of experimental communities, especially those in America, where land was readily available for communal purchase. In certain workers' associations, too, principles of common ownership actually operated, for example in some co-operative societies and in the French *sociétés de secours mutuel*. Here is yet another instance in which a particular value grew out of experience, an instance which tends to confirm the perceptive point made by Rosabeth Moss Kanter:

Utopian values may be after-the-fact explanations for social practices that arose accidentally, from expediency alone, to fit the needs of particular individuals, or to help maintain the group. A few nineteenth-century groups . . . first began to share property communally as the result of pressing economic circumstances rather than consciously to implement a set of coherent values; utopian ideals were later used to justify the practice.[12]

Communism could not be expected, though, to appeal to all workers. Many artisans placed great emphasis on the virtues of private property. In many skilled occupations workers usually possessed their own tools; and through apprenticeship schemes they could hope one day to achieve the status of master craftsman, employing a number of workers in a workshop. In such circumstances many groups of workers felt that they could legitimately strive to attain ownership of property. If one examines the working-class literature that emerged in the second quarter of the nineteenth century, one finds that private property was frequently seen as a fundamental right, and any opposition to private property was accordingly condemned as unnatural. Thus, to take an example, the important French working-class newspaper *Echo de la Fabrique* confidently dismissed all schemes for communal ownership as totally unrealistic, preferring to support the more moderate theories of Fourier.[13] And in America the disciples of Fourier, including Albert Brisbane, attacked the Owenites for their rejection of private property.[14] There was a fundamental conflict here between two concepts of economic equality. One emphasized the equal right of all men to own property, a right which, once operational, would inevitably lead to a certain amount of inequality of wealth, because some individuals would put their property to productive use, while others would not have the necessary ability or inclination. The second concept saw equality in terms of a pooling of property rights, a handing over of property to the community as a whole. It is therefore not very helpful simply to say that the early socialists were egalitarians. There were two quite distinct egalitarian traditions, one much more radical than the other.

3   *Religion versus secularization*

The question of religion posed major problems for the utopian socialists, One reaction was to see religion as a thing of the past, belonging to an age of superstition and no longer acceptable in the light of modern science. Such a view characterized much of Fourier's work, although it was modified as Fourier became interested in the possibility of love becoming a new kind of religious bond (an idea presented only very sketchily, and mainly in writings which remained unpublished during the author's lifetime). Owen, too, was associated with an attitude of hostility towards religion until the early 1830s, but he subsequently reconciled rationalism and religion to such an extent that he presented the 'new moral world' as the Second Coming of Christ. Other utopians, very much in the tradition of Rousseau and the French Revolution, remained convinced that religion was a social necessity. One possibility was that science itself could become the basis for a new religious faith (an idea developed in the early writings of Saint-Simon). Secondly, a new doctrine of social mysticism, more sentimental than scientific, could be formulated (this was the conviction of the Saint-Simonians). A third possibility was that Christianity could be reformed, brought up to date, and made scientific and more radical (this was the proposal of the later Saint-Simon, Cabet, and Weitling).

There were in fact so many versions of new, reformed Christianities and religions of humanity during this period that one must seek some social explanation of the tendency. To begin with, the expectation, shared by all these thinkers, of a completely transformed social existence clearly lent itself to a presentation in messianic terms. This was particularly true in the case of France, where utopian socialism often appealed to disillusioned Catholics. In Britain and America the religious ideas of the early socialists were undoubtedly influenced by the great revival of millenarianism – that is, the anticipation of the thousand-year reign of Christ on earth, with its consequent consolidation of peace, justice and fraternity – that occurred on both sides of the Atlantic at this time, and which found expression in numerous sects and movements of every kind. Many commentators have noted how the spirit and even the vocabulary of millenarianism became increasingly important ingredients in Owen's thinking following his return from the New Harmony community in America, and it is clear that this shift cannot be fully understood without reference to the more general rise of religious millenarianism which was then taking place, and to which Owen had to respond.

Another factor which must be taken into account is that to many working-class groups, especially in France, religion seemed to be as natural an institution as private property, and its demise was therefore unthinkable. Furthermore, the principles of harmony, association, community and co-operation represented a rejection of selfishness and individualism, and expressed a growing concern for humanity and the common good – values traditionally associated with the inspiration of religion, especially the Christian religion; and it is not surprising that during the period in question these principles appealed particularly to groups who already had some religious, usually Christian, outlook in common. There were, for instance, many religious sects who turned to utopian socialism mainly because their religious rights were not recognized in their own societies. Many of the groups who emigrated from Europe to America in order to form experimental communities did so in an effort to practise their own religions free from persecution. The Judaic element also played a part in the emergence of some socialist schools, most notably the Saint-Simonian movement after 1825. On the other hand, a distinctly anti-semitic attitude marked some aspects of Fourier's teachings, especially his vehement attacks on the commercial classes.[15]

The point is also worth mentioning that religion was often able to serve the crucial function of creating positive commitment to a socialist movement. It was a most effective mechanism for recruiting support and for creating that sense of attachment without which no movement can endure for any length of time. It is true, of course, that none of the new utopian religions was very successful; but what is important is that religion was often decisive in the formative, take-off, stage of modern socialism. Interestingly enough, the most successful early socialist movement, Cabet's Icarianism, was unashamedly based on a doctrine of the new Christianity, a doctrine which stressed, in particular, the primitive communism of the early Christians.

4 Revolution versus gradualism

It has already been remarked that the utopian socialists' insistence on harmony had certain counter-revolutionary implications. Many of them did indeed reject violence altogether. But one specific strand of the early socialist movement persistently advocated revolution: the tradition of insurrection stemming from Babeuf (leader of the Conspiracy of Equals, 1796), further developed by Barbès and Blanqui (who directed the Paris uprising of 1839), and adopted by Weitling. For many years,

particularly in France, communism was widely regarded as being synonymous with insurrection, and it was often contrasted with socialism
for this reason. Yet Cabet confused matters by putting forward a theory
of pacific communism: he wanted his movement to be out in the open,
legitimate and respectable rather than being hidden away underground
in the form of a secret society.

It is also the case that revolutionary methods were not in keeping
with the experience of certain groups of workers in the early nineteenth
century. Many workers, after all, enjoyed reasonably good relations
with their employers. The master–apprentice relationship in the workshop was frequently of this nature. In these circumstances revolution
seemed inappropriate. Only when the modern factory took over,
bringing with it a different set of industrial relations, did revolutionary
attitudes gain more widespread support. One of the most valuable
insights offered by economic and social historians is that the level of
workers' radicalism during the industrial revolution varied from area
to area and from industry to industry depending on the social structure
of the locality in question and the framework of industrial relations.[16]
A number of excellent studies of labour unrest in France, dealing particularly with the revolutions of 1830 and 1848 and the Lyons uprisings
of 1831 and 1834, show that it was among fairly specific groups of
workers and in distinct locations that revolutionary doctrines had their
greatest impact.[17] Often thinkers who normally rejected revolution
changed their outlook through their involvement in particular revolutionary situations. Thus the Saint-Simonian disciples, usually advocates of gradualism, became very conscious of the revolutionary fervour
of the workers in the 1831 Lyons uprising, and this prompted them to
modify their theories accordingly.[18]

There were other reasons, too, why many utopian socialists opposed
violent methods of change. There was a strong emphasis in their theories
on the social question as opposed to the strictly political, and so
political revolution could be dismissed as being somewhat irrelevant.
In addition socialism was often viewed as an experimental tradition, an
approach which encouraged groups to gradually build a socialist community, usually on a small scale; and this meant that comprehensive
revolution, involving the overthrow of an entire society, was quite
inappropriate.

5 Statism versus communitarianism

This leads on to another controversial issue: whereas some thinkers (for example, Saint-Simon and his disciples, Cabet, Weitling) envisaged their utopias in terms of complete societies under quite a high degree of centralized control, others (notably Owen and Fourier) emphasized the need for small-scale, decentralized, communitarian schemes. Thus there is a striking contrast between, say, Saint-Simon's vision of future industrial society and the Saint-Simonians' conception of 'universal association', on the one hand, and Owen's plan for numerous 'home colonies' or Fourier's Phalanxes on the other. (Fourier was most specific: every Phalanx should have between 1500 and 1800 people.) With Cabet and Weitling it has to be admitted that a contradiction arises, for although they advocated the transformation of whole societies, circumstances eventually persuaded them to put their ideas into operation at the communitarian level in the United States.

This disagreement has remained at the heart of disputes about the proper organization of socialist society right up to the present day. But it is doubtful whether it has been a source of more tension than during the early nineteenth century. At that time there was a direct and uncompromising opposition between those who urged total societal change and those who wished to achieve change through more modest schemes of experimentation. The latter view linked up most directly with those principles of association, community and co-operation discussed earlier, for it was at the local level or in a specific group of workers that those principles could be most meaningfully expressed. Also, it was widely seen to be more realistic to strive for social improvement through small communities than through large-scale organization. In America, of course, it was fairly easy to adopt this approach, since there was every opportunity to start new communities. In Britain and the countries of continental Europe, however, it was less easy. Owen probably had most success with his scheme for 'home colonies' in Britain; but even he considered the prospects to be better in America, in company with many other utopians who shared the view that socialist society could most easily be created on virgin soil.

6 Democratic versus authoritarian organization

Linked to this latter issue is the problem of whether the utopian socialists subscribed to basically democratic or authoritarian values. As was seen in Chapter 4, many commentators have argued that the vast majority of utopian schemes throughout history have tended to be authoritarian, chiefly because of the characteristic utopian emphasis on harmony, consensus, the avoidance of conflict and the rejection of individualism.[19] As far as the principal utopian socialists are concerned, it is undoubtedly true that with the exception of Owen the idea of democracy seldom entered into their detailed blueprints for future organization. On the other hand, there was a general awareness of the importance of certain freedoms, not only those of a legal-constitutional nature but perhaps even more significantly economic and social freedoms, which would nowadays be regarded as central to democracy. The Saint-Simonians, interestingly enough, with their constant emphasis on the need to preserve hierarchy in social and political organization, were frequently condemned by rival utopian groups for what were considered to be fundamentally illiberal attitudes.[20] In this respect, at least, one might say that some real concern was being expressed for values of a democratic nature.

Generally speaking, the democratic/authoritarian distinction reflected the communitarian/statist distinction, for it was the thinkers who were interested in small-scale experimentation, such as Owen and Fourier, who seemed to care most for democracy in the sense of individual and group self-determination. But perhaps even more significant is the fact that where there was some concern for democratic participation, this seemed to grow out of the actual experience of democratic methods in workers' associations, clubs, friendly societies, etc. Thus Saint-Simon and his disciples, who had no such experience, placed little emphasis on democracy. Owen, Fourier and also Weitling, however, whose doctrines were more closely linked to the activities of co-operative organizations, had much more of a positive contribution to make.

Factors which conspired against democracy in utopian socialist schemes were numerous and varied. The workers involved in these movements had little or no experience of political democracy at the national level. Their membership of a utopian movement probably represented their first mobilization in any real action group, and this meant that strong leadership rather than extensive democratization was likely to be emphasized. Furthermore, democracy was often equated with insurrection and militancy, characteristics which workers frequently wished to avoid. Jones and Anservitz have also shown the importance of charismatic authority in movements during this period, and it is certainly true, as they point out, that at times of social instability large groups of people often exhibit a remarkable willingness to support movements dominated by an individual leader or leaders who display charismatic qualities.[21] In the case of the utopian socialists, this aspect is very important precisely because so many of their doctrines assumed the form of religious instruction. Finally, one might add the sociological observation that any attempt to create a new scheme of social organization is likely to be more successful if it is carried through under strong leadership. There is abundant evidence to show that the most successful utopian communities in the nineteenth century were also in several key respects very authoritarian.[22]

It is hoped that this particular case study of the rise of socialist utopias in the early nineteenth century has served to highlight the inadequacies of analysing utopian ideas in purely logical and conceptual terms through such questions as: Were the utopian socialists right? Did they argue sensibly and coherently? Were their conclusions related to valid assumptions and verifiable observations? While this kind of approach is clearly of some use, and is indeed indispensable for certain purposes, it does overlook the fact that ideas often emerge and gain acceptance not because they are particularly logical or reasonable, but because they give expression to the deep-rooted aspirations of specific groups in society. There can be little doubt that the essential constitutive values of utopian socialism emerged primarily as the response of certain identifiable groups to the impact which socio-economic upheaval was having on their traditional ways of life.

The roots of transcendence: conflict, protest and hope

Further light is shed on this relationship between social situation and the emergence of utopian theories by taking up one of the key arguments of Mannheim's book, *Ideology and Utopia*. We have already referred, in Chapter 3, to Mannheim's view that the most important distinguishing feature of utopian thought is the way in which it completely 'transcends' the existing social situation through its *practical* capacity 'to shatter either partially or wholly, the order of things prevailing at the time'.[23] Utopias urge men to break out of the confines of actuality and establish a new world because the contents of utopias 'can never be realized in the societies in which they exist, and because one could not live and act according to them within the limits of the existing social order'.[24] At any particular time in any particular society it is unlikely that all groups will wish to reject the actual social situation and strive to bring about in practice a new, utopian alternative which of necessity requires the abolition of that which exists. It is to be expected that certain groups, perhaps just one small section of society, will exhibit this utopian propensity, while other groups, possibly constituting the majority of society, will resist change and will operate within 'the world-view characteristic of the period'.[25] As Mannheim points out, some sets of ideas may *appear* to 'transcend' reality in the sense that they point to the possibility of a transformed existence, but if, *in practice*, they simply integrate themselves into the social situation as it exists, they then remain ideologies rather than utopias. For example,

> As long as the clerically and feudally organized medieval order was able to locate its paradise outside of society, in some other-worldly sphere which transcended history and dulled its revolutionary edge, the idea of paradise was still an integral part of medieval society. Not until certain social groups embodied those wish-images into their actual conduct, and tried to realize them, did these ideologies become utopias.[26]

According to this argument, utopias are not to be defined simply as idealistic 'wish-images'; they are 'wish-images' which, *when put into practice,* shatter the existing social situation. Utopianism is the characteristic attitude of those groups in society which are so fundamentally dissatisfied with the existing order that they refuse to integrate themselves into it, and work instead to establish an alternative system in which they believe they (and possibly everyone else as well) can achieve complete happiness and fulfilment.

The kinds of dissatisfaction which lead some social groups to adopt a utopian response to their existing situation do not fit neatly into any one single category, but a study of the history of utopianism shows that they have tended to derive from an acute sense of oppression and alienation, and the awareness of being threatened by the pressure of socio-economic upheaval, and by the forces and activities stemming from the beliefs and activities of other, opposing, groups. The origins of nineteenth-century utopian socialism have already been examined as one particular case in point, and it has been seen there that the severe social dislocation experienced by certain sections of society under the impact of capitalist industrialism led directly to the formulation of utopian proposals for what was considered by these groups to be a much better, indeed perfectly harmonious, world. As the case of utopian socialism demonstrates, however, the fear of an existing social reality is not sufficient in itself to give rise to utopianism. What is also required is an accompanying conviction that this reality (evil) can be transformed into a new utopia (goodness) through some kind of practical programme of action. Without this conviction the fear of reality will find expression either in pessimistic despair and a deep sense of hopelessness, or in the quest for salvation not in this earthly life but in a heavenly existence beyond death. (In some cultures the doctrine of personal reincarnation has served to provide people with yet another route to happiness, but this does not really count as a vision of *collective* salvation such as is offered by the notion of a heavenly paradise.)

Historically, the conviction that something positive can be done to transform existing conditions of misery into a new world of true harmony and happiness has invariably spread as a result of the deliberate efforts of various individual thinkers or groups of thinkers who have assumed the mantle of leadership, and have usually presented themselves as great intellectuals, prophets, revolutionaries or even messiahs. In the Western world up to the seventeenth century the single most important source of inspiration for such leaders was what is often referred to as the 'eschatology' of Christianity, with its firm prediction of a final, thousand-year (millennial) state of earthly existence characterized by peace and universal brotherly love, and inaugurated by the Second Coming of Christ. Norman Cohn, in his book *The Pursuit of the Millennium*, has shown that until the fourth century Christian theologians usually accepted this doctrine of terrestrial salvation, and urged the faithful to expect the imminent establishment of the Millennium in their lifetime. However,

When in the fourth century Christianity attained a position of supremacy in the Mediterranean world and became the official religion of the Empire, ecclesiastical disapproval of millenarianism became emphatic. The Catholic Church was now a powerful and prosperous institution, functioning according to a well-established routine; and the men responsible for governing it had no wish to see Christians clinging to out-dated and inappropriate dreams of a new earthly Paradise. Early in the fifth century St Augustine propounded the doctrine which the new conditions demanded. According to *The City of God* the Book of Revelation was to be understood as a spiritual allegory; as for the Millennium, that had begun with the birth of Christianity and was fully realized in the Church. This at once became orthodox doctrine.[27]

The millenarian eschatology of early Christianity now became associated with heresy and dissent, and during the Middle Ages, as Cohn has revealed, it inspired numerous revolutionary movements. While this tradition deviates from the more modern concept of utopianism as we have introduced it, inasmuch as it involved notions of divine intervention in human affairs (the achievement of the Millennium could indeed be described as miraculous), it nevertheless paved the way for those more secular forms of utopian thinking heralded in the sixteenth and seventeenth centuries by works such as More's *Utopia*, Campanella's *City of the Sun* and *New Atlantis* by Bacon. Modern utopias have generally dispensed with the notion of divine intervention, and have urged men to rely entirely on their own efforts in striving for salvation; yet even so, elements of Christian millenarianism seem to have found their way into modern thought, for instance in the tendency, already discussed above, for some early socialist utopias to be presented by their authors as New or True Christianities. The idea of the Second Coming of Christ actually re-emerged in the first half of the nineteenth century as a key ingredient of many utopian theories.

The beginnings of a distinctively modern utopianism undoubtedly grew out of the extraordinary combination of socio-economic, political, religious and intellectual changes of the seventeenth century, although some anticipations are to be found even earlier. It is impossible to put an exact date on such a gradual change. For some purposes it seems convenient to take More's *Utopia* as the most significant literary landmark; yet the practical dimension of modern utopianism did not really emerge until a century later, when it could be seen to be embodied in the fervent egalitarianism of many of the radical movements which flourished at the time of the English Revolution. In the next chapter, when we come to examine the dynamics of modern utopian movements in more detail, we will take the momentous events of this era as our initial point of reference.

Suggested reading

An analysis of the social basis of utopianism ought to begin with K. Mannheim's *Ideology and Utopia*. Of the many more general works on the relationship between social movements and political ideas one of the best is R. Heberle, *Social Movements: An Introduction to Political Sociology*. This will give the reader a good, clearly written exposition of the kind of analytical approach to understanding the social context of ideas which is discussed in the above chapter. R. M. Kanter's *Commitment and Community*, although it is more specifically concerned with communes, also offers some valuable insights on the sociological understanding of utopian movements as an expression of protest and discontent. The significance of early socialism as a response to the development of capitalist industrialism is studied in more detail in K. Taylor, *The Political Ideas of the Utopian Socialists*. Although N. Cohn's *The Pursuit of the Millennium* is concerned with the Middle Ages, it offers many general insights into the social origins of millenarianism, mysticism and utopian revolt. Social historians such as E. J. Hobsbawm (*Primitive Rebels*) and E. P. Thompson (*The Making of the English Working Class*) have also shed valuable light on this issue, and they show how a Marxist perspective can be of use in this area of investigation.

6 Movements for utopia—1

If utopia is not to be brought about through divine intervention, how might man hope to achieve it? Two broad strategies for attaining utopian existence have found expression in Western secular thought. The first is based on the possibility of arriving at utopia in the course of a voyage of discovery to foreign lands. According to this viewpoint, utopia exists now, in the present, but in another place which we have yet to find. The second strategy involves transforming one's own society into utopia through the implementation of some kind of grand design for social improvement. According to this viewpoint, utopia does not yet exist in any place, but it will come into existence at some point in the future in this place, once certain measures have been taken. The distinction between these two approaches is that between spatially located and temporally located forms of utopia, and at this stage in our analysis it is important that the full significance of this distinction is appreciated.

Utopias in space and time

More's *Utopia* is a good example of the spatially located type. Written during 1515-16, in an age when great sea voyages were actually revealing 'new worlds' (America had recently been discovered), the book located utopia not in another time, but in another place: on an island close to the American continent (but separated from it by a man-made channel built on the instructions of Utopus, the conqueror of this territory). The word 'utopia' may have meant 'no place', but in fact this ideal society had to be located somewhere, and it was given quite a specific geographical context. Furthermore, at a time when there was a widespread expectation that many new lands were about to be discovered by heroic explorers, the suggestion that one such territory might really prove to be a utopia was certainly not considered to be unreasonable. But who, we need to ask, would benefit from such a remarkable discovery? Perhaps the explorers themselves would be fortunate enough to be accepted as citizens of this admirable society. This would be marvellous for them, but their fellow-countrymen in England (if we take this to be their country of origin) would thereby be excluded from sharing these benefits. Of course, they could always emigrate and hope to enter utopia in this way; or, alternatively, they might try to change their own society in accordance with the utopian model. The first possibility – mass emigration to utopia – is not quite so far-fetched as it might at first seem, and one can see that the American New World, for instance, has always exerted an attraction of this kind, particularly in the nineteenth century, when millions of Europeans took the decision to journey to what they considered to be a 'promised land' of hope and opportunity. Yet historically a much more important response has been the second of the two possibilities: the citizens of one country, say England, do not physically move across the seas to reach the newly discovered utopia, but reorganize their own society in order to establish a new, duplicate, version of the utopian model. Thus, even though More gave an account of a spatially located utopia, it obviously had certain implications concerning the possibility of an English utopia in a different temporal location, i.e. in the future. Such an emphasis was not made explicit by More, however. Nor was it made explicit by other writers of the sixteenth and early seventeenth centuries such as Campanella and Bacon, both of whom stuck rigorously to the notion of utopia being located at the present time but in a distant place. Gradually in the seventeenth century, however, the temporally located utopia gained an intellectual acceptance corresponding to the rise of new theories of social evolution and future progress. This was a far-reaching development in the history of ideas, and was an essential prerequisite for the emergence of what we now consider to be the modern phase of utopian thought.

Intellectual awareness of the fact that societies were not static, but were capable of evolving under the impact of human direction, heightened dramatically during the seventeenth century. Reason, as embodied particularly in the growth of scientific thought and the observable capacity of applied science to transform the natural world, was seen as the chief tool with which man could construct a better life on earth, and history accordingly came to be viewed more and more in linear terms, as a process of evolution towards great social improvement and possibly perfectibility. The whole notion of time and its social relevance assumed a new significance during this period, and the result was the emergence of 'an evolutionary image of society-in-time' accompanied by 'the perception of society as malleable, of human control of social change as possible'.[1] From now on it became much more reasonable to situate utopias at some future stage of development of one's own society than to insist that utopia was already in existence in an alien society across the seas. This does not mean that the spatially located utopia now became completely redundant. There are certainly important examples of this type right up to the present day, and in the early nineteenth century one of the most influential of all utopian works, Cabet's *Voyage en Icarie*, deliberately adopted the same island-utopia model utilized by More. Yet no one reading Cabet's book could doubt that the author intended it primarily as a demonstration of how France or England might be organized in future at the culmination of historical progress.

The idea of the essential malleability of 'society-in-time' was further reinforced by the political upheavals of seventeenth-century England, particularly during the period of the abolition of the monarchy and the establishment of the new Commonwealth (1649–60). The destruction of the old regime inevitably stimulated much discussion of possible alternative modes of organizing society, and one key ingredient in this discussion was the widespread conviction that the light of reason could show man how to achieve universal happiness on earth. Society was here looked upon as an artefact, the product of deliberate design and human labour, and the aim must be to produce a design which, in the vacuum left by the disappearance of traditional institutions such as the monarchy, would lead not only to a good commonwealth, but to the best possible commonwealth. Gerrard Winstanley's celebrated question, often quoted in accounts of the political thought of this period, sums up well the new attitude of hope which was now emerging: 'Why may we not have our Heaven here (that is, a comfortable liveli-hood in the Earth) and Heaven hereafter too?'[2] Winstanley's own Diggers or True Levellers embodied this philosophy in their bold combination of religious fervour and rationalistic communism. But they were by no means alone in their highly optimistic approach to social change, and numerous utopian sects and experimental communities flourished at this time. Many of these can be seen as a continuation of the older Christian millenarian tradition discussed in the previous chapter. Indeed, some element of millenarianism seemed to be involved in all such movements, including that of the Diggers:

It is well known that during and after the Civil War religious excitement ran high both in the Army and amongst civilians and that neither the Episcopalian nor the Presbyterian Church was able to canalize the flood of lay religiosity. Many felt that the time had come when God was pouring out his spirit upon all flesh. Ecstasies were everyday occurrences, prophecies were uttered on all hands, millennial hopes were rife throughout the population. Cromwell himself, especially before he came to power, was moved by such hopes; and thousands of soldiers in the New Model Army and thousands of artisans in London and other towns lived in daily expectation that through the violence of Civil War the Kingdom of the Saints would be established on English soil and that Christ would descend to reign over it.[3]

Utopia in time

1   The liberal view

If seventeenth-century England produced many notable utopian sects and communities, it did not, interestingly enough, produce many great utopian political writings. (James Harrington's *Oceana*, published in 1656, is one major exception, and it is a work which is also very important in terms of its subsequent practical influence, since many of its principles found their way into the American Constitution.) Nor did political theory yet take the new concept of society-in-time to its logical conclusion by disentangling it completely from the older millenarian tradition rooted in Christian theology. This task was accomplished in the following century by the thinkers of the Enlightenment, particularly those in France, who were largely responsible for putting forward grand stadial accounts of social development based on notions of secular and terrestrial progress. These thinkers – Turgot and Condorcet are probably the best examples – mapped out history in a completely new way by providing a conception of a gradual movement towards perfection through what was often called 'the progress of the human mind'. The seventeenth-century view of society as an artefact was now gradually superseded by the more sophisticated notion of society being a part of nature, and being subject to some kind of process of organic evolution or growth. From a sociological perspective what is particularly significant about this eighteenth-century transformation of the initial notion of society-in-time into the idea of a complex organic evolution of society is that it undoubtedly corresponded to the rise of what Mannheim calls 'the liberal-humanitarian stage of utopian mentality'.[4] This is a most important point, since so often utopianism is seen to be the prerogative (perhaps even the 'sin') of socialists, yet in fact the initial boost to the development of modern utopianism was provided not by socialism but by the rise of liberalism as a political force in the eighteenth century. (In recent years, as was demonstrated in Chapter 4, many liberal thinkers have put themselves forward as enemies of utopia, but this strategy cannot hide the fact that liberalism was itself at one stage rooted in essentially utopian motives.) Furthermore, it is doubtful whether one can fully understand the significance of socialist utopianism without first considering the utopian elements involved in liberalism, elements in relation to which so many socialists were later to develop their own theories.

The very term 'liberalism' reveals the force of its original utopian propensity: to establish a new social order based on a whole range of new liberties or freedoms as a means of attaining harmony and happiness. This vision undoubtedly arose in part out of aristocratic resistance to the pre-eminence of monarchy; but it was the new bourgeoisie in eighteenth-century Europe which did most to transform liberalism into a potent political force by striving for freedom 'in the sense of bursting asunder the bonds of the static, guild, and caste order, in the sense of freedom of thought and opinion, in the sense of political freedom and freedom of the unhampered development of the personality'.[5] Liberalism attacked the existing social order in an uncompromising fashion and put forward a conception of an alternative society, an ideal world in which reason would reign over human affairs. But, as Mannheim points out, this conception of an alternative society 'is not used . . . as a blueprint in accordance with which at any given point in time the world is to be reconstructed. Rather it serves merely as a "measuring rod" by means of which the course of concrete events may be theoretically evaluated'.[6] Liberalism presented a somewhat abstract and indeterminate view of the future. It did not doubt that history would lead one day to a state of social perfection, but exactly when and how the realization of such a state would be brought about was never made precise. Nor could it be made precise, since the whole notion of freedom seemed to be based on the individual's subjective sense of 'being free', which was in turn related to a strong emphasis on the importance of freedom of the will in individual moral choice. 'The progress of the human mind' was a certain principle, but one could not be sure at any particular point in time how much more progress had to be made before the ideal society became a reality. In the meantime gradual improvement, a relatively slow movement away from actuality towards the ideal, was the only strategy which seemed to conform to this philosophy. The ideal was important in as much as it provided a standard by which to identify certain changes as contributing to the overall pattern of progress, but it was not an ideal to be attained in full at any specific time. According to this criterion neither the American nor the French Revolution was seen by liberals to have actually established a utopian society, yet both events were regarded as land-marks on the path of progress towards the future realization of complete liberty (together with other related values such as equality and frater-nity), even though some liberals were seriously disillusioned by certain aspects of these events, in particular by the way the French Revolution quickly deteriorated into a violent 'reign of terror'.

2   *The socialist alternative*

Liberalism did, of course, achieve many of its specific practical goals, and did eventually succeed in overthrowing the traditional, rigid social order based on hierarchical feudalism. In this respect one might say that certain elements of liberal utopianism were realized. Yet by the early nineteenth century the ultimate goal of perfect freedom and unhindered reason remained as indeterminate as ever, and it was partly a frustration at the negative abstractness of liberal conceptions that motivated many thinkers during this period to put forward an alternative, much more concrete, conception that in retrospect can be seen as the initial phase of modern socialism. Some of the key constitutive values of early nineteenth-century socialism – those principles associated with thinkers such as Saint-Simon, the Saint-Simonians, Owen, Fourier, Cabet and Weitling – were discussed in detail in the previous chapter, and there is no need to repeat that analysis here. From one point of view those values would appear to have something in common with the bour-geois-liberal idea of history leading inextricably towards a future realm of freedom and reason. Socialists also predicted a future state of society in which man would achieve liberation and would be governed by the requirements of a new, thoroughly rational and thoroughly moral code of behaviour. But whereas liberals saw this process in terms of 'the progress of the human mind', and emphasized the growth of man's subjective sense of freedom and well-being in what Saint-Simon mockingly called an abstract, 'legal-metaphysical' manner,[7] the early socialists situated progress in the context of definite material circum-stances. For them the values of harmony, association, community and co-operation (as was seen in the previous chapter) were not vague ethical ideals to be realized at some indeterminate point in the future through the loosening of legal restraints, the establishing of declarations of the rights of man, and the winning of constitutional-institutional reforms. Rather the future utopia required quite specific – objective rather than subjective – changes in the material basis of society, changes which could only be brought about through the implementation of an overall, collective plan – a fairly detailed blueprint – of some description. It was in this respect that the very term 'socialism' emerged in the 1830s as the antithesis of liberal 'individualism'.

It can be seen that although early socialism grew out of liberal notions of progress and perfectibility, it rejected liberalism's abstract and legalistic interpretation of how such progress and perfectibility would be achieved. It wished to locate its utopia quite specifically as the outcome of a certain set of material preconditions which one could describe now (in the present) and which would come into existence (in the future) at a certain definite stage in the process of social change. Utopianism now became a vehicle for outlining a theory of the interconnectedness of all social, economic and political facts, and denied the possibility of attaining socialism in any one sphere without appropriate changes in the others. The triad of association, community and co-operation speaks for itself: the new emphasis was on understanding society as an integrated whole based on an interdependence of its various activities and areas of human behaviour. Utopia demanded a complete remaking of the whole social world. As Mannheim has put it, socialism urges us to

examine every event with a view to discovering what it means and what its position is in the total developmental structure. . . . The driving purpose here no longer consists in activity on the basis of random impulses toward some arbitrarily chosen here and now, but rather in fixing attention upon a favourable point of attack in the structural whole within which we exist. It becomes the task of the political leader deliberately to reinforce those forces the dynamics of which seem to move in the direction desired by him, and to turn in his own direction or at least to render impotent those which seem to be to his disadvantage. Historical experience becomes thereby a truly strategic plan.[8]

The 'strategic dilemmas' facing the early socialists have been considered in the previous chapter, and it was seen how much disagreement there was among these thinkers when it came to making their visions of utopia absolutely concrete and precise. One of the weaknesses of Mannheim's account of socialism is that it overlooks these variations and tends to deal with 'the socialist-communist utopia' as a whole without any differentiation between quite distinct approaches within the broader tradition (apart from an emphasis on anarchism's separation from other schools of thought).[9] This differentiation, we wish to argue, is vitally important, and for two major reasons. First, while it is true, as Mannheim, Bauman and others have argued, that modern socialism's sociological function has been that of the chief 'counter-culture' to capitalism, the primary 'active utopia' (Bauman's term) of modern times, one presenting us with the chief alternative to actuality,[10] the fact is that different individuals and groups have perceived socialism to mean very different things, and this variation does itself demand some kind of sociological explanation. Second, the rise of socialism has occurred simultaneously with the rise of modern mass society, and the resulting techniques of disseminating ideas, organizing parties and movements in support of those ideas, and stimulating a sense of commitment have clearly had something to do with the 'success' of some versions of socialism as opposed to the relative 'failure' of others. The fact that in practice socialism has frequently been successful in societies which have lacked a liberal-bourgeois capitalist basis is surely of the utmost significance here, and further reinforces the view that a sociological account of socialism's development as the major modern form of utopia must be differentiated into a number of different strands.

Early socialism and political mobilization in France

Some idea of the enormous complexity of the problem before us can be given by returning to the question of what social forces led to the initial emergence of modern socialism in the first half of the nineteenth century. Although, for some purposes, it may be convenient to refer to early socialism in very general terms as a single tradition, on closer inspection it needs to be broken down into a number of distinct movements with different sources of leadership, different organizational structures, and different techniques of creating and maintaining commitment. Some of these movements were conspicuously more successful than others in terms of their practical impact, and the reasons for this variation shed valuable light on the whole question of socialism's role as an instrument of political mobilization in modern society. Before we can say definitely that socialism is related to the activities of any particular component of the social structure (in the same way that we previously saw liberalism as the expression of the rising bourgeoisie), it would be wise to examine some aspects of the role of leadership, organization and commitment in determining what practical success the various socialist theories had in this crucial, formative phase, the phase of its 'take-off' as an effective movement.[11]

It must be stressed at the outset that the whole issue of early social-ism's significance as an agent of mobilization is very much a matter of scholarly dispute. Rudolf Heberle, for example, asserts that the early socialists 'did not create a real mass movement'.[12] Yet the most recent research suggests that at least one movement, Icarianism, *was* a mass movement; and the Saint-Simonian and Owenite sects, at the height of their appeal, also had large numbers of adherents. Yet even if one decides not to become involved in this rather vague debate on what exactly constitutes a mass movement, one cannot deny that some early socialist movements were more successful in mobilizing leadership and support than others, and Icarianism stands out as undoubtedly the most successful of all such movements.

Furthermore, not all early socialist movements appealed to the same groups in society, and none of them appealed to the newly emergent factory workers, a group still at a relatively underdeveloped stage in its growth, especially in the countries of continental Europe and in America. In the first half of the nineteenth century the working class still consisted mainly of artisans and handicraft workers, and this meant that early socialism could only draw its numerical strength from this sector. The point was made before that many of the key values of early socialism were derived from artisan experience, and this reinforces the view that the early socialists were in an extremely ambiguous position, combining both a consciousness of the old society (pre-capitalist or pre-industrial) and an anticipation of the new, however they might choose to define it.

What has to be stressed is that during this period large numbers of workers were willing to lend their support to movements offering security and salvation in a basically insecure world. Why certain move-ments attracted more support than others is a fascinating question, especially in relation to France, which was a battleground for numerous alternative utopian schemes. It may be useful, therefore, to proceed with some more detailed comments on the French situation. Icarian-ism deserves to be dealt with first, not only because it was the most successful early socialist movement, but also because we know more about Icarianism than about any other movement, thanks to the outstanding work of Christopher Johnson.[13]

Icarianism

The success of Icarianism is in some ways surprising, for the movement was rooted in the ideas of Cabet, who was one of the least interesting and least original of the early socialists. In its most successful phase Icarianism attracted a very large following, somewhere between 100,000 and 200,000.[14] As Johnson shows, it was the most conspicuously working class of all early socialist movements, although 'working class' here means artisan rather than proletarian. It must be admitted that the term 'artisan' is itself somewhat vague, since it covers a variety of occupations, from master craftsman to journeyman, apprentice and ordinary labourer. Johnson accordingly encounters some difficulty in giving a more precise picture of the basis of support for Icarianism. The statistical evidence he presents suggests that most Icarians were of fairly low status: there were more journeymen, apprentices and labourers than master craftsmen. In other words, the kind of independent artisan who might justifiably be described as 'petty-bourgeois' tended to be excluded.[15] Furthermore, Johnson is able to show that Icarianism was particularly popular among such specific groups as tailors, shoemakers and cabinet-makers.

A number of factors seem to have contributed to Icarianism's success. It was the most deliberately political of the early socialist movements, placing a great emphasis on active involvement in political affairs. It was very well organized, had a strongly charismatic leader in Cabet, utilized propaganda brilliantly, and assumed the persuasive form of a Christian sect. The combination of these factors enabled it to appeal most effectively to those artisans who were working in depressed industries and who were most severely threatened by mechanization and the introduction of capitalist forms of production. This appeal was strongest at times of economic crisis, when the declining position of the lower-placed artisans became most evident. Not surprisingly, support for Icarianism was concentrated in the largest cities (there was hardly any rural following at all). As Johnson points out, it is in the cities during the July Monarchy that 'one can discern the first steps in the "proletarianization" of the diverse groups of artisans'.[16]

The success of Icarianism confirms a view put forward by Heberle, who states that 'it is generally recognized . . . that the chances of an idea's becoming part of the creed of a mass movement depend not so much upon its intrinsic value as upon its appeal to the interests, sentiments, and resentments of certain social strata and other groups'.[17] In the case of Icarianism, as has already been pointed out, the movement's underlying ideas were hardly original and usually lacked coherence. Yet the movement had a staggering success. It did not survive increasing governmental persecution in the late 1840s, and there were also failures of leadership, most notably Cabet's decision not to continue the struggle in France but to emigrate with a band of followers to America. It may also be argued that Cabet failed to understand the revolutionary potential of certain elements of the working class, and in this sense his emphasis on respectable, pacific communism certainly appeared out of place by 1848. Yet in spite of these failings, Icarianism played a vitally important role in mobilizing large groups of workers into an organized movement.

Saint-Simonism

In considering Saint-Simonism we face the problem that we still know very little about the movement's social composition and the sources of its support. However, certain essential facts are established. Saint-Simonism flourished for only a short time as a coherently organized school, from the death of Saint-Simon in 1825 to 1833, when it was declared illegal. Under the Restoration Monarchy (to 1830) it could hardly be expected to enjoy any real success, but its appeal grew after the July Revolution of 1830, when it became associated with the republican cause. It managed to gain some 40,000 or so adherents,[18] and even after it was banned in 1833 it continued to have an influence, certainly up to 1848.

Like Icarianism, the Saint-Simonian movement enjoyed considerable organizational advantages. It was authoritatively and charismatically led, had numerous colleges, churches and missions throughout France and also abroad, and used propaganda with great effectiveness. It was, however, different from Icarianism in that it failed to exert a strong appeal to the working class. There were a number of reasons for this. It was very intellectual in orientation, basing its theories on extremely sophisticated and rarefied arguments which must have been difficult for some people to grasp, even though the Saint-Simonian leaders attempted to simplify the message for the uneducated and the less intelligent. The essential doctrine may have been known, as one commentator points out, 'to every educated person in Europe',[19] but then not every person was educated. Much of the doctrine's terminology was quite novel and therefore difficult to understand, and quite often Saint-Simonian ideas appeared extremely eccentric (Saint-Simon himself having been widely dismissed in his lifetime as a bizarre, even mad, thinker!).

Following Saint-Simon's conception of 'the industrial class', the movement attempted to unite all productive workers in society, including labourers, artisans, the 'captains of industry', farmers, artists and so on. Such an outlook could not be expected to appeal to the working class in the same way that Icarianism was able to do in the 1840s. In fact Saint-Simonism tended to appeal first and foremost to certain elements of the middle class who identified with the movement's 'bourgeois' notion of progress through industrial development and programmes of government-sponsored public works. A strong technocratic tendency drew many adherents from the ranks of businessmen and engineers, especially those from the Ecole Polytechnique. Industrialists who gained from the economic expansion of the 1830s admired the movement greatly, although the school's growing collectivist sympathies eventually led to a loss of support from this group. To a certain extent, also, the appeal of the movement had a generational basis. Young middle-class radicals were impressed by Saint-Simonism as a way of achieving an alternative society to the strongly conservative France of the 1820s. History furnishes us with many examples of utopian movements appealing particularly to alienated youth, and Saint-Simonism was very important in this respect during the late 1820s and early 1830s.[20]

Gradually, after 1830, the Saint-Simonians did attempt to appeal more directly to the working class. Their involvement in working-class communities and their participation in such upheavals as the Lyons uprising of 1831 encouraged the leaders of the movement to appreciate specifically working-class aspirations and to develop more of a revolutionary awareness. However, this came too late, for the movement was now being split through arguments over religious and moral questions. Its rejection of Christianity, its creation of a new religion of humanity, its proposals for a new moral code (including suggestions for a more liberal attitude towards sexual relations and the institution of marriage) – all these were out of touch with mass opinion. Furthermore, there can be no doubt that Saint-Simonism was pointing in the direction of a considerable degree of authoritarianism. As was mentioned earlier, there was a strong body of working-class opinion which believed that Saint-Simonism threatened to put an end to human liberty.

Fourierism

Like Saint-Simonism, the Fourierist movement is difficult to analyse because of the general lack of information concerning its social composition. We can be certain, however, that the movement was never as successful as Icarianism or Saint-Simonism, and this is not too difficult to explain. For one thing, it was the least political of the early socialist movements in France during the 1830s and 1840s. It also emphasized small-scale experimentation through a system of 'Phalanxes', and was persistently anti-industrial in its approach to social change, emphasizing a hatred of factories and commerce, and a defence of the traditional arts and crafts, agriculture and horticulture. Such an outlook managed to appeal to certain middle-class elements, to many intellectuals, and also to workers in agriculture (this last element was conspicuously absent in the case of Icarianism and Saint-Simonism), but not to any large sector of the working class. In organizational terms Fourierism had some success in the workers' co-operative movement in France, but generally speaking it was marked by 'petty-bourgeois' characteristics, for it was the more independent, property-owning tradesman or craftsman who was most likely to be attracted to Fourierist doctrine.[21]

The Fourierist movement also suffered from being badly led and organized. Fourier himself was content to sit and wait for benevolent capitalists to come and offer financial help so that his schemes could be put into operation. He was not a great charismatic leader, and his ideas were frequently bizarre, badly presented, indeed often incomprehensible. Propaganda was almost non-existent in the early stages. Only later, with the involvement of new leaders such as Considérant in France, and Brisbane and Greely in America, did Fourierism become more of an organizational force. This was particularly the case in America, where a national association was instituted to promote the creation of Phalanxes. With improved organization came a growing emphasis on the messianic qualities of Fourierism. 'First came Jesus Christ, then Fourier' was one slogan.[22] Thus, we have yet another instance of what would seem to be an inevitable tendency for early French socialism to merge into religion. In the case of Fourierism, though, the religious element was so artificial that it could not possibly hope to gain as much success as either Cabet's 'true Christianity' or the Saint-Simonians' new religion of humanity.[23] Splits in the Fourierist leadership also contributed to the movement's failure, especially in France. Only in America did it maintain any momentum, possibly because its emphasis on small-scale communitarianism was so acceptable among the pioneers and immigrants who wished to establish a new way of life for themselves.

The virtues of the Fourierist doctrine derived from two vital ingredients. First, it was not communist, and it thus offered an alternative for those groups who recognized the worth of private property and who believed that communism was bound to be violent and insurrectionary.

Second, it was always libertarian and anti-authoritarian in outlook, and this served to counteract the undeniable authoritarianism of some movements, most notably of Saint-Simonism. Fourierism was indeed so liberal and moderate that the French Government always tolerated it, and the social basis of support for the movement was also of such modest proportions that the Government never anticipated any Fourierist upheaval.

Early socialism and political mobilization in Britain, Germany and America

Owenism

We may now shift our attention from France to Britain, where Owenism was the most important early socialist movement in the 1830s and 1840s. Of all such movements Owenism was the one which tried hardest to come to terms with the realities of mechanization and factory production. Britain, of course, was more industrialized at this stage than France, Germany or America, and therefore early socialism had to respond to a more advanced stage of industrial development. Also, Robert Owen himself formulated his ideas through his experience in the factory situation, and he had a much better understanding of mechanization and the relationship between men and machines than most other thinkers.

Nevertheless, for many years Owen's ideas had little or no appeal to ordinary working men. Until the late 1820s his views were associated with paternalism and benevolent managerialism, and his absence in America for most of the period 1824-9 did not help matters. Only after his return to England did Owenism gain significant levels of working-class support, reaching a peak in 1834 after which date the movement declined as Owen broke with trade unionism, and as Chartism offered workers a more radical alternative.[24] Unfortunately, the extent of working-class support during the years 1829-34 is difficult to measure precisely. Thus, while some commentators have seen Owenism as a real mass movement,[25] others have rejected that view.[26] At some Owenite demonstrations there were probably as many as 100,000 participants;[27] yet the number of persons who actively took part in Owenite organizations, clubs, societies and trade unions was undeniably much smaller.

What is striking about the success of Owenism in the early 1830s, however one tries to measure it statistically, is that the movement appealed to a very broad group of people from the point of view of its social characteristics: middle-class philanthropists, utilitarians, enlightened capitalists, as well as the working class (although as with Icarianism, 'working class' here means primarily artisans and the more highly skilled labourers rather than proletarians). In part, this very broad appeal was due to the essential vagueness of Owenite schemes and also their flexibility. At the same time one must recognize that Owenism was able to direct its energies towards fairly specific institutional forms: co-operatives, trade unions, labour exchanges, 'home colonies' and so on. This gave Owenism a very valuable organizational structure within which to operate, although it also followed that any weakening of the structure (e.g. through the failure of trade unionism) inevitably weakened the movement. It is also important to note that these organizational forms were derived directly from working-class experience. Indeed, Owen frequently came to issue proposals for certain forms of association precisely because he knew that the working class had already demonstrated a willingness to support them. As Thompson has pointed out:

The germ of most of Owen's ideas can be seen in practices which anticipate or occur independently of his writings. Not only did the benefit societies on occasion extend their activities to the building of social clubs or alms-houses; there are also a number of instances of pre-Owenite trade unions when on strike, employing their own members and marketing the product . . . . The covered market, or bazaar, with its hundreds of little stalls, was an old institution; but at the close of the Wars new bazaars were opened, which attracted attention in philanthropic and Owenite circles, where a section of counter was let (by the foot) for the week, the day, or even part of the day . . . . By 1827 a new bazaar was in being, which acted as a centre for the exchange of products made by unemployed members of London trades . . . .
Thus the Equitable Labour Exchanges, founded at London and Birmingham in 1832–3, with their labour notes and exchange of small products, were not conjured out of the air by paranoiac prophets.[28]

Although Owenism was thus based on a body of working-class experience, one might argue that this experience was of more relevance to the older craft occupations than to modern, large-scale industry. The repeal of the combination laws in 1824 assisted Owenism because it permitted precisely the kinds of association which could help to enlist support for the movement; but even so Owenism did not develop any significant proletarian basis. One other important reason for this was that Owenism encouraged a politically moderate approach to social improvement. It followed that politically radical groups could find little of substance in Owenism, and after 1836 another vehicle for workers' demands – Chartism – was thus able to benefit from this weakness and managed to attract widespread support. Owen did not in fact lend any public support to the Charter until the very last year of his life (1858), and this actually made his approach much less convincing. There was the consequent irony that

while Chartism increasingly drew its support from the casualties of the industrial changes of the period, trade unionism developed either among craftsmen who were little affected by such changes, as for instance those in the service trades of London, or among workers who had actually benefited from change, as in the case of the new engineering tradesmen, the boilermakers, and so on.[29]

One other element in Owenism which deserves mention is the strongly secular basis it retained until the early 1830s. This contrasts greatly with the enthusiasm among French socialists for new versions of Christianity or religions of humanity. Owen's emphasis on rationality up to (and including) the years of success during 1829–34 led him to advocate a thoroughly secular perspective on social affairs. In later life he did become more interested in various forms of mysticism and the possibility of a rational religion, but the fact remains that as an organized movement Owenism derived much of its strength from its original opposition to religion. As Hobsbawm has written, 'the mechanics of the 1820s followed Robert Owen not only for his analysis of capitalism, but for his unbelief, and, long after the collapse of Owenism, their Halls of Science spread rationalist propaganda throughout the cities'.[30]

German artisan socialism

Turning now to German socialism during this period, we encounter a new factor: the most important movements were invariably established among *émigré* workers, particularly in Paris and London, and also for a time in Switzerland. While Weitling was undoubtedly the major theoretician, other leaders – for example, Schapper – contributed much in matters of organization. These German *émigré* groups were dominated, by artisans, and perhaps more than any of the other movements dealt with here their ideas reflected artisan experience of association in particular trades and crafts. Guilds persisted in Germany, and they influenced the German artisans in their approach to socialism. Most importantly, the gap between masters and journeymen in the guilds was seen to be widening, and this encouraged journeymen such as Weitling to urge the creation of new workers' clubs as an alternative to the guilds. During the 1840s the new clubs did much to stimulate a working-class (i.e. artisan) consciousness which finally came to fruition in the upheavals of 1848–9.[31]

German artisan socialism had a major impact on the development of the League of the Just (known after 1847 as the Communist League), in which a running battle was mounted in the late 1840s between the artisan view of socialism and the Marxist approach. There were many dimensions to this argument. The artisans, for instance, tended to reject large-scale mechanization, and they believed future society could restore workshop forms of production. Marx rejected this view and urged the necessity of accepting wholesale industrialization even if it meant the proletarianization of craft workers. Religion was also a controversial issue. For some artisan leaders, such as Weitling, socialist, and in his case communist, society had to be based on Christian principles. Such a view derived not only from theoretical arguments; it was also based on the experience of artisans in Germany, their existing knowledge of doctrines of millenarianism, and their emphasis on the one book with which they were usually familiar: the Bible. Yet some leaders, including Schapper, rejected this notion of a Christian socialism, and this rejection was also endorsed by Marx.

Another dispute centred on the question of revolution. Many German artisans in France were linked with the insurrectionary movement organized by Blanqui, and their whole approach to change was inspired by revolutionary fervour. This was the attitude of Weitling, but Schapper and others adopted a more moderate approach, believing in the virtues of pacifism in a similar way to Cabet. On this point Marx agreed with Weitling, qualifying it, however, by insisting that revolution could not be accomplished in the immediate future by artisans but must await the further development of capitalism and the growth of a factory proletariat. Such a warning was directed in particular at the situation in Germany, where, as Marx and Engels frequently pointed out, the attack on feudalism was just beginning, and hence socialist revolution lay far in the future. Not surprisingly, German utopian socialism was mocked as a form of 'petty-bourgeois' nostalgia by Marx and Engels, even though they acknowledged the contribution of such writers as Weitling to the socialist cause.[32]

Possibilities for the development of an effective socialist movement in Germany itself were continually weakened by emigration. In addition to the groups of workers, often journeymen, who made their way to such cities as Paris and London, thousands emigrated to Russia and America. The movement to America was especially noteworthy after the 1830s and early 1840s. Between 1846 and 1855 more than one million Germans emigrated to America, many of them small farmers who had been ruined by economic change in their native country.[33] This provided a strong basis for socialist activities in America, but did nothing at all for the progress of workers' movements in Germany.

Early socialism in America

The impact of early socialism in America is a huge topic, but because of the interest shown in America by many of the early socialist theoreticians a few general comments must be made here. To begin with, one should perhaps draw attention to the irony of a situation in which theories formulated in Western Europe, against a background of fairly specific social and economic changes, were put into operation in a society which had not undergone the same process of change, and where generally speaking industrialism was not causing the same dislocation that workers were experiencing in France, Britain and Germany. There were other distinctions too. Mechanization was generally beneficial to labour in America owing to the shortage of workers in many areas, and hence the opposition to the power of machinery voiced by some socialists was less appropriate. (The absence of any kind of Luddism in America is interesting in this respect.[34]) Communitarianism was more acceptable in America, as the long tradition of community-building since colonial times, much of it remarkably successful, demonstrated, and the availability of land for this purpose greatly assisted socialist schemes. This same factor suggested to many thinkers that the creation of a new society in America would not necessitate the destruction of the old regime (as it would in Europe), since there was in fact no old regime to destroy. The country was therefore considered to be particularly suitable for a peaceful, orderly approach to social change. It is also noteworthy that small-scale communities were economically viable in America, whereas they might not be in France, Britain or Germany. To take just one example, George Rapp's 'Harmony' community was widely regarded as an economic showplace.[35] The typical economic unit in America consisted of small, independent producers and property owners.

This combination of socio-economic factors, coupled with the political freedom and religious toleration which America seemed to offer, helps to explain the extraordinary proliferation of utopian experiments in the United States during the early nineteenth century, and it also enables us to understand why certain movements which were not successful in Europe made rapid progress on the other side of the Atlantic. The Fourierist movement, for example, did not meet with much success in France, but it did in America, where some forty Fourierist communities were established in the 1840s. In part, this was due to good organization and leadership, but perhaps even more important is the fact that the Fourierist view of society coincided with peculiarly American assumptions: the emphasis on small-scale units of production, support for agrarianism, anti-authoritarianism, a defence of private property and so on. In this respect Fourierism had more in common with the Jeffersonian view of democracy than even Fourier could ever have imagined.

Utopia *for* the working class

We are now in a position to summarize what we consider to be several key sociological features of the process by which socialism emerged as a utopian movement of great weight and influence in the first half of the nineteenth century.

1   Leadership was of great importance, in terms of both the intellectual stimulus and guidance provided by the major thinkers concerned, and also the organizational skills of those actively involved in efforts to gain and maintain support for the various practical strategies. This leadership, moreover, came predominantly from members of the bourgeois middle classes and even (in the case of Saint-Simon) from the aristocracy.

2   In this formative period socialism was certainly presented by its proponents as a doctrine intended to improve the condition of the lower social strata, but the working class in the modern sense of an industrial proletariat did not yet exist, and so the groups which committed themselves to socialism at this stage were a mixture of artisans, the more highly skilled labourers, agricultural workers, independent tradesmen and craftsmen, plus philanthropists and intellectuals from the bourgeoisie. As we have seen, almost every socialist school appealed to its own unique social constituency according to the sympathy its doctrines could attract and the effectiveness of its propaganda and campaign methods.

3   It follows that socialism already existed as a movement *before* the creation of a large industrial proletariat. It did not emerge as the direct expression of the modern working class, but as the expression of the ideas of middle-class intellectuals and leaders reacting to the plight of different groups of workers suffering under the impact of capitalist industrialism in a relatively early phase. As Lichtheim has observed, the fact that early socialism gained its most impressive momentum in France and not in England, i.e. in a relatively backward rather than in the most industrialized society, is significant because it shows that there was no direct relationship at this time between the stage of development of the industrial proletariat as a socio-economic group and the extent of socialist awareness.[36]

These conclusions are vitally important if we are to fully understand the way in which socialist utopian thinking began to exert an enormous practical influence in the Western world, and quickly established itself as *the* distinctive utopia of modern times. Although it is customary to relate socialism as a doctrine to the interests of the working class (just as liberalism was associated with the class interests of the bourgeoisie), we have argued that the formulation of socialism actually preceded the creation of the working class in the modern sense. One way to resolve this problem is to adopt the approach of Marx and Engels, already referred to in Chapter 3, and assert that the early socialism of the period 1800-48 was not an authentic, 'scientific' socialism, but was utopian in the specific sense of being fantastic, misguided and hopelessly idealistic. The authentic scientific socialism, it is argued by Marx and Engels, came later as capitalist industrialism developed to a higher stage and furnished thinkers such as themselves with concrete evidence of the material circumstances in which the proletariat proper had to live and work. Such a view, although Marxists continue to defend it to this day, must be criticized in at least one important respect: it does not account for the way in which the most basic principles of early socialism (harmony, association, community and co-operation) reappear in the thought of Marx and Engels, and how most of the key strategic decisions of Marx and Engels on industrialism, private property, religion, revolution, state power and democracy (the six strategic dilemmas discussed earlier) are all foreshadowed in the thought of Saint-Simon, Owen, Fourier and the other writers of the earlier period. Furthermore, neither Marx nor Engels could claim to be a member of the working class himself, a point which reinforces our earlier conclusion that the whole development of the socialist utopia of the nineteenth century (and we would insist that there is a substantial utopian element in the thought of Marx and Engels) owed much to bourgeois, middle-class inspiration. From this point of view it would seem only reasonable to characterize socialism as a doctrine *for* (rather than a doctrine *of*) the working class. Because of this the main priority facing the leaders of socialist movements has always been to convince the working class that its interests are best served in practice through a strong commitment to socialist ideals.

Suggested reading

The complex interplay of notions of space and time in utopian thought is a theme in many of the major secondary works on utopias, including F. E. and F. P. Manuel, *Utopian Thought in the Western World*. Some sociological perspectives are offered by R. Levitas, 'Sociology and utopia', *Sociology*, vol. 13 (1979). Any attempt to understand the rise and fall of particular utopian movements must take K. Mannheim's analysis (*Ideology and Utopia*) into account. Utopian movements in the age of the English Revolution are highlighted in A. L. Morton's *The English Utopia*. The utopian implications of liberal ideas of progress and perfectibility are clearly stated by the Manuels, while Mannheim attempts to put these ideas into their sociological context. On the general topic of early socialism, see further K. Taylor, *The Political Ideas of the Utopian Socialists*. Some of the best work on specific early socialist movements is concerned with the situation in France. See, for example, C. H. Johnson, *Utopian Communism in France*; and B. H. Moss, *The Origins of the French Labor Movement 1830-1914*. J. F. C. Harrison's *Robert Owen and the Owenites in Britain and America* can also be recommended.

7 Movements for utopia – 2

The repeated efforts made by Marx and Engels to draw a clear distinction between their own 'scientific' theories and the 'critical-utopian' ideas of the early socialists can be examined as an interesting epistemological problem, and such an analysis was undertaken in Chapter 3. But this distinction also needs to be treated as a matter of practical politics, a strategic weapon in the armoury of two thinkers who wished to convince the working class that they – Marx and Engels – had identified the 'right' path, the only path, which the working class must follow in order to achieve liberation and fulfilment, whereas Saint-Simon, Owen, Fourier and the other utopians had a completely false sense of direction. The utopians' criticisms of capitalism deserved praise, but their concept of how capitalism was to be replaced by a socialist alternative was totally unrealistic, quite impracticable, and unscientific in the specific sense that it failed to grasp the 'logic' of historical change, which Marx and Engels claimed to have discovered through their system of historical materialism.

Marx, Engels and utopia

It is well known that Marx and Engels frequently expressed a deep-rooted dislike of detailed blueprints of socialist society, regarding them as worthless products of intellectual speculation. This was an additional reason why they considered the early socialists to be utopian dreamers, and why they thought they themselves were *not* utopians. This attack on utopianism also reflects a distrust of all moralistic/ethical theorizing about the future, a style of theorizing which Marx and Engels deliberately attempted to eliminate from their own work with the result that, strictly speaking, *normative* considerations were dismissed by them as irrelevant in the face of the certain knowledge furnished by historical materialism. However, Marx and Engels did not actually succeed in this attempt to purge their work of all moralistic/ethical notions. This was due mainly to the fact that in order to try to attract the support of both bourgeois intellectuals and workers, they had to be able to present these groups with some sort of picture of what a *desirable* future socialist and communist society would look like. At all stages of history, major social and political movements have tended to require such an image in order to inspire widespread support, and Marxism is no exception to this rule. It is true that Marx and Engels never produced a single work or set of writings which examined this issue in great detail; but throughout all their works there is an emphatic commitment to a type of future socialist-communist society possessing certain unmistakable characteristics, the vast majority of them anticipated in the doctrines of the early socialists. Moreover, we would argue that without this fairly clear vision of a future society it is most unlikely that Marxism as a movement would have had such an enormous practical impact in the nineteenth and twentieth centuries.

Although Marx and Engels always declared a fierce hostility towards 'utopian' blueprints, it did not prevent them from making some quite specific and unambiguous predictions about the future in the statement of communist principles which they worked on during 1847-8 at the request of the newly formed Communist League (a successor to the League of the Just). Engels prepared a first draft, usually known as *Principles of Communism*, shortly after the first congress of the Communist League in June 1847, and in the following December and January Marx wrote the final *Manifesto of the Communist Party*. Both these texts, it must be stressed, were direct responses to a request for a clear programme of action; and there can be no doubt that the outlook of the Communist League, like that of the League of the Just before it, was firmly rooted at this time in the idea which had already been developed by the early socialists: that future socialist society could be described and could accordingly be seen to be ethically desirable (as well as being historically inevitable). Marx and Engels did not reject this idea, but willingly described key elements of a future society, although this fell short of being a very detailed picture. Nevertheless, the overall plan is there, and this is not really surprising since it is difficult to see how a party manifesto could have been produced without such a plan, especially during the turbulent upheavals of 1847-8, when the revolutionary struggle was generally seen by socialists of all schools in terms of the implementation of some strategy for achieving an alternative to bourgeois liberalism.

Engels set out his *Principles of Communism* in the form of a worker's catechism (a form of which was quite popular among socialist writers at this time, and which was used, for instance, by Saint-Simon in his *Catéchisme des Industriels*, 1823-4), and this enabled him to deal with twenty-five specific questions which he considered to be of importance in explaining the doctrine of communism formulated by himself and Marx, questions which he recognized would be of concern to those workers whose support was being sought. The first thirteen questions dealt mainly with the emergence of capitalist industrialism, and the role of class conflict in the various historical stages of the development of society up to the capitalist phase. The remaining twelve questions concentrated on the future development of capitalism into socialist and communist society: What will this new social order have to be like? Was not the abolition of private property possible at an earlier time? Will the peaceful abolition of private property be possible? Will it be possible for private property to be abolished at one stroke? What will be the course of this revolution? Will it be possible for this revolution to take place in one country alone? What will be the consequence of the ultimate disappearance of private property? What will be the influence of communist society on the family? What will be the attitude of communism to existing nationalities? What will be its attitude to existing religions? How do communists differ from socialists? What is the attitude of the communists to the other political parties of our time?[1] When Marx came to write his own version of the communist programme at the end of 1847, he decided to drop the catechism as a form of presentation (Engels too had become dissatisfied with it), and he found it necessary to depart from Engels's draft in numerous ways; but he did not hesitate to incorporate into his *Manifesto* answers to precisely the same kind of questions about the future which Engels had set out in the *Principles of Communism*. The second section of the *Manifesto* ('Proletarians and communists') discusses the future communist system and outlines many of the features which distinguish it from capitalism. In particular we are told that 'the immediate aim of the Communists is the same as that of all the other proletarian parties: formation of the proletariat into a class, overthrow of the bourgeois supremacy, conquest of political power by the proletariat'. Communist theory can be summed up as: the abolition of private property; this abolition will bring to an end bourgeois family relations; national differences and antagonisms will vanish; once having gained political power, the proletariat will take away all capital from the bourgeoisie, will centralize all productive instruments in the State, and will rapidly increase productive forces; precise measures will vary from country to country, but in the case of the most advanced nations some basic strategies can be stipulated.[2]

Perhaps most interesting of all is the very end of this section of the *Manifesto*, where a summary account of a future harmonious society is given which recalls both in tone and in terminology the aspirations of the early socialists. Particularly noteworthy is the elevation of the principle of association (which, as we have seen, was central to the early socialists' vision of harmony) to the forefront of this account:

> When, in the course of development, class distinctions have disappeared, and all production has been concentrated in the hands of associated individuals, the public power will lose its political character. Political power, properly so called, is merely the organized power of one class for oppressing another. If the proletariat during its contest with the bourgeoisie is compelled, by the force of circumstances, to organize itself as a class, if, by means of a revolution, it makes itself the ruling class, and, as such, sweeps away by force the old conditions of production, then it will, along with these conditions, have swept away the conditions for the existence of class antagonisms and of classes generally, and will thereby have abolished its own supremacy as a class.
>
> In place of the old bourgeois society, with its classes and class antagonisms, we shall have an association, in which the free development of each is the condition for the free development of all.[3]

In actual fact Marx seemed to stick remarkably close to the various images of future society presented in the writings of the early socialists. What he objected to in their work was not so much their ultimate vision of social harmony, but their characteristic reliance (apart from the occasional exception like Weitling) on gradual reform and non-revolutionary methods of achieving this harmony. 'They wish to attain their ends by peaceful means', he complained. They 'endeavour, by small experiments, necessarily doomed to failure, and by the force of example, to pave the way for the new social Gospel'. And perhaps the most unrealistic hope of all could be seen in the way in which they tried to realize all their 'castles in the air' by appealing 'to the feelings and purses of the bourgeois'.[4]

Thus, it would seem that Marx's relationship to the early socialists at the time of his writing *The Communist Manifesto* might usefully be explained in terms of the same problem of strategic value conflicts discussed previously in Chapter 5. Broadly speaking, Marx adopted the already established socialist view of the future as a stage when harmony, association, community and co-operation would be achieved; but he disagreed with his predecessors when it came to stating *how* this future stage was to be reached. He knew that his strategy could not be reconciled with what he considered to be their naive (because it was unscientific) conviction that an intensification of the class struggle could be avoided. For him the class struggle was everything, and a realistic as opposed to utopian (in the sense of impracticable) strategy demanded that the proletariat must liberate themselves *through* the class struggle and not by merely wishing it away.

Marx's attack on utopian socialism in *The Communist Manifesto* also had another practical dimension of particular relevance to the situation in Germany, a situation which was undoubtedly his main concern at this time. He was anxious to alert the German workers to the fact that a bourgeois-liberal revolution must be the next stage in German historical development, since Germany (unlike France and Britain) had not yet been through this phase – a phase which, according to the theory of historical materialism, would pave the way in due course for a proletarian-socialist revolution. In this respect it must be realized that *The Communist Manifesto* assumed the form it did partly as a direct result of the clash between Marx and Wilhelm Weitling over this question of a German revolution during 1846-7. Marx was anxious to dismiss Weitling's belief that communism could be established in Germany directly by the working class without a preparatory stage of capitalist industrialization and bourgeois democracy, since he realized there was a real danger that the League of the Just (soon to become the Communist League) would adopt this strategy in its new programme. Marx's tactical victory over Weitling was thus vitally important in that it enabled the distinctively Marxist strategy to find its way into the Communist League's first proper manifesto as 'official' policy.

After 1848 Marx and Engels issued many pronouncements on the subject of the future transition to socialism and communism. These pronouncements are to be found scattered throughout their writings, but occur particularly in those works which were prompted by circumstances demanding the resolution of detailed strategic issues, for example in *The Civil War in France*, occasioned by the experience of the Paris Commune of 1871, and the *Critique of the Gotha Programme*, which was a reaction to the joint programme of the two previously separate wings of the German socialist movement (led by Liebknecht and Lassalle), which in 1875 sought to establish a new united party. The world of practical politics required Marx and Engels, on numerous occasions, to answer quite specific questions about how communism would be achieved and how communist society would be organized; and, moreover, they also had to do this in order to combat the rival doctrines of other socialist thinkers, notably the anarchists, who during this same period were attempting to convince the proletariat of the validity of their own alternative approach to creating a better world. For a long time after 1848, in fact, the whole development of what we have regarded as the socialist counter-culture to capitalism centred on the Marxist–anarchist dispute, and some attention must now be given, therefore, to the nature of this dispute and the circumstances against which it took shape.

The anarchist challenge

Writing in 1929, Mannheim looked back on a century or so of socialism's role as a great practical utopian movement, and concluded that anarchism did not really belong to the mainstream of this tradition. He preferred instead to regard anarchism as the most recent manifestation of a quite distinct form of utopian mentality to which he gave the name 'chiliasm', a form which hearkened back to an older style of 'ecstatic' optimism displayed, for instance, in the attitudes of Thomas Münzer and in the Anabaptist sects of the early sixteenth century.[5] Mannheim described the essential features of chiliasm as follows:

The Chiliast expects a union with the immediate present. Hence he is not preoccuped in his daily life with optimistic hopes for the future or romantic reminiscences. His attitude is characterized by a tense expectation. He is always on his toes awaiting the propitious moment and thus there is no inner articulation of time for him. He is not actually concerned with the millennium that is to come; what is important for him is that it happened here and now, and that it arose from mundane existence, as a sudden swing over into another kind of existence. The promise of the future which is to come is not for him a reason for postponement, but merely a point of orientation, something external to the ordinary course of events from where he is on the lookout ready to take the leap.[6]

The chiliast may thus be seen as a passionate believer in the imminent transformation of the evil world into the world of harmony, a transformation occurring not as the outcome of certain determinate stages of social evolution, but as the result of 'a direct, explosive collision with history'.[7] For Mannheim what is most significant about anarchism is that it does not share the typical socialist–communist view of history moving in a determinate fashion towards the ideal society organized according to some overall, planned conception. Rather it relies on the chiliastic imperative to destroy the existing order at any time (but the sooner the better) and to achieve the ideal society through the act of revolution itself and without any planned system to take the place of the old. It is as though the emotional ecstasy of the revolutionary act will be sufficient to produce permanent harmony out of a momentary chaos. The new world will not require rational organization; it will be a spontaneous coming together of liberated individuals and groups motivated by a fundamental resistance to all notions of a single, rational order. Anarchism wishes to call a halt to any further evolution of society in the direction of increased collective rationalization.

Mannheim sees Bakunin as the arch-chiliast in his uncompromising glorification of the revolutionary deed, the art of destruction. 'The will to destroy is a creative will', reads Bakunin's celebrated maxim, quoted by Mannheim, and the point is elaborated in a series of short, sharp statements: 'I do not believe in constitutions or in laws. The best constitution would leave me dissatisfied. We need something different. Storm and vitality and a new lawless and consequently free world.'[8] And elsewhere he is reported to have confirmed: 'I believe in nothing, I read nothing.' If he ever did succeed in achieving his ambitions, would he know how to proceed? Certainly, he replied: 'I should at once begin to pull down again everything I had made.'[9] The sense of historical indeterminateness, which Mannheim regards as a key ingredient of anarchism (and which in part seems to recall the indeterminateness of liberalism), is certainly very much to the fore in Bakunin's works. Future society is seen as operating not on the basis of any particular set of authoritative rules, but according to numerous freely contracted mutual agreements between individuals and groups. There will be no government, no authority. The system will develop spontaneously; it cannot be determined now. No specific, objective conditions can be said to be necessary in order to build this system apart from the destruction, through revolution, of the existing capitalist regime.

For the purpose of our analysis, what is important about this dispute between Marxism and anarchism is that it reflects two different views of society evolving in time and of how an ideal society standing in opposition to bourgeois capitalism is to be established. In practical terms the clash of these two different views was vitally important in the development of nineteenth-century socialism because it led to a conflict between two fundamentally opposed strategies. In his *Modern Science and Anarchism* (1901) Kropotkin gave one of the clearest expositions of this disagreement:

So long as socialism was understood in its wide, generic, and true sense
– as an effort to *abolish* the exploitation of labour by capital – the

anarchists were marching hand-in-hand with the socialists of that time. But they were compelled to separate from them when the socialists began to say that there is no possibility of *abolishing* capitalist exploitation within the lifetime of our generation: that *during that phase of economic evolution which we are now living through* we have only to *mitigate* the exploitation, and to impose upon the capitalists certain legal limitations.

Contrarily to this tendency of the present-day socialists, we maintain that already now, without waiting for the coming of new phases and forms of the capitalist exploitation of labour, we must work for its *abolition*. We must, already now, tend to transfer all that is needed for production – the soil, the mines, the factories, the means of communication, and the means of existence, too – from the hands of the individual capitalist into those of the communities of producers and consumers.[10]

The dramatic sense of urgency – of not wishing to wait for a further historical development of capitalism – is very much in evidence in this passage, and again highlights what Mannheim sees as the basic chiliasm of the anarchist approach. From the point of view of studying utopian *ideas*, one could obviously assemble many arguments to support both the Marxist and anarchist strategies, and such an exercise would undoubtedly be revealing. But what seems to us to be even more important here is to look at the *practical circumstances* which actually led, in the course of the late nineteenth century, to the victory of Marxism over anarchism *as an effective movement*. And this kind of issue, as we have seen before, is to be resolved not through a study of the internal 'logic' of the rival systems, but in terms of their capacities to utilize leadership and organization in order to stimulate positive commitment in the struggle for a new social order.

George Lichtheim has suggested a two-fold characterization of the social basis of anarchism in the 1870s and 1880s.[11] In Western Europe the movement was basically a radical protest movement of impoverished artisans (and here he is thinking in particular of Belgium, Austria and Switzerland, although there were also remnants in France following the collapse of the Paris Commune. Many leaders of the Commune, it should be noted, were anarchist disciples of Proudhon). And in Spain and southern Italy it was mainly the downtrodden rural labourers who supported the movement. The industrial proletariat did not provide any significant social support for anarchism, but by this time were providing the chief constituency for the rise of social-democratic movements and parties, some of them (particularly in Germany and Austria) heavily imbued with the teachings of Marx and Engels, but interpreting those teachings in that spirit of parliamentary reformism which had been set out by Marx in his inaugural address of 1864 to the newly-formed International Workingmen's Association (the so-called First International). The picture was further complicated towards the end of this period, however, by the emergence in many Western countries of syndicalism as yet another alternative strategy, similar to anarchism in its rejection of political methods (and in the French case syndicalism, like anarchism, was rooted in the teachings of Proudhon), but relying on the exercise of force by trade unions, and therefore appealing directly to the industrial proletariat as a power base. As anarchism declined, towards the end of the century, syndicalism (and perhaps in the case of France and Spain one should say anarcho-syndicalism) took over as the main 'libertarian' alternative to Marxist social-democracy.

The desire to proceed immediately to the abolition of capitalism and the state (the latter seen as the embodiment of authority and hence as the chief threat to liberty); the belief that the new post-revolutionary society would be thoroughly decentralized and based on the local, predominantly rural community; the hostility to modernization, industrialism, technology, organization and bourgeois intellectualism: these were the main elements of the anarchist doctrine, and it is hardly surprising that they exercised their greatest appeal to the less well-off artisans and rural labourers, those groups who could easily imagine that they had nothing at all to gain from the new mass industrial society emerging in the nineteenth century. Some of these ideas were undoubtedly anticipated in the writings of the early socialists, and in particular in the theories of that great enemy of civilization, Charles Fourier. Just as Fourierism's appeal was mainly to the rural and lower middle-class victims of social change, so anarchism continued the tendency to cater for the aspirations of a declining, threatened and relatively small part of the class structure. Marxism, by contrast, saw progress in terms of the strengthening of a mass industrial proletariat, and the utilization of a highly developed capitalist system and state structure in the interests of the proletariat; and it was from this class that the Marxism of the 1870s and 1880s seemed at last to be drawing support. If one also bears in mind that the anarchists disliked the whole notion of utilizing large political parties and other 'legitimate' movements as instruments of organized activity, preferring to wait for the golden moment of heroic, direct action, one can see the greatly disadvantaged position they were in by comparison with the persistent Marxist emphasis on developing a proletarian 'class consciousness' through intellectual leadership and mobilization in national and international organizations. The Marxist willingness, after 1864 at least, to enter into the arena of parliamentary conflict within liberal democracies contrasted greatly with the anarchist rejection of all parliamentary methods. 'The anarchists refuse', Kropotkin wrote, 'to be party to the present State organization and to support it by infusing fresh blood into it. They do not seek to constitute, and invite the working men not to constitute, political parties in the parliaments.'[12] (Undoubtedly one important reason why syndicalism was later to prove more successful than the original anarchist approach was that it *did* utilize a formal, large-scale participatory institution, the trade union, as an instrument of change, culminating in the powerful weapon of the general strike; but even here 'contamination' by specifically political organizations was to be avoided.)

In Mannheim's view the dispute between Marxism and anarchism was of profound importance in the development of modern utopianism, since the defeat of anarchism (and of Bakunin's anarchism in particular) was also a defeat for the whole chiliastic strategy. Chiliasm did subsequently reappear in the doctrines of syndicalism, Fascism and even Russian Bolshevism, Mannheim seems to suggest, but he only mentions this in passing and does not take the analysis very far, insisting that it is in revolutionary anarchism that the chiliastic mentality 'is preserved in its purest and most genuine form'.[13] Bolshevism, of course, is particularly significant here, because of its practical influence in shaping the development of Russia and because of its impact on the Marxist movement more generally; and it is also, historically, a most remarkable expression of the utopian spirit. There are also important lessons to be learnt from an examination of Bolshevism in terms of the crucial role leadership and organization can play in ensuring the success of a revolutionary movement inspired by a doctrine which, from some points of view, might appear to have been inappropriate for a non-industrial, predominantly peasant society such as Russia evidently was in 1917. It is therefore very much a matter of looking at certain utopian outlooks deriving from Marxism and seeing how, in practice, those ideas were extended and modified by Lenin and his followers.

Lenin and the rise of Bolshevism

Marxism began to have an impact in Russia in the early 1880s, certainly after 1883 (the year of Marx's death), when George Plekhanov published his *Socialism and the Political Struggle* and, together with Vera

Zasulich and Paul Axelrod, founded the League for the Liberation of Labour, an organization established in Switzerland for the purpose of propagating Marxist ideas in Russia. From the very start Russian Marxists demonstrated their commitment to the belief that the process of historical development outlined by Marx – from feudalism to capitalism and then to socialism and communism – constituted an absolute law, and that consequently only a bourgeois-liberal revolution was possible at this stage in Russia (just as Marx, as we have seen, warned the German workers in 1847–8 of the need to strive for a bourgeois-liberal revolution in their country). When Plekhanov and Axelrod, in the 1890s, came to regard Lenin as a potential leader of the Russian Marxists, neither doubted that he too accepted the orthodox Marxist view of history. Yet Lenin knew that precisely because of Russia's economic backwardness and its predominantly peasant-based social structure, a Marxist movement in that country would make little sense without a new strategy of action fashioned deliberately for such circumstances. In particular he had to resolve the question of what kind of Marxist party organization was suited to a situation characterized by the absence of Western-type political institutions and by an oppressive Tsarist regime. This issue was tackled in Lenin's first important theoretical work, *What is to be Done?*, published in 1902, in which he rejected Marx's idea that the emancipation of the working class was to be achieved directly by the working class itself. The Social Democratic Party should not be a broad party of the working class, but rather it should be 'a small, coherent core of the most dependable, experienced, and hardened workers, which has trustworthy agents in the main districts and is connected, according to all the strictest rules of underground work, with an organization of revolutionaries'.[14] It was to be a party *for*, rather than *of*, the working class.

Lenin went on to argue that if the Russian proletariat could overthrow Tsarism, then the path would be open for an international revolution in the West. Such an overthrow was attempted in 1905, and although this revolution was not successful in its ultimate goal, it did lead to a number of bourgeois-liberal reforms: the granting of a constitution, the establishment of a parliament (Duma) and the formation of legalized political parties. Both Bolsheviks and Mensheviks now accepted the necessity of passing through a stage of bourgeois democracy on the way to socialism; but unlike the Mensheviks, Lenin argued that the Russian bourgeoisie was both unable and unwilling to complete this revolution by itself. In his view, the events of 1905 clearly demonstrated this inherent incapacity of the bourgeoisie, and consequently the proletariat itself must undertake the completion of the bourgeois revolution. Just how the proletariat was to do this was the problem dealt with by Lenin in *Two Tactics of Social Democracy in the Democratic Revolution*, written in the summer of 1905. The major condition to be fulfilled before the bourgeois revolution could be completed was an alliance between the proletariat and the peasantry. However, Lenin realized that such an alliance must be temporary, and that it would eventually have to be replaced by an alliance with the proletariat of Western Europe. Without the support of the European proletariat, a socialist revolution in Russia could not possibly be maintained.

In 1907 the Stuttgart congress of the Second Workers' International passed a resolution calling on all socialists to be ready, if war broke out, to exploit the resulting economic and political crisis in order to hasten the destruction of the social domination of the capitalist class. Lenin realized that war would provide the new crisis which Marx and Engels had viewed as a necessary precondition for revolution. It would present the opportunity of a socialist revolution in Europe which would enable Russia to pass on to her own socialist revolution. What Lenin did not foresee was the possibility of the Social Democratic parties of the West supporting their respective national governments when war commenced. Consequently, the events of August 1914 came as a great shock to the Bolsheviks, who viewed the behaviour of the Western socialists as tantamount to treason. The proletariat, which according to Marx was a potent revolutionary force, had proved not to be revolutionary at all. More than anything else, the First World War emphasized the particular state of affairs imposed on Marxism as it had evolved in Russia. How could Marxism be the object of unquestioning belief when Marx's predictions about the increasing poverty of the working class and the imminence of revolution had simply not come true? The crisis created in Russia by world war necessitated a new type of practical strategy; and it was Bolshevism as created by Lenin, and not Marxism in its original form, which eventually provided this strategy.

Lenin spent the years between the outbreak of war and the revolution of 1917 studying imperialist capitalism and its bearing on the socialist revolution. His major work during this period was *Imperialism, the Highest Stage of Capitalism*, written in Zurich between January and June 1916. Marx's predictions of imminent proletarian revolution had failed, argued Lenin, because capitalists, deriving high profits from exploitation abroad, had been able to pay high wages to the workers at home. But imperialist nations could no longer avoid wars between themselves, and such wars could only further the socialist revolution. By late 1916 Lenin thought that revolution was closer than ever, and when the Tsarist Government fell in March 1917, he was eager to return to Russia from Switzerland and resume political activity. Within a week of his arrival in Petrograd on 3 April, Lenin had rejected his long-held belief that the liberal-democratic republic was the only possible path to socialism, and had come round to the conclusion that Trotsky had reached many years before, namely, that the bourgeois and socialist revolutions would merge:

It is necessary to acquire that incontestable truth that a Marxist must take cognisance of living life, of the true facts of reality, that he must not continue clinging to the theory of yesterday, which, like every theory, at best only outlines the main and the general, only approximately embracing the complexity of life.... According to the old conception, the rule of the proletariat and peasantry ... can and must follow the rule of the bourgeoisie. In real life, however, things have turned out otherwise; an extremely original, new, unprecedented interlocking of one and the other has taken place.[15]

Between August and September 1917 Lenin was engaged in writing *The State and Revolution*, a work which occupies a very important place in the literature of modern utopianism because of the attention it gives to the issue of the state and its role in achieving socialism and, subsequently, full communism. Lenin argued that Marx had not said enough about the structure of the society that would succeed capitalism. However, by mid 1917 it was clear to Lenin that some sort of sketch of the impending changes in Russia was absolutely essential. *The State and Revolution* made it clear that the dictatorship of the proletariat would be, in effect, the dictatorship of the party. Lenin had always emphasized organization and discipline, and he realized that these would be the two essential qualities demanded of the proletariat acting as a ruling class. It would be necessary for the proletarian government to exercise strict control over the employment of labour and the needs of consumption. The dictatorship of the proletariat must not only organize a new economic and social order, but it must also hold down the exploiting class. The proletariat must destroy the existing state machine and replace it with a new one.[16]

The Bolshevik triumph in 1917 represents the end of a century-long phase during which the socialist counter-culture to capitalism emerged, gained influence, won various strategic victories and suffered many setbacks. The very terms 'socialism' and 'communism' were regarded as denoting thoroughly unrealistic conceptions of society when they were first used in the 1830s, but in 1917 an actual regime existed whose purpose was to demonstrate in practice how socialism and communism could be achieved. However, the fact that this regime was in a country in which capitalism had not yet achieved an advanced development raised obvious problems concerning its relevance as a 'model' of the ideal society, and this leads one to the whole issue of what happens to utopian visions of the future once they are supposedly acted upon in practice by those who actually hold power. It is an issue to which we shall return in Chapter 10, but we consider it more important, at this stage, to turn to another subject concerning the reaction of *non*-socialist thinkers and activists to the rise of socialism in the nineteenth century. Having given a great deal of attention to socialism and its utopian relationship to capitalism, we need to consider before we go any further whether there is any sense in which one can speak of other, non-socialist forms of utopianism during this period of history. Or is utopianism in the nineteenth century (and possibly in the twentieth century as well) simply synonymous with the socialist ideal?

Socialism's enemies: liberals, conservatives and positivists

To begin with, one can state with some assurance that the liberal-humanitarian brand of utopianism did not die out in the nineteenth century, although it lost much of its force because existing society actually came to approximate quite closely to the demands of liberal thinkers. It followed that liberalism as a tradition became orientated to a preservation of existing, newly-won freedoms and their consolidation rather than to a shattering of the existing order and its replacement by a new alternative. Liberals certainly continued to press for *greater* liberalism in economic and political arrangements, and the progress of liberal democracy was seen as a kind of path towards greater perfection; but the more these aims were considered to be compatible with the existing social framework, the more one could say that the utopian impulse in liberalism weakened. Utilitarianism, with its prospect of 'the greatest happiness of the greatest number', the principle formulated most clearly by Bentham and subsequently developed by John Stuart Mill, possessed a potential utopian dimension, but this was brought out not so much by liberals themselves as by the early socialists such as Owen in England and Saint-Simon in France, who were in fact greatly impressed by utilitarian arguments. John Stuart Mill, himself influenced both by early socialism, especially the French Saint-Simonian tradition, and by Bentham's utilitarianism, adopted a view of history which in many ways had more in common with socialism than with orthodox liberalism, but his practical recommendations usually compromised with the existing social system so much that one could hardly make out a strong case for describing him as a utopian. Nevertheless it is intriguing to look at his interest in a sort of 'qualified socialism', his belief in the possibility of a 'religion of humanity', and his relationship to French positivism as evidence of a propensity which certainly had *some* elements of the utopian impulse within it.

One of the most fascinating aspects of nineteenth-century liberalism was the way in which new theories of social evolution were incorporated in conceptions of society and politics which tended to defend rather than attack a framework of very gradual and moderate change. Herbert Spencer's evolutionary outlook and the whole late Victorian pre-occupation with social applications of Darwinism provide us with the best example of this trend. Spencer's concept of social evolution was in many ways more sophisticated than that of many socialists, yet it led him to the advocacy of what one commentator has described as 'the most simplistic and extreme version of *laissez-faire* individualism ever propagated'[17] – a philosophy of inaction, not action. Thus, although Spencer foresaw an ideal industrial society as the culmination of social progress, he did not see this as an alternative to existing actuality, but rather as an element already present in embryo within that society. To refer back again to Mannheim's distinction, this was most definitely an ideology rather than a utopia, although the ideology was presented in such a way that it claimed to offer the certainty of a new, transcendent harmony and happiness.

If there were remnants of the utopian impulse in liberalism in the nineteenth century, what can one say about conservatism, a tradition one can hardly ignore in this discussion, but one which is normally regarded as the absolute antithesis of the utopian outlook? If one accepts Michael Oakeshott's characterization of conservatism, for instance, one concludes that conservatism has no place at all for rational blueprints of the good society, and that it rejects the whole notion that one should try to move from the existing, actual society to an alternative which can be recommended as a clear improvement.[18] According to this view, conservatism is perhaps not even to be regarded as a coherent doctrine of politics at all, but is rather anti-doctrinal; and it is interesting to note here that in his own study of modern political doctrines in Europe, Oakeshott excludes conservatism precisely for this reason.[19] Yet historically the rise of liberal and socialist utopias presented conservatism with a challenge, a challenge it was forced to meet by producing its own alternative interpretations of the historical development of man-in-society, interpretations which Mannheim calls conservative 'counter-utopias'.[20] These counter-utopias, as one would expect, tended simply to justify the *status quo*, but they did so in quasi-rational, idealistic terms in order to emulate the modes of thinking of their opponents. Thus Hegel, in his association of the rational and the real, and in his dramatically conceived universal philosophy of history, took up the fight with the liberals on their own terms. It is true that British conservatism was slower to react in this way, and perhaps this is one reason why Oakeshott's characterization of conservatism is more of an anglicized, empiricist view than a continental, idealist one, but the British conservative tradition in the nineteenth century was certainly imbued with a new spirit of 'the meaning of history' and a rather romantic conception of how history led through its accumulated traditions to the existing state of society – the sum of man's most precious experiences. Some British conservatives, indeed, went so far as to emulate the early nineteenth-century socialist passion for blueprints, and one must surely regard, for instance, Coleridge's 'Pantisocracy' proposals and his *On the Constitution of Church and State* (1830) as examples of this trend. But the trend was even more pronounced at this time in France, in the Catholic writings of men such as Bonald and de Maistre, who reacted to the upheavals of the French Revolution by putting forward their own counter-proposals for establishing order and stability. As many commentators have observed, this specific conservative disposition actually influenced many of the early French socialists, in particular Saint-Simon and the Saint-Simonians, and also Comte.

The case of Auguste Comte and his positivist teachings brings us to one of the most interesting features of nineteenth-century utopianism. For while Comte is traditionally regarded as a conservative (he himself called himself *un conservateur* – see, for instance, his *Appeal to Conservatives* of 1855), there can be no doubt that he was the author of one of the most detailed utopias of modern times in his proposals for a 'positive polity'. Furthermore, he was not satisfied with the existing state of society, and so does not really fit into the conception of conservatism which is most widely accepted today. How, therefore, is he to be classified? He was certainly not a liberal or socialist, and frequently opposed both these schools of thought. We would suggest that Comte must be viewed as an exponent of a rather distinctive tradition of thinking – positivism – which represents a most unique alternative to bourgeois capitalism, but which at the same time opposes socialist collectivism. In other words, what we are arguing here is that there is already in the nineteenth century a utopia of a non-socialist type, and, we will go on to argue in Chapter 10, this positivist utopia has, in the course of the twentieth century, developed into a tradition of utopianism which can best be described as managerial and technocratic. Today, moreover, this tradition is very important because it is presented by its proponents as an alternative to both bourgeois liberalism and socialism. It has also become particularly fashionable since the Second World War to see managerialism and technocracy as the key features of a possible 'post-industrial' future.[21]

Comte's enthusiasm for the methods of positive science and the extension of those methods to the problem of managing society (the new science of social physics or 'sociology', a term he invented) was not new, and his initial views on this subject certainly grew out of the work he did in association with Saint-Simon towards the end of the latter's life. Thus, it may be that it is more accurate to regard Saint-Simon rather than Comte as the true founder of French social positivism. But it was Comte who was to develop the full theory of a 'positive polity' on the basis of his remarkable *Cours de Philosophie Positive* of 1830-42, and who attempted to show in detail how a modern society might be ruled according to the insights offered by science. His advocacy of rule by a new priesthood of intellectuals was in actual fact a mixture of technocracy and theocracy, since it involved the institution of a new religion of society to integrate man's physical and spiritual needs. Perhaps it would not be going too far to say that this was a form of French Catholic technocracy, although as T. H. Huxley once pointed out, the Catholicism had had the Christianity taken out of it. Modern technocrats, in the twentieth century, would perhaps reject such an alliance of religion and the rule of science, but this does not displace Comte from the broad technocratic tradition. Although private ownership of property would be preserved in the 'positive polity', owners would be subject to such rigorous managerial control that the system could hardly be called capitalism in the usual sense.

Comte's doctrine exerted a powerful intellectual appeal (and this is not surprising, since it was the intellectuals he was calling upon to assume power) in the nineteenth and, indeed, into the early twentieth century. Yet its practical impact was somewhat negligible for the reason which Aron has so clearly stated: 'The Comtist conception of industrial society has remained a kind of curiosity on the fringes of the rivalry among doctrines because none of the political parties, either on the right or on the left, has acknowledged it, with the exception of a few individuals.'[22] Only where positivism was able to link up with existing, established movements did it succeed in having a significant political role, as for example in English labour organizations.[23] Outside of Europe, where liberal-democratic political parties were not so crucial as agents of mobilization and activity, it was possible for Comte's doctrine to break through, and this partly explains the extraordinary influence of positivism in Latin America at the end of the nineteenth century.[24] But as far as Europe is concerned, other more powerful movements held the field and could not be broken into. Strangely enough in the twentieth century it has been exactly at those moments of disillusionment with traditional party politics that the techno-cratic utopia, foreshadowed by Comte, has once again been revived by intellectuals who see the world's salvation in the abolition of politics and the rise to power of scientists, engineers and other men of know-ledge. One of the continuing themes of modern utopianism – and of the imaginative dystopias such as *We, Nineteen Eighty-four* and *Brave New World* – has been the prospect for orthodox political institutions in an age when science and technology seem to undermine so many of our traditional political assumptions. This is a theme to which we shall return in our final chapter.

Suggested reading

G. Lichtheim's *Marxism* is still probably the best general text on Marxism's impact as a social movement. The utopian elements in Marxist thought are considered (from different perspectives) in E. Kamenka, *The Ethical Foundations of Marxism*; M. Lasky, *Utopia and Revolution*; K. Mannheim, *Ideology and Utopia*; and the appropriate chapters of F. E. and F. P. Manuel, *Utopian Thought in the Western World*. See also B. Ollman, 'Marx's vision of communism: a reconstruction', *Critique*, no. 8 (1977). On anarchism see both Mannheim's book and G. Wood-cock, *Anarchism*. More general perspectives on the major currents of nineteenth-century thought are offered by J. Bowle, *Politics and Opinion in the Nineteenth Century*, and S. Wolin, *Politics and Vision*. These books include material on liberalism, conservatism and positivism. On the latter subject an excellent analysis is provided by W. M. Simon, *European Positivism in the Nineteenth Century*.

8 Utopia writ small: communitarianism and its legacy

The image of utopia as a relatively small island or enclave jealously protected from contamination by the external world has persisted throughout the history of Western civilization. The city-states of ancient Greece and Renaissance Italy, the medieval monasteries, the lost islands discovered by the great explorers of the fifteenth and sixteenth centuries, the Fourierist Phalanxes and Owenite colonies of the early nineteenth century, the 'city beautiful' and town planning traditions of the later 1800s, the communal movements of the 1960s – all these traditions point in the direction of a utopianism based on small-scale communitarianism rather than the large, expansionist nation-states and Empires which have elsewhere come to be taken for granted as the 'normal' forms of political organization in the modern world. To many people, indeed, utopianism has always signified, first and foremost, the communitarian spirit, the desire to establish a closely knit, self-contained, family-like social unit based in a particular locality or territorial region. Utopianism thus becomes synonymous with hostility to the large, powerful nation-state, and is seen to involve an enthusiasm for the virtues of local self-government and that sense of parochial loyalty which so often seems to be lacking in this age which has witnessed the triumph of the huge, impersonal organization. The motto of this particular style of utopianism might well be summed up as 'small is beautiful'.

Because of this characteristic, it might be thought surprising that there is also a well-established school of thought, to which we have already given some attention in this study, which seems to equate utopianism and totalitarianism. Thus Popper, Hayek, Talmon and others are convinced that the emergence of the totalitarian police-state/mass-society (whether of the left- or the right-wing variety) was due in part to the influence of ideas stemming from the Western utopian tradition inaugurated by Plato and More and culminating, in the nineteenth century, in the ideas of the early socialists and Marx, and subsequently in Bolshevism and Fascism. Utopianism is here seen to be synonymous with precisely the same overpowering, large-scale, domineering control of man's activities which, according to our initial characterization, other commentators have recognized as the *antithesis* of the utopian-communitarian impulse.

Such confusion, it must be acknowledged, is not unusual in the study of political thought. It is in fact fairly common for certain key thinkers – Plato, Rousseau and Marx, for example – to be proclaimed by some commentators as heralds of true libertarianism, and to be savagely attacked by others as prophets of a cruel despotism. Utopianism as a genre fits well into this mould, and one can easily find support for two mutually exclusive interpretations of utopianism: the first treating it as an extremely liberal and voluntaristic tradition, emphasizing local independence and experimentation; the second (after Popper, Hayek and Talmon) insisting on the illiberal, totalitarian implications. The confusion is partly due to an ambiguity inherent in the literature of utopianism in its most modern form, certainly from the late eighteenth century onwards, an ambiguity arising because modern utopians have themselves been divided into, first, proponents of what might be called the utopian nation-state (or even a utopian international system) making use of large-scale productive techniques and uniting several million people in one highly integrated society; and second, proponents of the small-scale utopian community of just a few hundred or a few thousand persons living quite an independent, experimental style of existence, although they might possibly be subject to quite a considerable amount of authority and regulation within their community. This distinction is well illustrated by the case of early socialism, which was considered in Chapter 5, and it was there seen that the question of statism versus communitarianism was one of the chief strategic dilemmas facing the early British, French and German socialist thinkers. While Saint-Simon, the Saint-Simonians, Cabet and Weitling advocated the reorganization of entire national societies, Owen and Fourier did not wish communities to be larger than 2000 or 3000 people. Yet even Cabet and Weitling, it will be recalled, *in practice* found themselves involved in communitarian schemes in the United States (on an even more modest scale than those advocated by Owen and Fourier). And this brings us to one of the key points of this chapter. Much of the actual practice of utopian movements, even those aiming ultimately for the reorganization of large nation-states, has involved small-scale schemes of experimentation as a starting-point, a type of experimentation, furthermore, which, one might reasonably expect, would appeal to liberal democrats; yet in fact liberal democrats have tended to overlook this practical aspect of utopianism, preferring to dismiss all utopian schemes because they cannot easily be accommodated within the more conventional forms of liberal-democratic political organization. To make the matter perfectly clear: there is an orthodox view of communitarian experimentation, a view especially strong within the British liberal-democratic tradition, which states that communitarianism is not worthy of serious study, that it has clearly 'failed' to achieve significant practical results, and that those people involved in communitarian schemes are really eccentric 'outsiders' who have turned their backs on the more usual, and more effective, channels of political activity such as the large nation-centred political parties and interest groups of mass industrial society. What we wish to argue here is that such a view is not justified by the facts, that communitarianism has actually 'succeeded' in many ways, and that it has contributed much to modern political development.

The American experience

There can be little doubt that historically it is in America that communitarianism has had its greatest political influence. (And it is because of this that American liberal democrats have generally displayed more sympathy towards communitarianism than have their Anglo-continental counterparts.) When Arthur O. Lewis asserts that 'nowhere has the utopian ideal been more significant in shaping society than in the United States',[1] he is referring in part to the general idealistic spirit of progress that has motivated the initial creation and subsequent development of the United States; but more particularly he has in mind the dramatic and persistent influence of communitarianism in shaping American society. Furthermore, this influence was not confined, as some commentators have suggested, to the years prior to the Civil War. The research of Robert S. Fogarty has indicated quite clearly that communitarianism was not halted by the War but merely interrupted, and thus the more recent twentieth-century history of American communal experiments should be regarded as a continuation of the older tradition.[2] The sheer number of communities established in America is impressive: Fogarty's conservative estimate is that about 600 communities were founded between 1663 and 1950,[3] and to this figure must be added the staggeringly large number of new communes – probably several thousand of them – which arose during the utopian renaissance of the 1960s and 1970s, particularly in California and along the west coast. Fogarty is particularly anxious to reject the view that the creation of communities in America has gone in isolated phases, representing periods of wild, somewhat eccentric experimentation; rather he insists (and we would agree with him) that communitarianism has *always* been a perfectly normal ingredient of the American social and political culture: 'I am not convinced that there have been high periods and low periods, but rather that the urge to start new colonies - in a culture so intensely individualistic as ours - demonstrates, likewise, the felt presence of the cooperatively minded.'[4]

If, in America, utopianism has found so much fruitful expression because of a receptive *individualistic* culture, then this clearly is one response to the charge that utopianism is necessarily synonymous with totalitarianism. Certainly, some of these numerous American communities have been fairly authoritarian in terms of their internal organization, yet underlying the whole communitarian tradition, even in those cases of internal authoritarianism, has been a fundamental voluntarism which has meant that membership of these communities and support for them have invariably rested on express consent, a virtue which, from a liberal-democratic perspective, ought to be commended. The liberal idea of a freely concluded social contract is also peculiarly relevant to this kind of communitarianism, since the vast majority of communities can be seen to have resulted from contractual agreements between their original members which they were not compelled to enter into, but which they made out of deliberate choice. One might also add the more cynical comment that the ease with which so many communities have disintegrated confirms that in the last resort they have rested on free consent rather than imposed coercion. There is indeed a very high rate of collapse among American communitarian experiments. Relatively few have survived for any substantial length of time, and the vast majority have been of extremely short duration. It is these basic facts which have led to the widely expressed charge that communitarianism has 'failed' and must be discounted as a serious movement. Yet more recently, as a result of new historical and socio-logical surveys of communitarianism, this orthodox view has been seen by many commentators to be in need of revision.

How important is duration as a criterion for gauging the success of a utopian community? There can obviously be no final, objective answer to this question, any more than one can definitely judge an individual person's worth by the length of his or her lifetime. From some points of view it may seem that a community's life-span is the single most significant factor, and that broadly speaking those communities lasting the longest may be deemed the most successful. On the other hand, there are strong arguments in favour of placing much more emphasis on the 'quality of life' actually achieved in a community, no matter how temporary the community as a social institution. This is a view well represented in the outlook of Henry Demarest Lloyd, an American reformer of the 1890s who was greatly impressed by what he saw of life in the country's numerous communities:

> Only within these communities has there been seen, in the wide boundaries of the United States, a social life where hunger and cold, prostitution, intemperance, poverty, slavery, crime, premature old age and unnecessary mortality, panic and industrial terror have been abolished. If they had done this for only a year, they would have deserved to be called the only successful 'society' on this continent, and some of them are generations old. All this has not been done by saints in heaven, but on earth by average men and women.[5]

We may readily agree with Lloyd that one should not underestimate the achievements of small, short-lived communities which achieve the eradication of major social evils, for however brief a time. Yet at the same time, if evidence suggests that communities in general are incapable of surviving, of providing a reasonably permanent, stable, viable framework for social life, one would have to conclude that they should not be taken too seriously as a recommended basis for any future programme of action. We must surely look for some positive indication that *under certain favourable circumstances* small communities are a viable proposition and a realistic alternative to the more established and more widely accepted forms of social organization.

On this issue the evidence provided by the history of American communitarianism is especially important, since that history goes back much further than similar experimental traditions in other countries, further for instance than the *kibbutzim* of Israel, which are usually taken as the second great category of utopian communitarianism. Because there is a continuous communitarian tradition in America going back to the late seventeenth century, the results provide us with a marvellous living laboratory of the possibilities and potential provided by alternative life-styles and new forms of social, economic and political organization which in many respects undermine the assumptions of the modern, liberal-democratic nation-state. Furthermore, even in terms of the very basic criterion of durability – which, as we have seen, is not always as important as might be supposed – some American communities have indeed been very successful, more so in fact than some nation-states. (The durability of the nation-state in nineteenth- and twentieth-century Europe and in the Third World has been far from impressive.)[6] The following information concerning successful (in the specific sense of durable) American communities, taken from Rosabeth Moss Kanter's sociological study *Commitment and Community*, provides us with a good starting-point, and shows that even by comparison with some nation-states there have been several long-lived utopian communities:

The Shakers. 195 years. 1787–present. Grew out of a sect, the United Society of Believers, founded by Ann Lee. First Shaker Village established by Joseph Meachem after her death. About 500 original members; at height, 1830–1840, 6000 members in 18 villages throughout the northeast.

The Harmony Society. 100 years. 1804–1904. German separatists led by George Rapp. Settled first in Harmony, Pennsylvania, then New Harmony, Indiana, then Economy, Pennsylvania. 600–700 original members; 800 in 1811.

Amana. 90 years. 1843–1933. The Society of True Inspiration, a German sect. Settled first in Ebenezer, New York, then established seven communal villages in Iowa. 800 original members; 1800 in 1880.

Zoar. 81 years. 1817–1898. The Society of Separatists, a German group led by Joseph Bimeler. Settled in Ohio. 300 original members; 500 in 1853.

Snowhill. 70 years. 1800–1870. Seventh Day Baptists. An offshoot of the Ephrata Community in Pennsylvania.

Saint Nazianz. 42 years. 1854–1896. A Catholic commune established in Wisconsin by German immigrants led by Father Ambrose Ochswald. 28 original members; 450 in 1866.

Bethel and *Aurora*. 36 years. 1844–1880. Established in Missouri and Oregon, by followers of William Keil. Bethel was founded first; later Keil and part of the group moved to Aurora.

Oneida. 33 years. 1848–1881. American Perfectionists led by John Humphrey Noyes, implementing 'Bible communism' in upstate New York. For a time, branches elsewhere, principally in Wallingford, Connecticut. 40 original members in Putney, Vermont. 104 members in Oneida in 1849; 288 in 1880. (Thirty-three years is a conservative figure for Oneida's duration, for the core group actually started five years earlier in Putney, and when the community was transformed into a joint-stock company in 1881, it retained strong communal overtones and a residential base.)

Jerusalem. 33 years. 1788–1821. New York community established by followers of Jemimah Wilkinson, the 'Universal Friend'. 250 members in 1800. (Thirty-three years is a conservative figure for Jerusalem's duration, since a core of the community remained together another twenty-two years under the guidance of Rachel Malin, Jemimah's appointed successor.)[7]

To this list of the major communities founded between the American Revolution and Civil Wars (which are Kanter's main concern) we should also add two later examples, both still surviving today: the Hutterites or Hutterian Brethren (founded originally in about 1530 and in America since 1873), now with some 150 communities and 17,000 members; and the Bruderhof or Society of Brothers (founded about 1920 and in America since 1953), with three communities and about 800 members.[8] There is also a case for including the Icarian movement founded by Cabet as a fairly successful example of a durable communitarianism, although Kanter, for reasons which are not entirely clear, regards Icarianism as unclassifiable.[9] But the fact is that five Icarian communities of various kinds (none of them very large) did survive for half a century, from the initial settlement at Nauvoo, Illinois, in 1849, to the demise of the final breakaway group in Adams County, Iowa, in 1898. Icarianism was certainly beset by difficulties and schisms, but achieved much more in terms of durability than the short-lived Owenite and Fourierist communities.

Preconditions for success

The communities listed above, it will be observed, were predominantly of the sectarian type, based on some shared religious inspiration, and this sectarianism is undoubtedly one clue to their durability. However, religion was not always so crucial: in the case of Oneida the original religious basis was dispensed with in favour of a more secular programme: and as far as Icarianism is concerned, although Cabet taught his followers to subscribe to a doctrine of 'True Christianity', this was never formalized to any great extent, and the secular morality of communism was always given great emphasis. Furthermore, it has to be remembered, as Kanter stresses, that many *short-lived* communitarian schemes were also religious and sectarian, thus leading one to the conclusion that 'the difference between the successful and unsuccessful communes was much broader than religion alone', and consequently 'it does not seem that the presence of a religion or of religious origins *per se* made the difference between success and failure'.[10] What clearly was important in all the successful communes was that a strong sense of *utopian commitment* had been established among the members. This notion of utopian commitment, as we saw in Chapters 6 and 7, can be very useful in helping us to explain why some utopian movements are more successful than others, and, as Kanter shows in her book, it seems to be of vital importance in the study of communitarianism. It thus becomes a matter of seeking to understand what mechanisms communities may use in order to develop a sense of commitment among their members. Religion can be very important in this respect, but it is only one of several commitment mechanisms, and what is significant about religion is the practices it involves rather than a particular set of beliefs in God or concept of divine worship:

There are many social practices often associated with religion that were useful in building commitment. These practices include a comprehensive value system and a transcendent moral order with many moral principles, which easily give rise to spiritual differentiation. Religious groups often require shared beliefs and conversion to those beliefs, which may include belief in inspiration, revelation, or nonscientific sources of wisdom. Religious groups sometimes have charismatic leaders invested with extraordinary properties. Membership in such groups may involve sacrifice and deliberate rejection of the material world, along with confession and mutual criticism. Finally, ritual and symbolic, expressive ceremonies, including the use of music and singing, is often characteristic of religious groups. It is these specific practices, available even to groups that resist a deliberate focus, which build commitment, not the presence of a formally labelled religion.[11]

In the course of her analysis of utopian commitment, Kanter found it useful to distinguish three aspects of a community system involving the commitment of its members:[12] retention of members, that is, the continuing willingness of people to stay in the community, support it and perform their duties; group cohesiveness – the sense of collective identity and strength *vis-à-vis* external threats; and social control – the ability to regulate the community in an authoritative way through the command of obedience and respect. In theory, these three categories of commitment could involve different solutions, and perhaps not all members would exhibit the same level of commitment in each of the three cases. Thus, the question of utopian commitment has several dimensions, and one can say accordingly that the durability of a particular community would reflect several kinds of success in achieving and maintaining commitment. Personal commitment itself could be expressed in various forms, and might be instrumental, affective or moral. Instrumental commitment arises through a utilitarian calculation of the rewards and costs involved; affective commitment is much more a matter of emotional bonds; and moral commitment emerges through an acceptance of social norms and beliefs. Kanter goes on to argue that instrumental commitment tends to be related primarily to the aim of retention of membership; affective commitment supports group cohesion; and moral commitment promotes social control. It is argued, furthermore, that the success of a community will derive from its ability to promote one or more of these forms of commitment. Total commitment in a community would involve maximizing all three forms of commitment. Degrees of commitment beneath this maximum level could involve, perhaps, a moderate success in each of the three areas, or possibly high success in two areas plus very little success in the third, and so on:

Ignoring for the moment all the other diverse sources of influence on group life, groups in which people have formed instrumental commitments should manage to hold their members. Groups in which people have formed affective commitments should report more mutual attraction and interpersonal satisfaction and should be able to withstand threats to their existence. Groups in which members have formed moral commitments should have less deviance, challenge to authority, or ideological controversy. Groups with all kinds of commitment, that is, with total commitment, should be more successful in their maintenance than those without it.[13]

By what methods, then, may a community seek to promote instrumental, affective and moral commitments? Kanter suggests that there are six major 'commitment-building processes', and that it is the successful organization of these processes that marks the long-lived American communities from those of only short duration.[14] First, instrumental commitment is developed through the processes of sacrifice and investment:

Sacrifice involves the giving up of something considered valuable or pleasurable in order to belong to the organization; it stresses the importance of the role of member to the individual. Sacrifice means that membership becomes more costly and is therefore not lightly regarded nor likely to be given up easily. Investment is a process whereby the individual gains a stake in the group, commits current and future profits to it, so that he must continue to participate if he is going to realize those profits. Investment generally involves the giving up of control over some of the person's resources to the community.[15]

Second, affective commitment is developed through the processes of renunciation and communion:

Renunciation involves giving up competing relationships outside the communal group and individualistic, exclusive attachments within. Whatever fund of emotion the individuals possess becomes concentrated in the group itself, glueing all members together, creating a cohesive unit. It is to this unit alone that members look for emotional satisfaction and to which they give their loyalty and commitment. Communion involves bringing members into meaningful contact with the collective whole, so that they experience the fact of oneness with the group and develop a 'we-feeling'.[16]

And third, moral commitment is developed through mortification and transcendence:

Mortification involves the submission of private states to social control, the exchanging of a former identity for one defined and formulated by the community. Transcendence is a process whereby an individual attaches his decision-making prerogatives to a power greater than himself, surrendering to the higher meaning contained by the group and submitting to something beyond himself.[17]

It can be seen that Kanter's six processes of community-building are divided into three groups, and each group consists of one process of *detaching* the individual from external commitments which might compete with the community in question; and one process of *attaching* the individual through positive commitment to the community. Sacrifice, renunciation and mortification are three detaching processes, while investment, communion and transcendence create a sense in each individual of attaching to the community. We are thus led, in the course of Kanter's sociological analysis, to the following framework for examining the way in which utopian commitment in a particular community is created and maintained, and for comparing how this is done (or is not done) in several communities (the diagrammatic representation is our own):

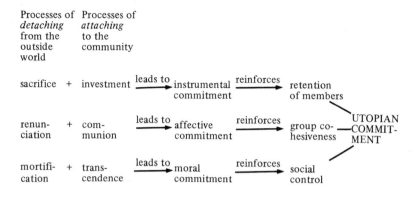

Successful, i.e. long-lived, American communities were able to promote the six commitment-building processes through a vast range of institutional mechanisms and social practices (although, of course, even they, in the end, usually found that they could not sustain these processes indefinitely). The unsuccessful communities, by contrast, failed to develop such mechanisms and practices at all, or at least did so only to a modest extent. This, it would seem, is the real key to the success of some American communitarian experiments and to the failure of others. Kanter analyses these mechanisms and practices in some considerable detail, and anyone interested in this issue should study her arguments at first hand.[18] For the purposes of this chapter some attempt will be made to summarize Kanter's most interesting findings, and we may conveniently do this under the six major headings corresponding to the six commitment-building processes.

1 Instrumental commitment

Sacrifice   It was found by Kanter that mechanisms of abstinence and austerity were much more common in successful than in unsuccessful communities. Members of the successful communities placed value on their participation because they knew it 'cost' them a certain amount of 'expense'. They made sacrifices for a cause, and the cause was thus made worthy and noble. Common sacrifices included abstinence from alcohol, tobacco, coffee, tea, rich foods or meat. Sexual abstinence through celibacy was practised at some stage in the history of all the nine successful nineteenth-century communities studied by Kanter. Many communities were exceedingly puritanical in their approach to personal clothing, jewellery and to 'worldly' activities such as sport, dancing and music. Successful communities tended to enjoy an austere life-style; they usually built themselves up from scratch, and members had to endure much economic deprivation. The sharing of hardship and struggle enhanced the level of commitment.

Investment   Successful communities were usually those which called upon members to make some tangible investment in the community's development. Members were expected to reside in the community's territorial area (non-residence was quite common in other, unsuccessful communities), to do useful work, and in addition were usually asked to have some financial holding in the community's economy. Productive property was invariably held in common, and personal property was often allocated according to some conception of overall social need. These commitments, furthermore, were often irreversible. Community, in other words, frequently meant communism.

2 Affective commitment

Renunciation   In successful communities a great premium was placed on individual integration into the collectivity through the renunciation of relationships with the external world and with subunits (e.g. traditional marital and family groups) within the community. The external world was often kept away through physical boundaries (such as geographical isolation or poor communication), and through internal self-sufficiency in matters of social, economic and political organization. Furthermore, the external world was kept away culturally by ensuring that the community developed its own distinctive norms of behaviour and belief in contrast to which the outside world was 'alien'. In addition regulations were often made to prohibit or limit emigration, even for brief visits. Within the successful communities it was usual for group solidarity to be emphasized rather than the value of the two-person union of one man and one woman or the traditional nuclear family. Celibacy might be one response to this issue; but another was the opposite extreme of 'free love' and a kind of 'amorous communism' and group marriage. Children were often brought up and educated communally rather than through the care of one particular set of parents.

Communion   Successful communities required the development of a strong sense of belonging to the community, of being part of a greater collective entity to which the individual could relate emotionally. Such a sense could most easily develop where the members shared a similar religious, social or ethnic background, where they had something positive in common before the community experiment began. The communities of Harmony, Amana and Zoar, for instance, were formed from groups of German sectarians. (The more recent Bruderhof tradition is another example.) Communal economic arrangements also contributed to the development of a shared identity and interdependence. This included an emphasis on work as a communal, shared experience – for instance through a rotation of tasks (in order to avoid narrow specialization), through tasks involving the entire community (e.g. harvesting) and through the abolition of individual wages. The physical arrangements of the community (e.g. residential and dining facilities) were also designed to bring the whole group into contact with one another. Community public assemblies were frequently employed to encourage joint decision-making. Rituals of celebration and common festivities and ceremonies added to the process of communion-building. One should also note that many communities suffered persecution (whether social, economic or physical) at the hands of the outside world, and this further enhanced community solidarity.

3   Moral commitment

Mortification   The distinction between private and public life was diminished, perhaps even eliminated altogether, in successful American communities. The individual's identity was defined through his or her success in living up to the norms and standards of the community as a whole. Systems of confession, self-criticism and mutual criticism were often used for this purpose. The individual had no private life; his behaviour was a group concern. Acts of deviance from community norms were 'punished', often through making a public example of the person concerned. On the other hand, exemplary conduct would be rewarded, perhaps through the deference and respect shown to such persons, or through the allocation of special privileges. Once again, the community's physical arrangements were important in that they left individuals little time for private activities.

Transcendence   Kanter found that transcendence required first and foremost 'the experience of great power and meaning residing in the community'.[19] Often this was made possible through the authority exercised by great charismatic leaders such as Ann Lee of the Shakers, George Rapp of Harmony, Joseph Bimeler of Zoar, William Keil of Bethel and Aurora, Jemimah Wilkinson of Jerusalem, John Humphrey Noyes of Oneida. But such individual charisma sooner or later had to be channelled into an ideological basis promoting the individual's sense of awe towards the authority of the group as a whole. Quite comprehensive, complex ideologies characterized all the successful communities except one (Bethel/Aurora), and invariably one feature of the ideology was a great reverence for certain types of individuals with the appropriate qualities such as wisdom or spiritual inspiration. Some kind of religious doctrine invariably lay behind this reverence. It was also common for all members of a particular community to regard themselves as being endowed with a special grace of spirituality simply by belonging to the group. Often a strict hierarchy of authority in a community (and the physical separation of great leaders from ordinary citizens) was accompanied by direct democracy through regular popular assemblies, a curious mixture of mysterious elitism and citizen participation. The division was usually that between elitism in major community decisions, and popular control over routine matters.

We have thought it useful to summarize Kanter's most important findings in some detail, because we believe that they are a most fruitful source of knowledge and understanding about one particular tradition of communitarianism, the American. But also, Kanter's approach offers a highly incisive set of analytical tools, a way of looking at all communitarian experiments in whatever period and location they occur in order to analyse their potentiality for success or failure. We do not wish to suggest, of course, that Kanter's is the only useful analysis of communitarianism. There are in fact many such works, and most of them seem to confirm Kanter's arguments.[20] But *Commitment and Community* is, we believe, the single most important sociological study, and the one which approaches the issues involved most systematically and in the most useful comparative perspective. At the same time there are certain issues which even Kanter's comprehensive survey tends to neglect, and one particularly important example is the relationship between communitarianism and the process of industrialization in nineteenth-century America. Although there is some discussion in her book of how industrialization and its associated technology, by changing the economic and social environment, made it extremely difficult for many communities to survive, and gave rise to many sources of conflict and disagreement within the communities (sources which could not easily have been anticipated when those communities were inaugurated),[21] nevertheless the specific question of whether communitarianism must have an agrarian basis if it is to succeed or whether it is compatible with an industrialized society is not given a great deal of attention. The fact is that the nineteenth-century American communities here regarded as successful were generally rural, village-type communities in which farming was the chief occupation. The one notable exception was Oneida, which under Noyes's leadership developed a strong manufacturing basis. Eventually all the other communities also developed some industries, but to a much more limited extent. This was also true of Icarianism. More recently, the Hutterites have avoided industry and have deliberately restricted themselves to agriculture, a policy which has actually proved successful since the Hutterites have survived as a communitarian system. The Bruderhof communities, originally agricultural, have managed in America to establish small manufacturing concerns for the production and distribution of educational toys. In a recent comparative investigation into the reasons for decline in nineteenth-century American communities Charles J. Erasmus found that 'an important initiating cause of breakdown was endorsement of progress through labour-saving mechanization'.[22] Such mechanization tended to undermine the agricultural subsistence and general economic self-sufficiency of these communities, and their separation and independence from the outside world, by encouraging specialization in the production of goods which they did not really need themselves but which they could 'export' at a favourable rate of return. At the same time a larger and larger proportion of the actual necessities they required was bought from outside because many of their own workers had been transferred to manufacturing, and because they could now afford to purchase more of the commodities in question than they could possibly produce themselves. Erasmus cites the particular example of the Amana community in Iowa:

At Amana, members found the demand for their woollens growing steadily with their reputation for high quality. Concentrating on its woollen mills, Amana was soon weaving far more wool than the community's three thousand sheep could produce.

Amana, like many of the other societies, gave increasingly less attention to agriculture as it expanded its manufactures. It came to depend more and more on the profits of its woollen mills to purchase the necessities no longer produced in the community. What did it give up? Despite a strong desire to be self-sufficient in agriculture and dairy products, by the end of the nineteenth century a year never passed that the society did not have to buy food supplies from outside to meet the needs of members and livestock. It had found that it was more economical to rent out its farm lands and enlarge its mills. And by the beginning of the twentieth century, it had given up many community crafts.[23]

Erasmus's view is that the collectivism so essential to the survival of the American communities was undermined by 'need elasticity permitted in the production sphere',[24] by which he means the tendency to develop methods of 'efficient' production geared towards a set of needs imposed by the materialistic outside world, thereby switching from subsistence to commercial production. And the switch to commercial production not only increased the communities' vulnerability to the fluctuations of the national (i.e. American) market, but also interfered with most of the commitment-building processes discussed earlier in relation to Kanter's analysis as material considerations achieved supremacy over other, non-material goals. Of the nineteenth- and twentieth-century American communities only the Hutterites have really demonstrated how to avoid this problem:

> While the Hutterites have not eschewed labour-saving machinery, they have so channelled it as to contain the progressive consequences that undermined our nineteenth-century utopias. More by accident than intent, Hutterite mechanization has kept within a Shaker Evans agricultural framework instead of following a John Humphrey Noyes industrialist expansion. Hutterites were not opposed to industrialization *per se*, for they had developed extensive craft industries early in their history. But by the time they arrived in the United States, the industrialization process with which Economy, Amana, and Oneida had grown up a generation or two earlier had now become highly competitive. The Hutterites took the more secure and profitable route for their purposes and developed eventually into modern, mechanized farmers.[25]

Israel: *kibbutzim* and *shitufim*

In the light of our growing knowledge of American communities, it is interesting to compare them with the *kibbutzim* of Israel, which are usually regarded as the second major category of practical communitarian utopias, and in some ways the most relevant category because they survive and flourish today and constitute, as a whole, the largest single communitarian movement ever. To be perfectly accurate one ought to distinguish between the thoroughly collective *kibbutzim* proper, and the semi-collective *moshavim shitufim*, which are of more recent origin and are much less well known, even in Israel. The *kibbutz* is a settlement in which communal life, work and collective ownership are developed to a very high extent. In the *shitufi*, by contrast, a system of collective work and ownership is combined with many elements of private family life, and it is thus less communal in character than the *kibbutz*. The first small *kibbutzim* started in Palestine in the early years of this century (the first was Dagania, founded in 1909) and their numbers gradually increased until, by the end of the 1940s, there were over two hundred. The first three *shitufim* appeared as a deliberate modification of the *kibbutz* between 1936 and 1938. No further increase in numbers occurred until after the Second World War. By 1968 there were twenty-two *shitufim*, and since then the number has grown to around forty. The *shitufim* also tend to be smaller in size than the *kibbutzim*. While the latter contain an average of about 400 persons, the *shitufim's* average population is about 250. In each case, however, there is a wide gap between the smallest and largest communities: the *kibbutzim* vary from 200 to 2000, the *shitufim* from 70 to 400.[26]

By any reasonable standard of duration (Kanter, for instance, suggests twenty-five years; Erasmus suggests thirty-five)[27] both the *kibbutz* and the *shitufi* provide us with examples of 'successful' communities. Yet there are already signs that pressures similar to those which we analysed earlier in relation to American communities are now affecting Israeli communities. Erasmus found that 'the *kibbutz* is already contending with all the symptoms of breakdown or transformation that beset our nineteenth-century utopias', and 'the *moshav shitufi* shows many of these same symptoms to a more advanced degree'.[28] In some ways, perhaps, this may seem surprising, since the *kibbutzim* and *shitufim*, especially the former, were at first characterized by many features which helped to build very high levels of commitment to the communitarian enterprise - higher indeed than in the case of many of the American experiments. In part this commitment derived from the *kibbutz's* incredibly strong ideological foundations, a factor which, as we have seen in Kanter's analysis, is supremely important in stimulating a sense of moral commitment. These ideological foundations, in turn, were a mixture of socio-economic, political, religious and national ideals. Zionism - the quest for a Jewish national state in Palestine - was one key ingredient, and this intense patriotism often (although by no means always) linked up with an enthusiasm for doctrines of socialism and communism. Many of the first pioneer immigrants spoke and wrote about the ideas of the nineteenth-century utopian socialists and their influence on American communitarian experiments. Others were more interested in Marxism, and some in anarchism. In all cases socialism's promise of equality, in a world which had amply demonstrated its persecution of the Jews and a vigorous anti-semitism, was generally held to be an essential element in the Zionist movement.

There were also considerations of a more practical kind which generated strong instrumental and affective commitment to the *kibbutz* idea in the early years of this century. Group solidarity *vis-à-vis* the outside world was obviously emphasized by the reaction against persecution and anti-semitism to which reference has already been made. The outside world was evidently hostile and alien and must be renounced. Furthermore, the early immigrants to Palestine usually had a pre-existing cultural background in common based on their shared experience of oppression and discrimination in Russia and Eastern Europe. The intense economic hardship in these early days of settlement also made for affective commitment to communal arrangements (Kanter's sense of 'communion') for the simple reason that at that stage no viable alternatives could be envisaged. As one commentator has put it; the main priority

was to find a form of settlement for Jews which was both practical and efficient. After the bitter experiences of the early, privately owned individualistic settlements, the pioneers turned to collective living, believing that the collective built on mutual aid would succeed where individual enterprise had failed.[29]

It can also be seen quite clearly that immigration to Palestine and participation in the settlement of Palestine involved both sacrifice for a cause and investment in future socio-economic development, and that instrumental commitment was thus greatly enhanced. The investment of human labour was always regarded as being especially important, and the idea of a 'religion of labour' was commonly used to denote this investment.[30] Interestingly enough, since many of the early immigrants were young middle-class intellectuals, the emphasis on physical labour which new circumstances required frequently called for a dramatic change in life-style.

Having considered some of the most important factors which have assisted the growth of the *kibbutz*, it must be stressed that the total population of the *kibbutzim* has never been very large. As a percentage of the total Jewish population of Israel a high point was reached in 1948, the year of the establishment of the state in Israel, when some 7.9 per cent of the population lived in *kibbutzim*, about 54,000 people in all, living in 150 *kibbutzim*. Since that year the number of inhabitants of *kibbutzim* has doubled, and the number of *kibbutzim* has increased by 50 per cent; but their significance has actually diminished if one looks at the percentage of the Jewish population living there. This was only 3.0 per cent in 1968, and it has since declined even more.[31] The reason for this change has been the mass immigration to Israel which has occurred in the post-Second World War period, and which has brought about a massive increase in the total population of the country. Not only has the whole idea of the *kibbutz* been much less appealing to the new immigrants than it was to the early pioneers (the latter, it must be remembered, came mainly from Russia and Eastern Europe, where the idea was popular, while the more recent immigrants have come mainly from America, Western Europe, Asia and Africa, where the idea was much less firmly established); but also the *kibbutz* has become less attractive as an economic unit as the virtues of capitalistic enterprise and social individualism have been seen to be quite compatible with Israel's general progress as a prosperous and powerful nation. The development of modern industry and technology can be seen to have posed many of the same problems for Israeli *kibbutzim* as it did for American communities, and to have prompted some tendencies which may be regarded as symptomatic of decline. The economic basis of the *kibbutzim* has had to change. The principle of *kibbutz* self-sufficiency through mixed agriculture has gradually given way to more and more mechanization, productive specialization and external trading for the purpose of increasing profitability. Industrialization has been accepted in the *kibbutzim*. It is estimated that about half of all *kibbutzim* income is now derived from industry; in some *kibbutzim* this figure is as high as 90 per cent. In order to sustain this process *kibbutzim* have had to employ more and more outside labour. By 1970 over half the workers employed in *kibbutzim* industries were non-members.[32] Needless to say, this development has been seen by many as a departure from the original spirit of true collectivism and self-reliance.

Another firmly instituted form of departure from the *kibbutz* ideal is represented by the *moshav shitufi*, which retains a collective economy but maintains the traditional nuclear family and its associated upbringing and education of children. It is a mid-point between the *kibbutz* and the private *moshav ovdim*; and its growing popularity in recent years reveals yet again how the original full doctrine of collective life has been modified under modern conditions. In this respect the social composition of the *shitufim* is revealing, since their population is mainly from European, American or South African Jews, and, since the late 1960s, ideologically fervent young Israelis from urban areas.

The absence of the original East European element which supported the first *kibbutzim* is thus striking.[33]

Internal conflict and demoralization in both *kibbutzim* and *shitufim* have undoubtedly heightened as a result of industrialization, modernization and rising affluence. Disagreements over issues of equal distribution and the consumption of more and more wealth, and the permissibility of some private property and private living accommodation have been common, as have arguments over the issue of equal effort through work. People have left the *kibbutzim* in large numbers since 1945. In the 1950s the defection rate was nearly 10 per cent per year, and there are now probably three times as many ex-inhabitants of *kibbutzim* in Israel as there are actual inhabitants.[34] The practice has also grown of members of *kibbutzim* taking jobs outside the *kibbutz*, sometimes for a large part of the week. A growing disinterest in participation in communal decision-making has been noted, especially in the larger *kibbutzim*, and the role of the general assemblies (composed of all members over 18 years of age) has in some respects declined in favour of expert and specialized administration. There have also been problems concerning the relations between *kibbutzim* and between *shitufim*, and the relationship of both to the Israeli national state. As we have seen, one very important factor which distinguishes Israeli *kibbutzim* from their American communitarian counterparts is that they have always been part of a larger national movement. However, disagreements between different *kibbutzim*, often reflecting profound ideological divisions, have resulted in several different national organizations of *kibbutzim* being established, some more centralized than others, and the original ideal of a single, integrated movement has never been realized.[35] These national organizations have assisted their member *kibbutzim* in many ways, not least through the granting of financial help and technical aid. It must also be borne in mind that the *kibbutzim* are also brought together through their relations with the Jewish National Fund (*Keren Kayemet*), an organization through which the Israeli nation owns the land which the *kibbutzim* in turn rent at a very moderate cost. (All other property in the *kibbutz* is owned by the members collectively.) While this external assistance may have contributed to the success of some *kibbutzim*, it has also undermined some elements of their independence and may have contributed something to a growing feeling in some quarters that the Israeli state and the National Fund are too closely involved in *kibbutzim* affairs, a feeling which has inevitably heightened during the years of the Arab–Israeli military conflicts. It is interesting to note that the *shitufim* began by being quite independent of one another and of other external organizations, but they too have since developed a common organization to deal with matters of general concern.[36]

Design utopias: garden cities and beyond

In considering the legacy of communitarianism, some mention must also be given to the long tradition of town planning, especially significant in Britain, America and France, which has absorbed many of the ideas and aspirations which belonged originally to the political utopians of the nineteenth century. The whole idea of planning the physical environment for new communities, of course, was very central to the ideas of Robert Owen, Charles Fourier, Etienne Cabet, their followers and other utopian socialists in the nineteenth century. But even before then a tradition of physical planning for the ideal town or city may be traced back through works such as More's *Utopia* and the ideas of Renaissance architects in Italy and philosophers in ancient Greece. As the profession of town planning has gradually developed in modern times, utopian thinkers passed on some of their key ideas to planners, and there has thus been established a notion of physical design for utopia which overlaps with the literature of social and political theory. Had town planning as a profession not developed rather separately from radical political movements such as socialism, it would probably be rather difficult to separate the two traditions today; but in fact the professionalization of planning served to depoliticize it in certain respects, and it became more closely linked to architecture than to political movements. Although a full examination of utopian planning is beyond the scope of the present survey,[37] some general points of interest may be made concerning its relevance for the student of politics.

First, the great planners have not written simply about matters of architecture, geography and spatial organization. They have also realized the importance of social, economic and political issues in determining the quality of life, and have attempted to accommodate this view in their theories. Howard in Britain, Lloyd Wright in America and Le Corbusier in France are probably the outstanding examples of this approach, and it is much to be regretted that the student of politics is rarely encouraged to look at their writings. Ebenezer Howard's book, *Garden Cities of To-Morrow*, for example, first published in 1898 (as *Tomorrow: A Peaceful Path to Real Reform*), is essential reading for anyone interested in tracing the filiation of utopian communitarian ideas after Owen, Fourier and Cabet. It is interesting to note that Howard had been very impressed by communitarian ideas and experiments in America, and became a self-confessed utopian after reading Edward Bellamy's best-selling novel, *Looking Backward.*

Second, the utopian planners have dealt with a very important problem: how to achieve utopia in an urbanized society. We have seen that much of the American and Israeli traditions of communitarianism was based on an extremely small-scale, rural agrarianism. Planners such as Howard, Lloyd Wright, Le Corbusier, Geddes and Mumford have tried to show how ideal towns and cities of quite a substantial size might be established relevant to the requirements of urban-industrial societies. Often the proposals involved integrating town and country in a single community, as in Howard's garden city idea, which was intended to be suitable for an area of 6000 acres (1000 urban and 5000 rural) with a population of some 30,000 persons.[38] In *The City of Tomorrow* Le Corbusier was concerned less with establishing new towns than with transforming existing ones and even large cities with several million inhabitants. No one seriously concerned with the problems of urban society and politics can afford to ignore this branch of the literature.

It is also noteworthy, with respect to the twin forces of industrialization and urbanization, that in the nineteenth and early twentieth centuries numerous attempts were made, particularly in Britain and America, to design and build communities which would integrate residential and leisure requirements with the functional needs of new industries. Many of these efforts followed more or less directly in the footsteps of Owen's experiments at New Lanark and the communities established by his followers. In Britain such model manufacturing towns as Saltaire, Port Sunlight and Bournville were testimony to a widespread conviction that workers and their families could be provided with ideal environmental conditions and amenities. Thus the worst evils of capitalism could be combated through philanthropy, while the capitalist industrial system itself (in terms of its basic economic and political structures) would survive.

Third, utopian planners have been extremely influential, and their ideas have helped to shape the physical environment in which we live. Many new towns have been built, and existing towns and cities rebuilt, according to ideas put forward originally by men like Howard, Lloyd Wright and Le Corbusier, and these ideas were invariably regarded at first as thoroughly unrealistic. Howard's bold garden city proposal, for instance, led to the formation of the Garden City Association and to the establishment of two garden cities in Britain at Letchworth and Welwyn. Just recently there has been discussion of a possible third garden city.[39] It is a tendency of students of politics to ignore the spatial characteristics of societies and the physical environment, but these clearly do a great deal to determine how happy (or unhappy) people are. A critical analysis of the actual experience of the social consequences of physical planning in the past should thus help us to approach the problem of utopian design for the future with more certainty than was previously possible. What has to be realized is that the existing physical structures and layouts we see around must not be taken for granted. They could have been very different. They have evolved as they have because some persons at a particular time committed certain ideas to paper and gained support for them. As urbanization spreads, a greater and greater proportion of our physical landscape is determined for us in this way, and it follows that it becomes more difficult (as well as more and more expensive) to change. Ironically, therefore, as we learn more and more about what the characteristics of a good physical environment are, the feasibility of establishing such an environment in practice may decline rather than increase, if only for reasons of cost and implementation. The present plight of decaying inner cities in Western societies is a case in point; even though there is almost universal agreement that a serious physical decline in the state of inner cities has occurred, the task of bringing about a radical improvement in this state is clearly defeating even the most affluent, resourceful and technologically advanced nations. This dilemma is illustrative of the kind of difficulties public policy-making in a liberal democracy frequently encounters, difficulties stemming from the problems of collective choice and rationality which we will discuss in more detail in the following chapter.

For all the reasons stated above, the utopian planning tradition – so often ignored in the academic study of politics – deserves serious attention. It may not normally be regarded as the subject matter of politics, but such a distinction is merely an academic one and does not have to be adhered to. For many purposes students of politics ought not to regard themselves as narrow specialists, but should be bold enough to embrace a broad humanitarian concern for such issues as the arts, architecture, the quality of the physical environment and so on. The more orthodox political concerns such as forms of government, methods of decision-making and the role of political parties and pressure groups are not always quite as important as they might seem, and at times the urgent questions seem to revolve around rather different issues, such as: How large should the ideal community be? What will it look like architecturally, and in its spatial balance between town, country and the facilities for man's various pursuits and activities? How will people be housed and where will they work? What allowance will be made for transportation? Will the city be an aesthetically beautiful place? Thinkers such as Owen and Fourier spent a great deal of their time thinking and writing about such issues, and in the history of political thought they have earned for themselves an important place. Contemporary political theorists, faced with the urgent and apparently insurmountable problems of highly urbanized, industrial and technological societies, would do well to shift their attention to such avowedly utopian issues.

Suggested reading

As will be realized from the above chapter, we attach considerable importance to R. M. Kanter's approach in *Commitment and Community*. A good general study, including much material on communitarianism, is C. J. Erasmus, *In Search of the Common Good*. More specialized works are (on America) R. S. Fogarty, *American Utopianism*; M. Holloway, *Heavens on Earth*; G. B. Moment and O. F. Kraushaar, *Utopias: The American Experience*; V. L. Parrington, *American Dreams: A Study of American Utopias*; (on England) W. H. G. Armytage, *Heavens Below*, and D. Hardy, *Alternative Communities in Nineteenth Century England*; (on Israel) M. E. Spiro, *Kibbutz: Venture in Utopia.* On design utopias and utopian planning see L. Benevolo, *The Origins of Modern Town Planning*; R. Fishman, *Urban Utopias in the Twentieth Century*; and H. Rosenau, *The Ideal City in its Architectural Evolution*.

Part Three

In defence of utopia

9 Is utopia really necessary?

Ah, but a Man's reach should exceed his grasp,
Or what's a Heaven for?

ROBERT BROWNING, *Andrea del Sarto*

In this chapter we return to the question of utopia's function as political theory and its unique, distinguishing properties. Some new ways of locating utopianism within modern social and political thought are suggested, which will serve the double purpose of justifying the utopian approach. The question of whether utopias are realizable is then discussed, and finally arguments are advanced for the present need for utopian thinking in politics.

In general, utopias enrich our understanding of the world by offering a global, or total, view of ideal social organization and operation, by contrast with the more partial, schematic views proffered by political theory. This is not to suggest that any model of the world or the world as it might be can avoid abstraction and selection – a full description of the world even at one moment in time would be infinitely long – but that utopianism takes an integrative rather than a partial view and attempts to make explicit the interconnections of the various elements of the ideal society.

Utopia and happiness

The defining characteristic of utopianism is that it is a political theory specifically directed towards the creation of human happiness. Most utopias aim at the provision of well-being in a way that does not set the individual above the community or vice versa, and makes virtue secondary to, or coincident with, happiness.[1] It is instructive to compare the utopian perception of happiness with the utilitarian definition, the maximization of average utility (or, in unrefined versions, the maximization of total utility). The stipulation of 'average utility' appears to be a concession to egalitarians and humanists, a hypothetical device unlikely to be realized and subject to all the problems surrounding averages, which can conceal a wealth of inequalities: happiness in the fully utilitarian society would no doubt remain highly variable between individuals and a matter of *sauve qui peut*.[2] But utopians make explicit the ways in which welfare is to be distributed with, in most cases, the guarantee of a minimum of welfare for all - a necessity on which the utilitarian cannot insist within his own logic. The community orientation of utopianism makes it possible to prescribe supra-individual sources of additional happiness such as the happiness generated by living in a society of happy people.

In his search for happiness, the utopian is unlike the rational man of the exchange theory of politics, being a maximizer, not a mere satisficer (one who stops acting when he has satisfied his expectations).[3] But he departs from utilitarian rationality too, being a perfectionist rather than a mere maximizer: that is, he seeks a fixed, definable, perfect goal, not the infinite increase and acquisition that maximization implies.[4] But in following the rationale of perfectionism, he encounters some of the problems which also haunt the exercise of utilitarian rationality, the puzzle of how to find the most efficient means to an end, and how to choose the end when there are *several* competing ends which are incompatible, and perhaps incommensurable in terms of utility or happiness. In striving to be the best of worlds, utopia must, logically, seek to maximize or perfect all available goods - an obvious impossibility since many are directly mutually exclusive (we cannot have both certainty and surprises) or indirectly so (more equality, less freedom, some say). The utopian, like every moral agent, has to order his priorities among the values which he wishes to instate, and his ordering will therefore be disputable. Even a utopia of abundance is bound to fall short of the counsel of perfectionism which requires it to perfect or maximize every possible good, since some goods are permanently in short supply, such as youth, and scarce positional goods will have to be fairly distributed. In each utopia we can perceive the effects of the utopian's choice between incompatible alternatives - the sacrifice of privacy for the sake of social stability by More and Campanella, the sacrifice of technological devices and high consumption levels made by Fourier and Morris in order to eradicate alienating labour. The making of such choices does not reflect the shortcomings of the utopian mode, but the nature of a world in which simultaneous, universal maximization of all goods is not achievable.

A salient question here is whether the diversity of goals and values which people espouse is the necessary product of intractable human diversity and a good in itself,[5] so that the deliberate selection of some values or goals at the expense of others would condemn some people to relative unhappiness in utopia - or whether the existing variety of tastes and values reflects a blind search for perfection which the utopian, with his revelation, can cut short. Utopian answers to this question range from the assumption that men are fundamentally similar and can be treated similarly (More), or that they differ in regular and class-ifiable ways (Plato) to the view that they are plastic and so can, by implication, be trained to like whatever they get (Owen and Skinner). Utopias based on such assumptions would tend to diminish the variety and plurality of life on the supposition that they could provide a unique, universal prescription for the Good Life. Alternatively, there is Fourier's appealing solution which avoids the horrors of imposed uniformity. Fourier rejoices in the innate diversity of men's temper-aments and invents a utopia which caters for all possible desires simul-taneously. His theory proposes that reputedly incompatible values *can* be reconciled if the utopian takes a sufficiently libertarian approach. Ultimately, the ordering of priorities between goals and values and the selection of particular values to be achieved in utopia rests on the utopian's view of human nature and his conception of happiness.

But critics have maintained that most utopians define happiness wrongly or pursue it by means which real people would repudiate, such as imposed equality, and from this hypothesis stem their accusations of authoritarianism. The implication is that the utopian is just like any other dogmatic moralist who wishes to impose 'higher' ends on other people. Yet most utopians do not intend their values to be 'higher', improving (in the sense of compelling people to be what they would not naturally be) or imposed. Abensour argues that the *volonté de bonheur* of the utopian socialists constitutes a break with the idealist philosophy which prescribed higher ends[6] – that is, ends we would usually *not* choose for our own happiness; and it is true that virtue as a concept disappeared from post-Enlightenment utopias except as an accessory to happiness.[7] Owen typifies this new approach in his argu-ment that altruistic behaviour is desirable because it enhances one's own happiness.[8] Certainly, utopian recipes for happiness are not always immediately appetizing, and this has given rise to considerable criticism. But what is true is that some of the innovatory values which utopians promote as means to happiness need time to penetrate our conscious-ness and to become *felt* needs. In this process of innovation lies the importance of utopianism: as Horsburgh argues, the creation of new value-conceptions is an important long-term validating function of utopianism.[9] Utopians take a fuller and richer view of happiness, well-being and satisfaction than other political thinkers, who tend to take a stipulative, non-exploratory view of the ends of human life

based on existing behaviour patterns. For many utopians the concept of
desire is all-important – a novel concept which, when introduced into
political theory, must be dealt with by novel means.[10] The focus on
happiness therefore indicates the important function of utopianism in
political theory when the latter is defined in its most generous sense,
as by Plamenatz, as the 'philosophy of life'.[11]

Possible worlds

Someone seeking a narrower, more 'scientific' definition of political
theory might reject the justification of utopianism given above as too
vague and normative. If we confine ourselves to a stricter specification
of the purpose of political thought, the use of utopian models can be
justified on different grounds as 'thought experiments'; they can be
viewed as a subspecies of the counterfactuals popular in philosophy
and in historical studies. In disciplines where the subject matter pre-
cludes the use of experimental techniques, the counterfactual provides
a 'thought experience' instead. Historians systematically remove
important factors in a given historical configuration in order to assess
what might have happened in the absence of particular causes; thus,
they can define the relative importance of various other factors. The
counterfactual process thus results in the creation, in thought, of
'possible worlds': these can be divided into two kinds. There are 'parallel
worlds', resembling our own except in one major respect (or perhaps
more), and 'branching worlds', worlds which might have developed had
history taken a different course in the past, such as the world which
would exist today had the French Revolution not taken place. Philosophers invoke the device of possible worlds in the analysis of the
properties of objects, the essential properties being defined as those
which hold in all possible (conceivable) worlds.[12] Thus, the creation
of a possible world via counterfactual assumptions enables the theorist
to gauge the importance of certain factors or the necessary or sufficient
nature of particular attributes of a state of affairs or an object. The
utopian may follow either the philosopher's approach or the historian's
in his conjectures about how society might differ from the given
world, and how it might improve.

　　There has been much debate over the proper distance from our own
world which counterfactuals may assume without becoming absurd.
(Would a counterfactual hypothesis which began 'If a race of men with
wings developed . . .' be of any use theoretically?) Elster points out that
a meta-theory is needed to specify the interrelations between the

elements of a given world and the acceptable dimensions of differen-tiation,[13] and this is certainly true of utopianism. We need some criterion to disallow bizarre inventions from counting as utopian political theory. To delimit the acceptable range of utopian possible worlds, the meta-theory would probably be one which specified certain constants of human nature and necessary features of human life, thus ruling out wild fantasy and exotic science fiction from the arena of utopian theory. The problem for utopians is that meta-theories of what is possible and necessary in human and social life differ, and people may disagree over which utopias are 'possible' – that is, which deserve theoretical con-sideration as possible worlds.

It has been argued that a world could not differ from ours in *only one respect*, since the parts of the world are so strongly interlinked that a single difference could not exist in isolation. Leibniz held this view of the elements of the universe. The same problem arises when the philosopher considers the identity of an object, and whether one attribute could be changed without fundamentally altering that object. But this view that everything is indissolubly interconnected has the unacceptably fatalistic consequence that nothing can ever be changed without changing the whole given universe, and has therefore been rejected, by and large, by advocates of possible world analysis. Kripke's suggestion that a possible world is a *skeleton* world, with certain fixed points ('rigid designators') and some differing elements suggests itself as the most useful approach in considering utopias as possible worlds.[14] It is then feasible for the utopian to depict a world with some major changes without having to assume that the rest of human behaviour and society would also be changed out of all recognition, a world which is still comprehensible to his audience.

Utopias, then, may be viewed as parallel possible worlds differing from the existing world in one major dimension (such as the absence of private property) or more, from which a number of related differences spring. Similarly they can be seen as counterfactual experiments intended to gauge the dispensability of various social factors, to show that society *could* operate without private property, just as the world could have continued without the French Revolution – but differently. The invention of a counterfactual utopia also enables us to exclude the inessential properties of society and to designate what remains as essential. Thus, most utopias constitute thought experiences which eliminate perceived causes of social evil and reconstruct a possible world without these. But just as the specification of a particular counter-factual possible world is a source of controversy among historians and philosophers, so the delineation of a particular utopia evokes strong criticism from those who deny the chosen dimensions of variation, or who assert that the utopia is not *proximately* but only *remotely* possible in relation to our own world[15] – that it is too far removed from existing society to be a useful thought experiment or a realizable project.

One theoretical criticism often made is that a utopia presupposes a world branching from our own sometime in the past which the process of history since then makes irrecoverable. This is reinforced by the practical criticism that the realization of such a utopia is not feasible in the absence of that earlier branching or that we have moved beyond the point where it is a *possible* world. These points were made against nineteenth-century utopias which sought to counteract the effects of industrialization, and are still made against today's proponents of alternative technology. But in fact some utopians considered guilty of this fault took pains to show how the branching might have occurred or might occur, and to show that the worlds which they described were indeed feasible. In *News from Nowhere* Morris painstakingly describes the socialist revolution and consequent reversion to a craft and agricultural society, while in *Erewhon* Butler gives a satirical account of the destruction and outlawing of machinery – a possible world at one remove from Luddism? If the critic's argument holds good against certain such utopias, in any case, the conclusion is not that such worlds are conceptually impermissible, but rather that they are possible worlds at *more than one remove* from our own: even high technology could be destroyed or forgotten in a process of several stages. Those who consider the 'branching worlds' criticism to be conclusive against certain utopias are perhaps too confident of the irreversibility of 'civilization' and 'progress'. However, the majority of utopias do not require historically counterfactual suppositions of earlier branching worlds because they start from a given society and negate the features of that society which are stipulated not to be fundamental to the nature of human society; thus, they depict parallel possible worlds. The terrain of criticism therefore shifts to whether such features are or are not inessential.

Almost all criticism of utopianism rests on the assertion that men *could not* behave in certain ways, or that certain institutions are indispensable to human society and that certain worlds are therefore *a priori* impossible. But if the critic argues that society would fall apart if egoistic and acquisitive men had to live in a world without private property and incentives, the utopian can counter that human nature and behaviour would be quite different in a world not dominated by property relations. The critic often retreats to the argument mentioned above, that all parts of the world are so inextricably connected that the utopian's proposed changes would be impossible: society without aggression, egoism, private property, marriage and so on would be inconceivable. But the employment of utopias as counterfactual thought forms should surely have the salutary effect of causing us to question such assertions and encouraging disbelief in the 'necessity' or 'naturalness' of features of a given society: utopia, like the counterfactual, emphasizes the *contingency* of the existent, and acts as a distancing device.

To categorize utopias as parallel possible worlds begs certain questions: what if they are only possible (realizable) *at several removes*? Elster in fact suggests that 'the essence of the Utopian approach to politics' is to claim that what can be done in two steps can be done in one,[16] a proposition which he treats as self-evidently false. On this definition most utopias are not possible. He argues, by analogy with the changes in scenery which occur as we climb a hill, that the accomplishment of the first stage of a move towards utopia (the shift from the present world to 'Possible World No. 1') may reveal so many attractive new alternatives that Utopia, *qua* 'Possible World No. 2' (which is only possible with respect to the present via the realization of Possible World No. 1), will soon be discarded. The wise utopian would rethink his possible world whenever the contours changed. However, many utopians - for example, Plato - would claim to have discovered the essence of the Good Life, so that their possible world is claimed to be the *Best Possible World* from any perspective - that is, with respect to any given world presently conceivable. (All these ideas of 'possible' and 'conceivable' must be understood to be qualified by a supposition that dramatic or cataclysmic changes affecting the nature of human life do not take place: that interplanetary travel is not perfected, and that nuclear war does not occur.) Elster's criticism of the utopians who dogmatically cling to their ideal in the face of changing contours and possibilities is sound, but his rejection of utopian thinking in general on these grounds is not: many utopians who did not have an absolutist epistemology like Plato's or a fixed idea of perfection were willing to concede the possibility of change in their utopias. Also, the political thinkers who draw on utopian ideas do not use them as blueprints which must be followed to the letter, but as suggestive devices which help us decide in which directions change should take place.

Criticisms of utopia are subject to some confusion because of the failure of many utopians and/or critics to specify whether the utopian possible world is to be considered as a thought experience, an exploration of possibilities, or as a realizable strategic objective. Some utopias fall into the first category and some into the second, according to the intention of their authors, but also according to the reaction of their readers, so that a criticism aimed at utopianism in general is bound to be wide of the mark in many cases. A utopia conceived with speculative intent cannot be condemned, as it would be by Elster, for being at several removes from existing society, although this point would hold against one which presented itself as a political programme for immediate implementation. The use of a utopia for theoretical exploration and consciousness-raising purposes, as envisaged by Horsburgh, should no more be challenged because it is possible only at two or three removes from the present than a historical counterfactual should be impugned *ab initio* on the grounds that the French Revolution did in fact take place. Of course, there will always be critics whose preconceptions rule out particular counterfactuals or particular dimensions of utopia, but, as Horsburgh points out, what is politically impossible for the politician is politically and conceptually possible for peripheral groups who can have longer-term aims than someone at the centre of power.[17] The rejection of a utopia by a theoretical critic or by a political activist (and 'rejection' is something different in each of these cases) is not *prima facie* grounds for dismissing it altogether.

In conclusion, the consideration of utopias as possible worlds suggests a systematic role for utopian thinking in political theory. Conceptualizing utopianism in this way should forestall some of the criticisms improperly directed against it on the grounds of its unreality and unrealizability.

Utopia and rationality

By treating utopian theory as a sub-species of counterfactual thinking, and as a unique form of possible world, we hope to have shown utopianism to be close in spirit to, although far older than, currently fashionable forms of social and philosophical theorizing. It is now respectable to contemplate the nature of possible worlds. But a further and different justification of the necessity and the rationality of utopian thinking can be offered which draws on the debate on the construction of social welfare functions via a suggestive use of Arrow's General Possibility Theorem. As will be recalled, Arrow shows that the aggregation of individual preferences or interests cannot usually lead to a collective interest or social choice under certain reasonable conditions because of the problems of intransitivity of choice and the difficulty of comparing utility interpersonally. He concludes that 'the only methods of passing from individual tastes to social preferences which will be satisfactory . . . are either imposed or dictatorial'. He also adds: 'If consumers' values can be represented by a wide range of individual orderings, the doctrine of voter sovereignty is incompatible with that of collective rationality.'[18] Although the conditions under which Arrow's Possibility Theorem holds are strict, we can argue on this basis that, in a heterogeneous society with a variety of tastes and preferences, the people could never 'choose' an ideal society through the aggregation of their individual preference orderings. The delineation of a utopia in everyone's interests, and *a fortiori* its implementation, would have to be 'imposed or dictatorial'. In this connection we may also consider the arguments of Olson concerning the need to induce, oblige or coerce individuals, and in particular the would-be free-rider, into contributing their due share for the provision of collective or public goods: without such coercion, many aspects of social welfare would perforce be ignored.[19]

In Arrow's terms, then, the utopian could be regarded as the spokesman for collective rationality, the creator of the social welfare function, and, in Olson's, as someone trying to organize the provision of the ultimate public good: the ideal society. In the circumstances it would be irrational for him to attempt to consult and aggregate the preference orderings of the potential inhabitants of utopia in drawing up his plans, particularly if he follows Rousseau, Fourier and Marx in believing that corrupt social institutions pervert men's desires and hence their preference orderings. But even if he merely takes men's present interests as permanent, the problems of intransitivity and the conflict of preferences would make accurate aggregation impossible. Also, at the risk of seeming paternalistic, we would suggest that the Good which utopia incorporates has dimensions beyond men's immediate, felt desires, and that this Good could be referred to as the 'collective rationality'. The method for devising a theoretical utopia is therefore the elaboration of collective rationality (or the common good) as analysed by the utopian, and the method for realizing this objectively and benignly defined collective good must be its imposition without consultation of personal preferences, since these would lead in diverse and contradictory directions. 'Imposition' here could range from implementation without consultation or acquiescence of individuals to coercion if necessary. But coercion need not be physical or violent: it may, as Olson suggests, consist of fines or the threatened loss of privileges of those disinclined to co-operate. Admittedly, any imposition of utopia without unanimous consent would violate Pareto optimality, but this constraint is inimical to any social change or improvement and cannot be accepted as a permanent absolute veto. A privileged section of the population in existing society surely cannot be granted the right to veto utopia for others in perpetuity just because their vested interests would be threatened. Some notion of majority interest must be invoked against this manifest injustice. Seen in the light of Arrow's conclusions, a new justification for the utopian method of proceeding against that of liberal democracy emerges, which must be applied both at a theoretical level (the right to proceed with conviction rather than gingerly, tentatively, open-endedly) and at a practical level (the right to impose policies if they can be shown undeniably to promote the collective good).

No doubt some will choose to find frightening shades of totalitarianism in this tentative justification of the utopian's role, as in Rousseau's account of the General Will, but it must be conceded that large sections of modern society, particularly in a Welfare State, operate on such principles without provoking intolerable intrusions into individual freedom. The justification of this approach to policy-making is that collective or community rationality on a large scale is being substituted for a collection of subjective individual interests; and this takes place, on a limited scale, in the provision of a health service or motorways and similar goods paid for by taxes. In other words, given that there are supra-individual goals, a utopian approach (which, if enacted, would override some individual choices) is the most rational strategy. The utopian attempts to create a rationality of the whole community, superseding that of the individual, to whose partiality and self-interest politics is a constant prey. His is probably the only possible approach to thoroughgoing social change, since the dominance of expressed interests, ideology and Pareto-type constraints would prevent change coming about in any democratic fashion. The operation of individual rational choice in a given community could never achieve utopia (although this would not be true of people *opting* to join a new community). These observations are intended to justify the theoretical attitude of utopians – but the argument drawn from Arrow seems to apply to the practical transition to utopia, where it justifies an imposed solution, and could also justify the continued imposition of the utopian's own ideas as the laws and constitution of utopia until the utopian citizens have been re-educated. It remains to convince those who deny the existence of a collective interest, or who argue 'better spontaneous misery than contrived, artificial happiness' – an argument most recently produced against the utopia of B. F. Skinner. The latter is a precarious value judgement; the former is based on an analysis of politics which is contradicted daily by political practice, even in the most *laissez-faire* of countries, and both seem vulnerable in the face of the promise of a planned concrete improvement of collective well-being.

This discussion leads finally to the question of whether utopias, with all their fictive and fantastic elements and lack of verifiability, can be termed wholly rational political theories. Every utopia, beneath the verbiage, seeks to lay bare an inexorable social logic. This is most clearly observable with regard to nineteenth-century utopians such as the early socialists, who present their utopias in the form of social knowledge, 'the social science' (Saint-Simon) and 'the Science of Society, the Rational System' (Owen). The favoured method is deduction from basic assumptions about human nature, these often being *soi-disant* 'insights' from which the proper character of social institutions is derived. This is seen by such utopians as the exposure of a logic innate in human nature. 'One best mode of social existence is deducible from the principles of (human) nature', wrote William Godwin.[20] Although earlier utopians were less conscious of method, more conscious of the need to entertain, an invariable pattern manifests itself: the analysis of human nature and needs, and the devising of social forms to accommodate these. To the modern empirical social scientist, this manner of proceeding is curious and fallible because of the paucity of observation and the derivation of *prescriptive* conclusions which are unverifiable, and which depart from the convention of scientific objectivity. Much could be said, elsewhere, in defence of social theorizing being *engagé*: utopianism, despite its idiosyncrasies, forms part of a respectable tradition in that respect, *pace* the empiricists.

Utopias can be seen as highly rational social theoretical models when the fictional elements are pared away. They proceed from a minimum of premises, excluding the contingencies of history and circumstance which obscure the vision of the social scientist, and construct models for the production of happiness, usually with admirable economy of means to ends. Such models can be viewed in many ways: as ideal-types for conflict resolution or peace or happiness, as speculation about possible worlds and 'lateral possibilities' (a provocative pleasure we rarely allow ourselves, even though futurology is in fashion – why not laterology?), as a special category of normative political theory, or as alternative models of society which we should seek to realize. Furthermore, it can be argued that all hope of rational and planned socio-political change in the collective interest comes from the rationalistic and normative approach which utopians choose to employ.

The realizability of utopia

A book which deals with political theory and practice must try to bridge the gap between utopia as a theoretically and politically possible world by discussing the realizability of utopias. It has been argued that utopian models are useful for the theoretician, but how can they be regarded by the political practitioner? Can the same model serve a purpose for both? The answers to such questions are essential for situating utopianism intellectually and politically, for its function changes according to whether we see it as an intellectual catalyst or as a realistic programme for political change. Different answers will emerge according to whether we interrogate utopian theory itself, or whether we look at historical evidence about attempts at the realization of utopia. But first we must ask of utopian authors themselves: to what extent did they believe in the realizability of their projects? Any attempt to generalize is rapidly defeated by the individual diversity of the authors. Owen and Fourier considered their schemes immediately realizable if only a sufficiently powerful or wealthy promoter could be found. But while all utopians (except those, like Butler and Swift, who employ satirical inversion) *prefer* their ideal societies to the existing state, some, such as More, seem to offer them to the world as pieces in an intellectual game, whose influence is therefore bound to be indirect at most. By contrast, the purpose of Morris's *News from Nowhere* is, presumably, to romanticize and popularize Marxism, thereby giving an already established theory a legendary status which might facilitate its realization. Evidently, the relations of utopian authors to their productions are strongly idiosyncratic and their intentions for them are legion.

The commentators on utopianism who have sought to find unifying or common principles in this diverse literature, and to discover essential properties of utopianism, have not come to any agreement about the realizability in principle of utopias. Mannheim defines the subject matter in such a way that it is those ideas which *tend* to be realized, but his collectivist definition of the utopian mentality would exclude a number of schemes which generally fall into the utopian category. For Marin, the realization of utopia would be its self-abnegation, for it would lose its crucially ambiguous situation in the Nowhere. He argues that, in order to become revolutionary praxis, utopianism has abandoned the ambivalence of fiction and been transformed into theory.[21] This characterization implies that there is a radicalizing mentality which now manifests itself in utopian fiction, now migrates to theoretically directed praxis.

A certain set of explanations or definitions of utopianism, among which Marin's should be included, leads to the conclusion that utopias are by definition unrealizable. Mucchielli's 'myth of the ideal city', which each man carries in himself, is another expression for infinite yearning and perhaps for the infinite human desire for unattainable perfection which will inevitably recur no matter what state of social ideality is achieved. But Mucchielli's account is better characterized by saying not that utopia is unrealizable, but that it will never be recognized as such even if realized; its role is to inspire political movements, heroic and otherwise. Again, if we take the generic explanation offered by Servier, that the utopian form expresses a profound and subconscious desire for a return to the 'female principle' as conceived by Jung, there is no possibility of satisfying that regressive desire since, according to Jung, the female principle is eternally lost – or rather, the virgin-mother is situated at the end of the perpetually desired journey. So the deepest intention of utopianism is permanently unrealizable. Likewise, those critics who characterize utopia as the product of an individual with particular psychological problems are deliberately excluding it from the realm of realizability, for the implication is clearly that normal people could and would not live inside the invention of a diseased mind.

A constructive approach, by contrast, appears in Friedman's *Utopies Réalisables*, where he offers conditions for the realization of utopia. Armed with these, we could test particular utopias for realizability by seeing to what extent they satisfied the criteria. He also makes the important point that modern utopias are not more developed than 'primitive' utopias: More cannot be said to be sophisticated by comparison with Plato.[22] This suggests that *time* is not a disqualification for the realizability of utopias, a point which would have been laughed to scorn by relativists a few years ago but which is in some respects substantiated by the present 'back-to-nature' and alternative technology movements. It seems that the theoretical structures of sociopolitical organization embedded in most utopias have cross-temporal relevance even if, time-bound as we are, we are unable fully to understand their significance in the author's time. It follows that it is not absurd to consider that a suitable community could be organized on the abstract principles expressed in the *Republic, mutatis mutandis*, and indeed Wells's *Modern Utopia* adopts and adapts these principles. If, as has been suggested, utopias deal centrally with a political constant, the problem of order, there is no *a priori* reason why, despite social advances, one solution should not have lessons to offer to people living in another time. However, utopia seen as a prescription for the Good Life may be more time-bound, as conceptions of human happiness and fulfilment change over time.

A different conceptualization of utopianism which has an interesting bearing on its realizability is Servier's view that utopianism is characterized by a rational perception and rational knowledge of the world,[23] a point not entirely reconcilable with his Jungian account! This is reminiscent of what Engels said of the utopian socialists: 'The solution of the social problems . . . the utopians attempted to evolve out of the human brain.'[24] Even before the rationalism of the Enlightenment, utopians were seeking logical solutions to social evils, whether by direct inversion or by the projection of lateral possibilities. If, following Servier, we redefine utopianism as man's attempt rationally and totally to reconstruct *his own artefact*, society, the project becomes one that is essentially realizable in principle.

But this does not follow if one adheres to the view that organic and historical forces govern society, which cannot be rationally ordered. Just such an account of society is given by Oakeshott in his critique of rationalism, which was discussed in Chapter 3. Oakeshott's strictures against rationalism can be read as an assertion of the unrealizability in principle of any utopia, because the principles which it seeks to apply are defective, ignoring the weight of history and 'practical knowledge'. His conclusion is that any attempt to realize utopia would necessarily be disastrous. There is, then, a consensus among most commentators, whether hostile or sympathetic, of the right or of the left, that utopias are unrealizable in principle because of the special characteristics of utopian thought – although different critics identify these differently.

The discussion of whether utopias are realizable has so far paid more attention to their nature *qua* theory than to political feasibility. When we shift our attention to the receptiveness of political reality to utopian change, the answer alters correspondingly. The meanings given to 'unrealizable' and 'impossible' must first of all be scrutinized. 'Unrealizable' could mean 'technically impossible': Huxley's *Brave New World* is happily unrealizable at present because we have not perfected the 'Bokanovsky process' for cloning human beings. Alternatively, it could mean 'politically impossible' in a situation where there was no power or support for the achievement of the goal in question. Impossibility can further be specified with respect to time and place, as Horsburgh argues. Few utopias could be definitively labelled 'never possible anywhere', and this would probably reflect their technical rather than their political impossibility, since even the most harebrained schemes have often proved politically realizable, although many might be regarded as *impossible at present, in this country*.[25] This does not foreclose the possibility that they will be realizable, and even realized, elsewhere now or here later, because of changing conditions and values. The remotely possible world would thus become proximately possible without any major upheaval and, as Horsburgh maintains, the utopian, peripheral as he may be politically, has a crucial role to play in introducing at the margin of politics the new conceptions of socio-political values which will slowly be assimilated and will prepare the way for a society closer to his ideal. Horsburgh suggests, in effect, that utopias *are* realizable, although not in the totality of details originally conceived by the utopian. This reinforces the suggestion that the notion of realizability has to be qualified in another direction: realizability in principle or in spirit must be contrasted with realizability *in toto*, the former being more probable and more feasible as a political aim, since it allows for the inevitable difference between theoretical blueprint and social practice.

Historical evidence suggests that societies do indeed change in accordance with utopian ideas even though a utopia is rarely instituted in precisely the form that the utopian or visionary envisaged. Many religions, notably Christianity, which were originally dismissed as utopian and even persecuted, actually gained converts and have become influential or dominant, displacing rival religions and ideologies, and producing social reconstruction. Socialism, widely condemned as utopian prior to 1848, has been applied, and now socialist regimes govern a large part of the world. This is not to say that there exists somewhere a truly Owenite or a truly Saint-Simonian society, any more than that the Anglican Church embodies all the doctrines of Christ's teaching, but merely that elements of utopian doctrines *have* been applied, and some socialist principles *have* been realized. Indeed, many aspects of modern society, such as planning and welfare institutions, are in accordance with utopian predictions.

So, even if we conclude that utopias are not realizable as totalities because of their theoretical nature, their production and the study of utopianism can be justified on the grounds that they are a useful source of socio-political truths and inspiration. A decision to extract or extrapolate from them in this way clearly contravenes the original intention of the utopian who claims to have produced a coherent, interlocking scheme of perfection. But the hippies of Big Sur saw no methodological objection to borrowing selectively from Fourier, and often it is a healthily innovative practice to remove key ideas from their context even at the risk of methodological impiety. There are, however, dangers in this process because some ideas are truly inseparable from particular premises and will be distorted without these qualifying conditions: thus, Rousseau is treated as a totalitarian by some critics because they ignore the social preconditions for the General Will which he stipulated. So random borrowing risks discrediting the utopian and dissipating the virtue of his ideals.

There are at present a number of 'life experiments', particularly in France and the United States, which draw on the principles of nineteenth-century utopian socialism with some success, and so bear witness to the continuing relevance and partial realizability after their own time of at least some utopias. What these experiments and the experience of history make clear is that all utopias, although conceived as totalities, are in constant need of revision, since utopian thinkers cannot possibly predict all sources of human dissatisfaction, or all social and technical developments. If Saint-Simon's blueprint for an 'industrial society' were applied to the letter in France today, there would be numerous problems caused by factors which he could not have predicted, factors such as alienation caused by work in industry, conflict between consumer and producer groups, inflationary tendencies in the economy, and so on. These would necessitate the modification of crucial elements of his scheme. The application of a utopian theory will always entail some degree of revision, even if it is applied in its own time.

Strictly speaking, one might say that *all* utopias are realizable in principle as long as there are no technical requirements which cannot be met, and politically realizable if they gain enough support among groups with political power. The extent of a utopia's political realizability thus changes according to circumstance: as Friedman argues, the preconditions for its realization are adequate mobilization and support, plus the necessary power among its adherents. The realization in its totality of a utopian scheme is unlikely and probably undesirable – attempts to create copybook Marxism have quickly come to grief. When we say that utopias are realizable, then the word 'realizable', must be construed undogmatically, and qualified in the ways already indicated. This conclusion is crucial for arguing the importance of utopianism in political thinking and practice, quite apart from its usefulness in critical political theory.

The necessity for utopia

The analysis of the special function that utopianism has in political thought has been developed in the course of this book: some final comments of a more general and more speculative kind are now appropriate.

Whatever one's reservations about recent attempts to analyse the nature of utopianism semiologically or psychologically, such accounts enhance our appreciation of the special role of utopianism in social theorizing, since they illustrate the breadths and depths which are touched by such theories. We would suggest that the utopian form is uniquely able to reintegrate parts of human life that have been deliberately sundered from the political outlook or compartmentalized. For example, utopia can provide a politics which takes into account unconscious or subconscious desires, as in the supposed reinstatement of the 'female principle', or can illustrate the connection between a tranquil, orderly life and aesthetic surroundings, a point ignored by much political theory. Symbolically or otherwise, utopianism can cope with human problems which are too broad and insoluble to be dealt with in political theory, yet which are a determining factor in our socio-political organization. The problem of death, for example, is constructively considered in Herbert Read's *The Green Child* (1935) and in Butler's *Erewhon Revisited* (1901), and many other utopias suggest ways of integrating death into life which seem more ideal than our own. The pointing up of these neglected elements in a utopia may have a corrective effect on other political thinking even if the utopian whole is rejected. In a similar vein it can be argued that the utopian, in offering a vision of society as a functioning totality, enables us in our imagination at least to reintegrate the parts of a life that has become both complex and fragmented; this vision is valuable, even if we are not able to translate it into action which operates effectively on the social whole, as the utopian would wish.

Finally, we would like to offer a positive defence of the use of the utopian mode of thinking today, which also justifies the consultation of past utopias in the course of present political activity. The special virtue of utopianism is, as has been said, that it takes a global view of the reorganization of society, in its constructive mode. In our current state of semi-permanent economic crisis the adoption of a utopian approach is urgent for theorists and practitioners of politics who wish to improve on the existing free-for-all-but-freer-for-some-than-others. Undoubtedly, on practical grounds alone, the 'authoritarian' method of the utopian *can* be justified. Where there are scarce resources with no imminent likelihood of abundance, men must accept an authoritative allocation of resources by criteria agreed to be fair, or which people would agree to be fair in the absence of vested interests; this imperative becomes compelling in the face of threatened scarcities, and even the most libertarian liberals now countenance some such control because refusal would constitute mass suicide. Authoritative allocation can be justified, we would argue, in all cases where one man's appropriation of an extra portion may detract from another man's chance of enjoying an adequate portion, as in any zero-sum game. Property is the paradigm case, but the formula might apply equally to the right to have a large family, and to other matters which liberals would consider to lie in the private sphere. Even where abundance of material and other goods could be attained, the ultimate limitations of space and human mortality may justify some degree of directed allocation.

The zero-sum formula that we are suggesting is reminiscent of Mill's enabling criterion for individual liberty (which forbade interference except when direct material harm was threatened), but has the opposite, *disabling* emphasis, and rests on the strongly un-Millean supposition that all individuals and activities in society are indissolubly interconnected and interdependent, so that 'private' or 'economic' decisions cannot be taken in isolation. Given that the problem is one of scarce resources, it would also be logical to extend the principle of authoritative allocation from distribution to the process of production, so that a social contribution could also be required from everyone. The formula leaves many problems unsolved: questions of which goods count as scarce, and which distributive criteria and values should apply, must still be answered painstakingly. Such an allocative formula might be *imposed*, but it need be neither arbitrary nor unjust.

In a shrinking world there are cogent reasons exogenous to political ideology for accepting social planning on the basis of such a formula. Planning is not utopia: nevertheless, the arguments for planning may be the thin end of the wedge in persuading liberal democrats to abate their hostility to the utopian approach. Also, the extending scope and predictive power of the social sciences now make future-thinking, including utopianism, a more respectable and less speculative and hubristic enterprise than it seemed previously. It is feasible, using economic projections, to devise a Good, in terms of resource use and corresponding social organization, for the next generation, and perhaps to manufacture a utopia – not in the sense of 'a perfect society', but a utopia which is the best of all possible worlds in the circumstances.

The persuasive force of the above arguments rests on the practical problems which the world now faces, but the totalistic and sometimes *dirigiste* approach of utopianism has better justifications than those of expediency: it represents a method of attaining social justice which does not rest on the precarious basis of individual choice. Fourier, for example, solved most problems of distributive justice by predicting abundance (other utopians, conversely, have postulated the absence of greed), but this failed to solve the problem of permanently scarce resources, which he was obliged to solve by authoritative allocation. So, regarding sex, he decreed that the sexually talented lovers of the 'Angelicate' group should sometimes give their favours to the less well endowed, who under *laissez-faire* would have gone without. Liberals would find such an intrusion of authority into the most private area of sexual choice highly offensive and perhaps bizarre. But Fourier's treatment of sex nicely epitomizes the central preoccupation of utopianism, namely, the contention that men owe the Good Life to their fellows individually and collectively, and are owed it likewise; they ought therefore willingly to sacrifice a measure of personal freedom and convenience to realize that utopia. Beneath this assertion lies the conviction that men are sociable creatures in the same small boat, which the canoe-paddling liberal may dispute. This utopian conception of altruism radically opposes the egoistic premisses of the dominant liberal ideology and makes the liberal fear that utopianism equals coercion and the loss of identity. But if this notion of collective mutual responsibility and the wholeness of society which is at the basis of all utopias can be justified, as we think it can, then utopianism as theory and practice can also be defended.

Suggested reading

Justifications of utopian thought are offered by many commentators, often in the guise of a theoretical account of utopianism. Especially important are: E. Bloch, *Geist der Utopie*; K. Mannheim, *Ideology and Utopia*; H. Marcuse, *Eros and Civilisation* and *Essay on Liberation*; L. Marin, *Utopiques: Jeux d'Espaces*; R. Mucchielli, *Le Mythe de la Cité Idéale*; J. Servier, *Histoire de l'Utopie*. See also P. Tillich, 'Critique and justification of utopia', in F. E. Manuel (ed.), *Utopias and Utopian Thought*. H. J. N. Horsburgh offers an illuminating analysis of the merits of utopianism *vis-à-vis* what generally passes today as political 'realism' in 'The relevance of the utopian', *Ethics*, vol. 67 (1957). For a provocative treatment of the whole issue of the realizability of utopias see Y. Friedman, *Utopies Réalisables*.

10 The utopian impulse in twentieth-century politics

The suggestion that there has been a decline in utopian thinking, perhaps even the complete disappearance of utopian thought, in the twentieth century has already been examined, and we saw that while there is some evidence to show that there has indeed been a certain decline, there is certainly no justification for heralding the 'end of utopia', since many utopian writings have been published, and if anything, since the 1960s, there has been a revival of such work.[1] As we have repeatedly emphasized during the course of this book, not only are we interested in utopian ideas as ideas, but also we wish to show how those ideas have a practical impact through their embodiment in political movements and activities of various kinds. Hence the questions of how far utopianism has actually served to shape the practice of politics in the twentieth century, and how far we may reasonably expect it to do so as we enter the twenty-first century are of obvious importance in the context of our investigation, and it is to the consideration of these issues that we wish to turn in this concluding chapter.

The quest for utopia: a contemporary dilemma

In Chapters 5 to 7 we saw that in the nineteenth century the emergence of socialism and communism as organized movements could be regarded as the expression *par excellence* of the utopian impulse, an impulse urging large groups of people towards a rejection of liberal-capitalist industrialism, and its replacement by an alternative form of society rooted in a comprehensive 'counter-culture'. At first the whole idea of a socialist or communist society (as put forward in the works of the early socialists up to about 1848) was treated as far-fetched and unrealistic. But after 1848, as socialist and communist movements and parties were formed and gained strength, subsequently participating in government or forming governments of their own, and even undertaking successful revolutions, socialism and communism became accepted as facts of political life, and it became less common to regard them as utopian in the sense of unrealistic, although some people still wished to dismiss individual socialist or communist thinkers as utopian in this sense (as, for example, in the distinction made by Marx and Engels between scientific and utopian socialism), and even more severe critics might still argue that the whole of socialism and communism represented unattainable goals.

From our point of view the really important question about socialism and communism is: what has happened to their utopian (in the sense of 'counter-cultural') element *since* the rise of powerful socialist and communist movements, and their entry into the realms of government and authority? In very general terms one can say with some confidence that events have confirmed Mannheim's predictions of 1929, as set out in his book *Ideology and Utopia.*[2] Mannheim observed that as utopian movements develop and enter the arena of political struggle, they gradually lose their uncompromising opposition to the existing social situation and become more and more conservative in outlook. In part this is because society actually changes according to the wishes of the ascendant utopian movement. Liberalism, for instance, actually achieved many of its aims, aims which originally stood in utopian opposition to the traditional, feudal type of society, and with the achievement of these aims liberalism inevitably became more and more predisposed towards a defence of the new existing society, i.e. it became more and more conservative and (in Mannheim's analysis) ideological. Likewise, socialism and communism, in the nineteenth century, stood for a transcendence, an overcoming of liberalism and capitalism: but with the achievement of certain socialist and communist goals the original utopian impulse was displaced by a new conservatism. This applies wherever socialism and communism succeeded as practical movements, in Soviet Russia as much as in social-democratic Western Europe. But the tendency of utopian movements to become more and more conservative is also due to the kinds of compromises made in the course of political struggle. A pragmatic concern with isolated issues and detailed decisions replaces the total, utopian emphasis on complete change:

The more actively an ascendant party collaborates in a parliamentary coalition, and the more it gives up its original utopian impulses and with it its broad perspective, the more its power to transform society is likely to be absorbed by its interest in concrete and isolated details. ... The utopian striving towards a goal and the closely related capacity for a broad perspective disintegrate in the parliamentary advisory council and in the trade-union movement into a mere body of directions for mastering a vast number of concrete details with a view to taking a political stand with reference to them.[3]

It follows from this last point made by Mannheim that one might reasonably expect a utopian movement in a liberal democracy to have to face more difficulties and be confronted by a greater need to compromise its position than a similar movement in an authoritarian, one-party system. In some respects this is true, since, to take just one example, the socialist party in a Western democracy cannot assume that it can retain governmental power for more than a few years, and must always think about the problems of winning elections before it can implement its policies. It thus becomes quite difficult for a socialist party to actually put into operation its total, comprehensive vision of a socialist society. To make the point even more explicitly, there can be no doubt that in the early nineteenth century, before mass democracy was achieved, it was in some ways *easier* for a thinker such as Robert Owen to put his ideas into practice, since he could try directly to persuade those in power, whether in government or in business, to help him implement those ideas. An individual prime minister or monarch favouring the theories of a utopian socialist in the nineteenth century might very well succeed in putting such theories into practice quite easily. Perhaps the best example of this actually happening is the way in which, in France under the Second Empire, many ex-Saint-Simonians won their way into governmental circles, and, with the gracious help of Napoleon III (dubbed 'Saint-Simon on horseback' by Sainte-Beuve[4]), Saint-Simonism became the semi-official doctrine of that regime. How much more difficult it is today for a movement or group to get its way. While personal influence is still a factor in politics, the mechanisms of liberal democracy, such as elections and parliamentary debate, have to be taken into account, and often force a party to modify its original aims. Such mechanisms, of course, do not face parties where there is no official opposition, as, for example, in the one-party states of the Soviet Union and Eastern Europe. Yet even here opposition of an unofficial kind does exist, and the prevailing view among students of communist politics seems to be that conflict between different interest groups is a key ingredient of decision-making in these one-party systems, a conflict which quite frequently produces the need for compromise of the same kind that we observe in the Western democracies.[5]

Mannheim also put forward another explanatory hypothesis which deserves attention in this context. He referred to a 'peculiar structural determinant' at work in forcing a relinquishing of the utopian impulse: 'The broader the class which achieves a certain mastery of the concrete conditions of existence, and the greater the chances for a victory through peaceful evolution, the more likely is this class to follow the road of conservatism.'[6] Conservatism, in other words, becomes more of an acceptable strategy if it can be seen that peaceful, rather than revolutionary, change, is likely to lead to the desired results; and this in turn is most likely to arise where the movement concerned represents a very large social constituency as opposed to a small, elite group, and when it actually becomes the ruling element in society. Liberals (first of all) and socialists (later) came to occupy positions of power previously held by conservatives, and in each case the eventual result was that the new holders did themselves assume conservative dispositions.

What has tended to happen, then, during the twentieth century, is that, first of all, various societies have actually come to assume the features of the kind of socialist or communist utopia embodied in the visions of nineteenth-century thinkers (from the Western democratic Welfare State to the several varieties of Marxist state in the Soviet bloc), and thus 'the historical process itself shows us a gradual descent and a closer approximation to real life of a utopia that at one time completely transcended history';[7] and secondly, socialist and communist movements, by gaining power and by becoming part of the established structure of government and authority, have lost their utopian intensity and have generally become more conservative. It follows that there are two possible paths of development in future: either utopianism as an active, practical political force comes to an end, and actually extinguishes itself completely; or new forms of utopianism emerge representing yet another 'counter-culture', in opposition both to liberalism and socialism-communism, opening up the possibility of another stage in the historical transcendence of existing reality, i.e. a form of society which is not only post-liberal and post-socialist, but perhaps even post-industrial.

Writing in 1929, Mannheim was evidently very concerned that the first of these two alternatives was the one which was actually developing. 'We approach a situation,' he warned, 'in which the utopian element, through its many divergent forms, has completely (in politics, at least) annihilated itself.'[8] And later he refers to 'the complete disappearance of all reality-transcending doctrines – utopian as well as ideological' which has taken place in Europe.[9] Such a disappearance, he asserted, amounted to 'the complete destruction of all spiritual elements'.[10] Yet at the same time the raw material existed, he believed, for a revival of utopianism, a revival which might assume one of two alternative forms, each depending for its power on a specific supporting group in society. 'On the one side are those strata whose aspirations are not yet fulfilled, and who are striving towards communism and socialism.'[11] The lower strata of society are crucial here, because it is their demand for greater well-being that is seen as the generator of the socialist-communist utopia. If their demands can be fulfilled through a peaceful evolution of existing society, their original utopianism is likely to decline. If, on the other hand, their well-being cannot be achieved and sustained through evolution, but requires revolution, then the old strength of their utopianism will emerge again. And the second alternative arises out of quite a different group in society, a group which could be labelled 'intellectuals' but which demands a more careful definition:

We are not referring here to those who bear the outward insignia of education, but to those few among them who, consciously or unconsciously are interested in something else than success in the competitive scheme that displaces the present one. No matter how soberly one looks at it, one cannot deny that this small group has nearly always existed. Their position presented no problem as long as their intellectual and spiritual interests were congruous with those of the class that was struggling for social supremacy. They experienced and knew the world from the same utopian perspective as that of the group or social stratum with whose interest they identified themselves. This applies as well to Thomas Münzer as to the bourgeois fighters of the French Revolution, to Hegel as well as to Karl Marx.

Their situation always becomes questionable, however, when the group with which they identify themselves arrives at a position of power, and when, as a result of this attainment of power, the utopia is released from politics, and consequently the stratum which was identified with that group on the basis of this utopia is also set free.

The intellectuals will also be released from these social bonds as soon as the most oppressed stratum of society comes to share in the domination of the social order. Only the socially unattached intellectuals will be even more than now in increasing proportions recruited from all social strata rather than merely from the most privileged ones. This intellectual section of society . . . is becoming more and more separated from the rest and thrown upon its own resources.[12]

Mannheim thus presents us with, first, the possibility that under certain circumstances the socialist-communist utopia will be revitalized, and, he adds, that this might also have the effect of stimulating counter-utopias (it will be recalled from Chapter 7 that such counter-utopias are characteristically conservative); and second, the possibility that intellectuals, alienated as it were from the dominant socialist-communist utopia, and by implication from other previous forms of utopia, will seek to formulate a new alternative utopia of their own. In actual fact this second possibility is not described very coherently by Mannheim, who deals with the issue very briefly, and devotes more time to the prediction that intellectuals might 'retreat' from the world in various ways than he does to the more positive alternative of a new intellectual utopia. Nevertheless, there is at least the hint that intellectuals might produce a new utopia different from the socialist-communist type.[13]

Today, fifty years after Mannheim produced his book, it may well be that insufficient time has elapsed to enable us to develop the historical perspective necessary in order to judge the merit of his argument about the possibility of a revitalization of utopianism. Yet it is perhaps worth the effort, even at the risk of coming to premature judgements, since we need to try to make some sense of the major political trends which have developed over the last half-century, a period in which mankind has come face to face with problems and dangers of a momentous kind, and in which major challenges to prevailing modes of political thinking have arisen. During this period socialism and communism have continued to develop, and new political movements have emerged which at first sight appear very important, and yet are so different from other existing movements, that they need to be classified afresh and explained in some sort of analytical fashion. And it seems especially important, from the point of view developed in this book, to try to investigate the nature of these new movements in relation to the utopian tradition. Are they characterized by any element of utopianism at all, and, if so, how does this element stand in relation to liberalism, socialism-communism and conservatism? Or is it possibly a completely new element? Are any of these movements expressions of one or other of the two alternative forms of revitalized utopianism posited by Mannheim?

We need to consider, first of all, what has happened to the socialist-communist tradition under the new socio-economic, technological and political conditions of the twentieth century. Then we need to look at other movements which might be deemed to have utopian implications: Fascism; technocracy (very important because of its intellectual component); conservatism and liberalism (to see how they have fared and whether they have reacted to socialism and communism by producing counter-utopias); the communitarianism of the 1960s and early 1970s (especially important in America); a movement which is difficult to classify, but which for the sake of convenience we will refer to as the ecological type, since it emphasizes issues of ecology and environmental balance; and, finally, feminism. This list of eight major headings is not exhaustive, nor are the individual headings mutually exclusive. Individual readers will no doubt wish to modify some of these headings, and may have additional ones to suggest. We merely offer it here as a fairly useful, introductory (but tentative) way of beginning to look at recent political movements in the more advanced societies (both East and West) which may or may not embody significant elements of the utopian impulse. Inevitably we must restrict ourselves to fairly concise summary accounts. Our main hope is that the points we raise will stimulate interest and encourage debate.

Socialism: a continuing evolution

In its early phases of development, in the nineteenth century, socialism exhibited a strong utopian element in the sense that its proponents sought to show how radical, qualitative change in the structure and organization of society could be achieved. 'Socialist society', however difficult it was to define in specific terms, was generally regarded by all socialists as being a totally new stage of historical development, a stage in which society's whole way of life would be transformed, major social evils would be eradicated, and such paramount virtues as harmony, association, community and co-operation would prevail. From the 1880s onwards the question of *how* such a new society was to be achieved continued to provoke much disagreement, but the extension of voting rights and the emergence of nationally organized socialist parties *in fact* led socialism in the direction of parliamentary politics, reformism and gradualism, although strategies based on revolution and other forms of direct action did not cease to be promulgated in many quarters. In the majority of Western countries new socialist parties evolved programmes based on the assumption that massive electoral majorities were bound to give them a clear mandate on the basis of which they could proceed to establish socialism through the use of legislative power. This was a dramatic shift from the standpoint of most socialist theorists prior to the 1880s, since none of them had envisaged the transition to socialism taking place in this way through the machinery of parliamentary government.

In retrospect it can be seen that socialist 'revisionism', as it later came to be called, was mistaken in its assumption that massive parliamentary majorities would easily be won by the new socialist parties, and in its faith that a transformed society could be established through imaginative use of the legislative process. Nor did the early twentieth century's growing confidence in scientific rationality and planning prove to be the panacea which many socialist thinkers, especially during the severe economic crisis of the 1920s and 1930s, expected it to be. We should not, of course, underestimate the contribution of socialism to the establishment of the modern Welfare State, with its comprehensive system of social services, social security and income maintenance. But it has to be realized that these achievements, however valuable, do not automatically amount to what earlier socialists envisaged as the necessary change in the nature of society and its power structure. Indeed, one might reasonably argue that in most Western societies in the late twentieth century there is still a conspicuous lack of harmony, association, community and co-operation, and there remain deep gulfs dividing rich and poor, the privileged and the underprivileged; and that as long as such features remain one cannot reasonably claim that socialism has 'succeeded'.

It is interesting to look at the ways in which Western socialist parties have characterized the features of the socialist society they have been aiming to create, and also at precisely how they have expected this new society to develop out of the existing non-socialist, essentially capitalist system which precedes it. Generally the emphasis has been on what William Morris described as the *machinery* of socialism, that is, the organizational forms and structures which socialists perceive to be necessary as a framework for promoting greater equality and social justice.[14] Thus there has been a great deal of socialist debate about the ownership and control of industry, the mechanism of planning and economic intervention, the provision of social security benefits, and so on. But, as Morris feared, socialism has failed to link such an emphasis to the need for a radical change in the *attitudes* of members of society, and especially of the working classes, whose *desire* for equality and a transformation of society largely for their benefit has to be nurtured and encouraged to develop. The result is that Western societies have witnessed the spread of a great deal of socialist machinery, in Morris's sense, but the 'faith in the possibility and workableness of socialism' and 'the courage to strive for it and labour for it . . . so that the due impetus might be gained for the sweeping away of all privilege'[15] have *not* succeeded in permeating the very fabric of society, thus paving the way for a really radical movement of opinion. By the 1950s and 1960s the established socialist parties had done a great deal to introduce organizational changes in society, and many 'revisionists' felt that these amounted to the abolition of capitalism. The argument that capitalism had now given way to a new system was in fact put forward quite seriously by such writers as Crosland.[16] This idea was never able to gain universal credence within socialist parties, but it did serve to stimulate fierce argument about the future goals socialists ought to be striving for.

From the late 1950s onwards existing 'models' of socialism in practice, whether those in the Western countries or those deriving from the Soviet-style 'totalitarian' system, were taken as evidence by more and more socialist movements (mainly outside the major parties) that there was still a long way to go before a truly socialist society could be deemed to have arrived. Usually referred to collectively as the New Left, these movements attempted to establish new political organizations expressive of a revitalized socialist vision. One of the most significant features of the New Left was that it consisted mainly of *youth* movements, and, furthermore, members tended to be drawn from the better-educated, middle-class groups. Here, then, was a radicalism of the middle class, highlighting modern conditions of changing class structure in which protest brought together individuals who 'had shared . . . the historically unique experience of growing up without the direct knowledge or threat of physical deprivation – or political repression'.[17] Bauman draws our attention to 'the increasingly intellectual-elitist status of the more radical offshoots of the contemporary socialist utopia', and to the fact that 'the thin stratum of the educated middle class' which dominates this radicalism frequently has few, if any, practical links with the actual victims of the injustice and exploitation which are being condemned.[18]

One particularly significant feature of the New Left is its attempt to expand the focus of radical criticism of contemporary society beyond a mere call for higher living standards and greater material equality, so that it encompasses an awareness of the need to overcome human alienation in all its forms, and to create conditions in which the human personality can develop fully and hence promote true, all-round well-being. Although, in the end, the New Left did not offer any serious threat to the established political parties and institutions, and although the promise of revolution (reaching a peak in the 1968 upheavals in Paris and the widespread student unrest of this period) declined fairly quickly into ineffectiveness,[19] one should not underestimate the impact of these new trends on socialist thinking. Since the 1960s an impressive reawakening of interest in socialist utopianism has occurred, mainly due to the stimulus provided by the radical ideas and movements of that time. Furthermore, the utopian impulse has come to infiltrate approaches to socialism which previously tended to resist it, most notably the Marxist approach. Partly due to a process of re-interpreting the works of Marx himself (especially in his early, philosophical writings), partly due to a revaluation of the actual experience of life in those Eastern European societies claiming to be Marxist, Marxist thought in many intellectual circles has come to accommodate essentially utopian thinking about the future, very much along the lines William Morris was hoping for at the end of the nineteenth century. One of the most significant contributions in this respect, to which we have already referred, is that made by Marcuse. There has also been a strong impact made by dissidents from Eastern Europe, at least one of whom - the East German writer, Rudolf Bahro - has produced a work now generally regarded as utopian in its perspective on the future prospects for a truly humanistic communism: *The Alternative in Eastern Europe.*[20] Another interesting development has been the widespread tendency to 'rediscover' the utopian socialism of the nineteenth century, from Saint-Simon, Owen and Fourier to Morris, and to try to derive insights from these thinkers which may be applied today in efforts to promote socialist transformation.[21]

Fascism and technocracy: in defence of capitalism?

The Fascist movements which arose in interwar Germany and Italy undoubtedly displayed some of the characteristics of utopianism, most notably in their conception of history leading to a future golden age, a conception which, in the case of German National Socialism, was almost millenarian in its prophecy of a Third Reich. It is, admittedly, tempting to suggest that a philosophy advocating violence and involving hatred towards particular racial groups should on no account be deemed utopian. (This point was made in Chapter 1 in relation to the problem of classifying *Mein Kampf* as a utopian work.) Yet from a more sociological point of view, as Mannheim demonstrated, it becomes more important to consider whether the movement in question served *in practice* to transform and transcend the prevailing social system, i.e. in this case the bourgeois-capitalist system.

Inasmuch as both Soviet Marxism under Stalin and Western Fascism under Hitler and Mussolini instituted totalitarian state systems which by any standards seem the antithesis of liberalism, it would appear logical to conclude that if we can call Soviet Marxism utopian in its basic tendency, then we must do the same with Fascism. Furthermore,

Fascism, like its Soviet counterpart, emerged as a mass movement demanding extensive social change. Yet at the same time there was an ambiguity in the social basis of support for Fascism, because a strong element in this support came from the bourgeoisie, who thought it possible to *defend* their interests by assisting the Fascists in their fight against the threat of communism. Thus it would appear that the relationship between Fascism as a movement and the class structure of society is very complicated, and more difficult to unravel than it is with many other movements. Heberle suggests that

tentatively we may say that Fascism and National Socialism arose among the disillusioned and uprooted elements of the urban middle classes (we use this rather vague term intentionally), found support among the economically insecure farmers, and came into power through an alliance with certain elements among the bourgeoisie who hoped to use the Fascists' forces against the socialist-communist labour movement.[22]

One of the reasons for this curious relationship between the Fascist movement and its social basis was that Fascism as a theory denied the existence of class differentiation and class struggle, thus opening itself to support from many different quarters. Even in its opposition to communism, Fascism denied that it was assuming a class standpoint. And there is the further irony that although Fascism fought against communism, it did not hesitate to make use of similar state and party structures. Heberle notes that the organization of the Italian Fascists was largely based on the Bolshevik model, that the National Socialists were influenced by both,[23] and that in the case of Germany the party was bold enough to use the actual term 'socialist' in its title.

We are thus led to the observation that Fascism, in its approach to the socio-economic arrangements of society, did *not* in fact seek to make fundamental alterations. It sought, rather, to allow a new elite to take hold of the state and govern, but to do so *within* the general bourgeois-capitalist framework. (Hence its appeal to many bourgeois elements.) It established a new, totalitarian state system, but in terms of class structure it retained a hierarchy bequeathed from bourgeois capitalism. This is why Mannheim, in 1929, characterized Fascism as 'the exponent of bourgeois groups' with 'no intention of replacing the present social order by another'.[24] Mannheim was, of course, writing before the establishment of the Fascist-totalitarian state in its most developed form, and one wonders whether, ten years later, he would have still insisted so much on the similarities between Fascism and the bourgeois social structure. This issue is exceedingly complex and has caused much disagreement, yet in recent years there has been much academic support for the argument that Fascism was an outgrowth of bourgeois aspirations.[25]

It is also worth taking note of Mannheim's observation that the Fascist theory of history was so vague and so irrational that it could hardly be called utopian in the more specific sense of a determinate prediction about achieving a new society. Indeed, he went further and compared the Fascists' emphasis on the deed – the *Putsch* or spontaneous rising – as a means of gaining power with the anarchists' emphasis on an immediate explosive revolt. Fascism, like anarchism, he believed, was a form of the chiliastic mentality.[26]

We have thus seen that it is by no means easy to classify Fascism in any straightforward fashion as utopian or non-utopian. But on balance its refusal to contemplate any major unheaval in the social structure and its doctrinal irrationality suggest that it did not seek to transcend the bourgeois-capitalist system. In Mannheim's terminology, perhaps one can say that there were utopian elements in Fascism, but that in the end these were dominated and overruled by ideological factors.

A similar ambiguity characterizes the phenomenon of 'technocracy'. This term refers to a form of social organization in which technicians – technical experts specialized in science and technology – occupy the dominant positions. The word was first used in the early 1930s in America when an engineer, Howard Scott (a follower of Thorstein Veblen), founded the Technocracy movement in the hope of raising technicians to become a new ruling elite.[27] Since that time, however, the term has been used more widely to refer to doctrines and movements espousing the supremacy of technical efficiency over other criteria of decision-making. Such an attitude, as we have seen already in this book, has characterized several different branches of political thinking, and consequently one can point to technocratic tendencies in the work of numerous individuals and schools of thought from Bacon to Saint-Simon, Bellamy, H. G. Wells, the Fabians, Lenin, B. F. Skinner and so on. Technocracy, then, is present to varying degrees in many traditions of political thinking in the modern world, and is certainly not monopolized by any one tradition. Yet since the early nineteenth century, we would argue, there has been quite a distinct technocratic movement gradually growing more and more separate from the liberal and socialist-communist schools because it has rested increasingly on the aspirations of quite a distinct social stratum: the *savants*, to use a French term popular in the nineteenth century to denote this group (see especially the work of Saint-Simon and Comte), or technical intelligentsia (the 'intellectuals' referred to by Mannheim). It is when the intellectuals develop a sense of their own identity *vis-à-vis* the rest of society, and when they feel that they must develop a new technocratic doctrine to promote their own interests, that they can be seen to be moving towards a form of technocracy which might justifiably be called utopian.

A technocratic impulse which does *not* set out to shatter the existing social order can hardly be called utopian. Howard Scott's Technocracy movement, for instance, or the Synarchists in France, or even the Industrial Party in Russia – all of them products of the socio-economic crisis of the 1930s – would not really qualify as fully-fledged utopian movements, since they all sought to give technicians power *within* the framework of advanced capitalism (in America and France) or of emergent communism (in Russia).[28] A change of ruling group, as we saw in the case of Fascism (which was, interestingly enough, a product of this same historical period), is not sufficient to be labelled utopian. What true utopianism requires (following Mannheim) is a total transcendence of the prevailing order.

Such transcendence was promised by Auguste Comte's positivist doctrine, and this is why, in Chapter 7, we argued that positivism could reasonably be described as a unique form of utopianism, although in some ways this must be qualified because Comte's proposals for elevating capitalists to positions of power (although subordinate to the *savants*) might be considered something of a compromise with bourgeois liberalism. This is not surprising, since Comte's doctrine was formulated at such an early stage in capitalism's development that it was bound to rely to a certain extent on the continuing progress of that system. But what *is* important is that positivism as a doctrine, with its faith in organizing society according to expert knowledge and ranking society according to the same provisions, represented the start of a trend which, in the late nineteenth and twentieth centuries, has offered the intelligentsia a rationale for attempting to change society so that they, rather than the bourgeoisie or the lower classes, dominate. It is, in other words, precisely the kind of rationale which might nowadays be taken by the intelligentsia as a basis for a political movement if (as is certainly possible) they become more and more set apart from liberalism and all forms of socialism and communism.

Ironically, perhaps, the best known technocratic movements and regimes are imaginary and universally horrific: those of the *dystopian*

novels such as *We, Nineteen Eighty-four* and *Brave New World*. No one
who reads these fictitious glimpses into our technological future could
doubt that we have passed beyond liberalism and socialism. In practice,
of course, no such movements have yet arisen, although some observers
(extreme pessimists) have argued that the process of transition to
technocracy is actually under way. In most of these cases, however –
and one might cite James Burnham's *The Managerial Revolution* or
J. K. Galbraith's *The New Industrial State* as examples – it is less a
question of a conscious, centrally-directed movement towards technocracy; rather it seems to be a trend conspicuous by its lack of overall
leadership and explicit long-term purpose.

In order to pass from the realm of science fiction into real life, a
crucial precondition is necessary for technocracy's future development
as a form of utopianism. The intelligentsia must grow in size, consciously
detach itself from other social classes, and formulate a clear conception
of its own social interest and how to achieve it. Perhaps this will never
happen. But some observers do identify this kind of trend in the
process of 'post-industrial' change, as more and more people come to
work in technical, white-collar employment, and as scientific knowledge comes to occupy a position of supreme importance in the
economy and general organizational structure of the advanced societies.
Daniel Bell, for instance, offers us the prospect of technocracy as one
potential future of the post-industrial society he sees emerging, especially
so as he believes an 'end of ideology' is occurring, in the sense of an
end of the political debate between traditional doctrines such as liberalism and socialism. Yet even Bell acknowledges that technocracy is a
possible rather than a *probable* future.[29] In the light of our own analysis,
what needs to be stressed is that until the social basis for a thoroughly
utopian technocratic movement arises, the idea of technocracy will
remain either completely fantastic or an element within existing
capitalist or socialist societies.

Conservatism, liberalism and the counter-utopian prospect

The chief functional characteristic of conservatism has always been that
it is a doctrine defending the interests of a ruling elite within a hierarchical system of social organization which is seen to be under attack from
both liberalism, with its promise of a rational individualism, and socialism and communism, with their prescriptions for a collectivist equality.
Inevitably, the actual constitution of the ruling elite which is defending
its interests through a conservative disposition has changed during the

past two centuries or so. As one commentator has put it, the evolution of modern society has seen a succession of elites – first of all landed interests, then commercial, and most recently managerial – each of them adopting a conservative outlook towards the rival claims of liberalism and (later) socialism and communism.[30] From our point of view what is most interesting about conservatism is precisely that it has always been present, attacking *all* forms of utopianism which uphold a rational reordering of the social system. In the twentieth century, although Western political systems have undergone the transition to liberal democracy, and have witnessed the attainment of many liberal and socialist goals, ruling elites (defined not only in terms of the composition of government, but also the bureaucracy and holders of economic power) have resisted change, and in political systems which encourage a diversity of party affiliations and interest groups, conservative parties and movements have managed to retain a hold on power, albeit through a gradual acceptance of the Welfare State and techniques of economic management established originally by liberals and socialists.

As Mannheim pointed out, conservatives may be anti-utopian, but the success of their rivals, who *do* put forward utopian solutions, encourages them to formulate 'counter-utopias', explanations of the existing, prevailing power structure in terms of its historical desirability, seeing it as the culmination of valuable cultural and spiritual traditions – partly irrational in contrast to the liberal and socialist emphasis on reason.[31] In the nineteenth century this 'counter-utopian' approach frequently assumed the form of a romantic, idealist defence of the existing state, as for instance in the ideas of Hegel and the French Catholic counter-revolutionaries. In the twentieth century there has been added an emphasis on the way in which, *in practice*, liberalism, socialism and communism (especially the last two) lead to what conservatives see as undesirable results: ignorant government, lack of national identity, a lowering of spiritual standards, and, ultimately, the great evil of totalitarianism which, according to Talmon, Popper and Hayek, is a direct result of rational, utopian social engineering.

A certain amount of modern social theory, particularly in the sociological study of elites and their role, has given an additional, intellectual impetus to quite distinctive twentieth-century forms of conservatism. Thinkers like Mosca, Pareto and Michels have been responsible for establishing the view that all societies have a functional necessity for elites whatever their declared political doctrine says about equality, and this kind of theorizing has rightly been seen as a way of discrediting liberal and socialist-communist theories of equality. And even the tradition of technocracy, discussed previously, has played a role here through its emphasis on the need of a modern industrial-technological (or even post-industrial) society for a qualified, meritocratic group of specialist leaders. If such a group were to gain power (and some observers, as we have seen, would argue that there is already a technocratic elite in the advanced societies), then its defence of its social supremacy could quite easily assume the form of a new kind of conservatism.

One can also discern a clear conservative disposition in the growth of some parts of modern sociology, especially in the concern of some theorists with issues of social order, cohesion, stability and functional performance. Whereas, in the nineteenth century, it was usual for the founding fathers of sociology to be interested in the organic development of society through history, i.e. sociology was often linked to historicism and the philosophy of history, twentieth-century sociology has been led into areas of detailed concern for particular parts of the social system, and for issues relating to the need for 'equilibrium' and 'system maintenance'. We have seen what Mannheim described as the emergence of a 'sceptical relativism': 'Instead of the conception of progress and dialectics we get the search for eternally valid generalizations and types, and reality becomes nothing but a particular combination of these general factors (cf. the general sociology of Max Weber).'[32] It has even been argued explicitly by some observers, notably by Dahrendorf, that the preoccupation of some sociologists with utopia must be resisted at all costs, and that – to use Dahrendorf's phrase – it is about time sociology emerged 'out of utopia'.[33]

To a certain extent conservatism's respectability has gained from the obvious disappointments of life under regimes declaring themselves to be liberal, socialist or communist. If such regimes prove not to be as utopian as was first thought, then conditions are ripe not only for new radical utopias, but also for a revival of conservative counter-utopianism. Such a revival could indeed be said to have occurred in many parts of the Western world since the early 1970s as a reaction against established socialist parties in power developed, and as socialism came to be associated with over-centralization, bureaucratization and excessive government spending. The conservative counter-utopia of less government, less bureaucracy and cheaper (and more efficient) administration, of a world in which greatness is restored to declining industrial societies like Britain through intelligent, masterly leadership carries with it a power which should not be underestimated.

If, as we have suggested, there has recently been a further evolution of socialist utopianism and the rise of a new conservative counter-utopianism, what, it seems important to ask, has been the fate of liberalism? As we saw in Part Two of this book, liberalism originally emerged as a movement which could reasonably be described as utopian, since it sought to show how society could progress towards a future age of reason quite distinct from the old hierarchical order of feudalism. The liberal view of progress, though, was always somewhat indeterminate and vague, relying on a belief in abstract conceptions of freedom and justice. What has happened in the twentieth century is that Western societies have undoubtedly undergone forms of reorganization which reflect the impact of liberal thought, so that we readily refer to these societies today as liberal democracies and recognize that they are based on a system of pluralism and interplay of interests such as liberalism recommended; yet at the same time, of course, new forms of collectivism have emerged which reflect the rise of the socialist-communist utopia as a direct challenge to the liberal order. Exactly how far Western societies have moved on the path from capitalism, through the mixed economy, to what might be called social democracy is difficult to say with certainty, yet there seems to be substantial agreement that liberal movements have everywhere (with the possible exception of the United States) declined in force and vigour, and the clearest indication of this is the way in which liberal parties have generally lost support and, in Western Europe, have tended to become subordinate to both socialist and conservative groups.

This decline of liberal movements reflects a decline in the role of the bourgeois middle class as a radical force in modern politics, since it was always the ascendant bourgeoisie on which liberalism relied for its stimulus. This social decline began, indeed, in the nineteenth century, when many elements of the bourgeoisie exhibited a remarkable willingness to compromise with the forces of conservatism, even if it meant actually joining conservative parties and movements. In England, for instance, liberals

could afford to discard their radical language because the middle class did not have to engage in a protracted struggle with the forces of the old order. Landed groups accepted an erosion of their economic supremacy in return for a retention of their political, but especially ideational dominance. . . . An idiosyncratic blending of the old and new was the consequence. Towards the end of the century sections of the industrial and commercial elites deserted the ranks of the Liberal Party for those of the Conservative Party.[34]

And, of course, the threat of emergent socialist and communist movements further promoted this growing conservatism of the bourgeoisie. In terms of political theory, in the late nineteenth century a kind of romantic, idealistic and neo-Hegelian conservatism made its way into liberal writings, as was the case in England with the work of T. H. Green and Hobhouse.

At the same time one must recognize that liberalism has always contained an element of a kind of rational utilitarianism which is almost socialistic; and in the twentieth century this element has led some liberals to advocate degrees of government intervention in economic management and welfare provision which are barely distinguishable from the proposals of some socialists. Thus, one can see that the distinctiveness of the liberal idea has been surrendered in the twentieth century to both conservatism and socialism, the former gaining from those liberal circles most concerned with the preservation of bourgeois ascendancy in some, although not all, areas of social life, the latter gaining from those liberals who have been willing to extend their rationalism as far as a form of democratic socialism combining socialist policies with a liberal-democratic political system.

In intellectual terms all this does not mean that there have been no important liberal contributions to twentieth-century political theory. Indeed, some of these have been considered in Chapters 2 and 4; but, especially in very recent years, either these contributions have had little practical influence at all, or their influence has been firmly within the counter-utopian conservative school. Hayek's defence of the free market, for instance, whether or not one chooses to define this as liberal or conservative, has been embraced most fervently by conservatives rather than liberals. A great deal of liberal writing, also, has assumed the form of critical attacks on utopianism and on totalitarianism (see Chapter 4), and this approach also merges with the conservative case against social engineering. If liberalism has retained any vigour, it has been in its contribution to very specific issues, particularly those concerning political-constitutional matters, human rights and freedoms, and moral responsibility. Discussions of these questions in many Western countries have certainly involved many substantial inputs from liberalism; but what has been lacking is liberalism's former concern for establishing society *as a whole* on a new rational basis. This line of attack has been so much the prerogative of socialists and communists that it takes a brave liberal indeed to engage in this debate in the late twentieth century.

Communitarians, ecologists and the future of industrial society

One direction in which middle-class radicalism did develop in the 1960s and 1970s, notably among the younger generation, has already been mentioned: the New Left. At first sight it might appear that the communitarianism of this period, especially prominent in the United States but also a feature of many Western European countries and even Japan, was simply one strand of this New Left tradition. But such a conclusion would be wrong, since the communitarianism of the 1960s and 1970s was notable for its widespread rejection of comprehensive, all-embracing doctrines of man and society, whether liberal or socialist. Kanter has summarized this important shift as follows:

Today there is a renewed search for utopia and community in America – for alternative, group-oriented ways of life. But overwhelmingly, the grand utopian visions of the past have been replaced by a concern with relations in a small group. Instead of conceptions of alternative societies, what is emerging are conceptions of alternative families. Whereas communes of the past were described in books about socialism, communism, and co-operation, communes today are increasingly discussed in books about the family. . . .
    The contemporary commune movement is characterized by a diminishing scope. By and large, contemporary communes encompass fewer visions of social reconstruction, fewer hopes for permanence, fewer people, fewer demands on those people, and fewer institutions, than did the utopian communities of the nineteenth century.[35]

Nevertheless, although Kanter refers to the 'diminishing scope' of modern communes, one is struck by the very large number – several thousand – of communes which have been set up by small groups of predominantly young, well-educated, middle-class people in an attempt to achieve a new form of 'the good life'. And among some of these groups there is undoubtedly the view that the communes *can* provide a viable method of changing the whole of society eventually through the force of example.

    Communes in the late twentieth century, existing within the framework of highly advanced urban-industrial and technological societies, obviously face many difficulties, difficulties which, as we saw in Chapter 8, contributed to the breakdown of many earlier, nineteenth-century experiments. In particular, it is extremely difficult for communes to establish themselves as isolated units cut off from the rest of society, and it is virtually impossible for them to emerge as efficient productive organizations fulfilling their own economic needs or indeed their own welfare requirements. Some communes may try to find suitably remote rural locations and may develop a 'back-to-the-land' philosophy, but others are more willing to accept the conditions of an urbanized society and set themselves up within urban areas. We thus have the interesting phenomenon of urban communes which, as Kanter notes, is a new development, not present in the last century.[36]

Perhaps one may criticize the first category of communes for committing themselves to a somewhat backward-looking, nostalgic view of pre-industrial, pastoral society. Is this not indeed a kind of 'opting out' of reality, the advanced industrial society, and a totally fanciful and unrealistic attempt to restore something which cannot actually be restored? This is certainly a criticism which can be justified from certain points of view. Yet another argument would be that such a philosophy might also look *forward* to a possible *post*-industrial society made necessary by the collapse of our present highly technological system, which could be criticized for being not only dissatisfying and alienating, but also doomed to failure because the levels of economic growth on which it relies cannot possibly be sustained.

Many modern communes are quite anarchistic in organization, in the sense that they often lack sophisticated methods of regulation or control of behaviour, and frequently there is an emphasis on members 'doing their own thing' and discovering their own personal routes to self-fulfilment. Even the issue of survival and durability is not always taken too seriously, and it is accepted that the commune may only last a short while, or that members may leave to engage in a new communal venture somewhere else. Communes, according to this outlook, are simply one part of life's rich and varied pattern, and they serve a useful purpose if they assist individuals to develop and to learn about themselves and other people in preparation for life elsewhere.

Kanter also draws attention to yet another form of commune, quite unique to the post-war period and especially the 1960s and 1970s, which provides us with an example of how communal life can be accommodated within modern industrial society: these are the communes established to provide a service of assistance towards specific groups in the larger society, usually groups with specific problems such as poverty, mental illness, physical disability, drug addiciton and so on. Not surprisingly, quite a lot of these 'communes with a mission' are staffed by religious groups, and many of them see themselves as agents of Christianity. In America there is probably a greater freedom for such groups to operate than in many other

Western societies, and so one cannot say that they are likely to be a major characteristic of all societies, yet the American examples provide us with an indication of their potential. Some communes of this kind do see themselves as a means of transforming society as a whole through their influence. Hence many of them are controversial, and their activities encounter opposition precisely because they assume an 'imperialist' role. Such a controversial organization is Synanon, founded in 1958 for the provision of therapy for drug addicts by Charles Dederich, a former alcoholic, with a 33 dollars unemployment cheque. By 1968 Synanon had over 1200 resident members, many urban communities from California to New York to Puerto Rico, and over 6 million dollars' worth of property. It now runs its own schools and numerous business organizations.[37] One can hardly imagine a more 'successful' utopian movement, yet, typically, this kind of development goes virtually ignored by students of contemporary political affairs.

The question of man's relationship to the natural and man-made environments has assumed particular importance as the advanced industrial societies have attained high levels of production and consumption, and as factors such as world population growth and rapidly escalating energy requirements have come to threaten the world's existing economic, social and political framework. Pessimists have responded to these developments with gloomy predictions about the survival capability of the world, and of the advanced industrial societies in particular. Yet there has also been an optimistic strand of thinking which puts forward more positive views about the feasibility of achieving a new form of society based on an ecological balance between man and his environments. What is perhaps even more interesting is that ecology has stimulated political activity among leaders and citizens in many Western countries, and that in some countries ecology parties have been formed, already achieving some modest success at elections. Within the space of a relatively short time, ecology has become an important political issue.

The term 'ecology', it must be recognized, covers a variety of somewhat different approaches. Not all of these approaches have had a direct political impact, and some have tended to be concerned almost solely with quite specific issues such as the use of nuclear energy. Yet at least one branch of ecology has taken the question of political activity very seriously, and has always concerned itself with the issue of reorganizing society *as a whole*. This branch has been labelled the 'tribal' wing by one commentator, who summarizes its main features as follows:

The 'tribal' wing represents one of the more radical environmentalist tendencies. It is also well established, dominating the pages of the journal *The Ecologist*, and complexly elaborated upon. 'Tribal' ecology offers an interpretation of human history, an explanation of nature and evolution, a critique of industrial society (including the Soviet variant), an aggressive epistemology, and a set of predictions and prescriptions (e.g. *A Blueprint for Survival*). If we were to divide environmentalists between the 'tidy-uppers' and the 'steady-staters', the 'tribalists' would fall unquestionably within the second category. But their aim goes far beyond the establishment of the 'steady-state' economy. The 'tribal' wing looks to the ultimate dismantling of industrial civilization as the solution to the ecological and social problem. The 'steady-state' of the 'tribalists' is effectively a neo-tribal complex of small, self-sufficient communities held in equilibrium, not stasis, by the workings of family, tradition and a new (religious) world-view.[38]

In other words what we have here is yet another variant of the post-industrial approach to social change, yet in fact it is rooted in a very romantic notion of the virtues of primitive, *pre*-industrial (tribal) society, a view which, as we have seen, also stimulated some elements in the communitarian movement of the 1960s and 1970s.

Although quite detailed accounts of the future ecologically stable society are available, not only in 'scientific' studies such as the *Blueprint for Survival*, but also in fictional works such as Ernest Callenbach's novel *Ecotopia*, there is at the same time a lack of clarity in writings of this kind about *how* the transformation to the new society is to be achieved. In the *Blueprint for Survival*, indeed, there is a conscious emphasis on the need to plan what is ecologically necessary in the long term rather than to discuss what is politically feasible in the short term, an approach which has much in common with the utopian style of political thinking defended in this section of the book, and outlined in summary form in the last chapter.

If ecological thinking, almost of necessity, has been extremely intellectual, then one wonders what social basis could develop in order to sustain ecology as a practical movement. Scientists generally have been unwilling to assume a practical role, and it is interesting to note that when *A Blueprint for Survival* first appeared, scientists frequently spoke of their desire to enter politics, but in fact have been extremely reluctant to do so. The intellectual content of ecology has tended to demand a predominantly middle-class response in supporting ecological parties and organizations, but with the general trend in the advanced societies towards more white-collar employment, ecology may find that such a social base is readily available. As yet, however, it seems that ecology's general reluctance to regard existing political elites as a means of instituting change is a disadvantage. There are times when it seems that all politicians and all traditional party doctrines from left to right are dismissed by ecologists as unnecessary and as a hindrance to further progress.

Socially, then, it is too early to say whether ecology can emerge as an effective utopian movement. If the advanced industrial societies cannot sustain present levels of economic growth, if a real crisis develops, then it may be that the ecological solution is the only one that can help mankind. If, on the other hand, the existing, large political parties discover methods of overcoming the socio-economic difficulties that have beset the Western world in the 1970s, then it may be that ecology will remain a relatively small, intellectual, fringe group. It may also split up into groups concerned with more specific issues. The anti-nuclear-power/nuclear-weapons lobbies offer the best examples of this, since, as the 1980s commence, it is perfectly clear that the issues concerned are ones on which public feeling is fairly strong. At a time when, for the first time in human history, the human species is faced with extinction through the use of mankind's own scientific and technological knowledge, it may be that the apparently utopian demand for the elimination of nuclear weapons is an essential precondition if a more harmonious and stable world is to emerge in the twenty-first century. Our very survival may depend on it.

Feminism and the liberation of women

The argument that in modern society women tend to be subject to various forms of oppression, degradation, general inferiority of status and severe inequality of opportunity has found widespread expression in social and political theory. Proposals for radical change in society, with the aim of transforming the position of women, are not the exclusive property of any one school of thought; but generally, in modern times, such proposals have been located on the left of the political spectrum. For a long time in the nineteenth century, calls for the liberation of women in the broadest sense tended to be associated with early (utopian) socialism and (later) with movements influenced by Marxism. Other, non-socialist, thinkers may have contributed to the spread of feminist ideas (John Stuart Mill's work on the subjection of women is a good example), or to the particular cause of women's voting rights, but it was more usual for total condemnation of women's inferior position to be voiced within socialist theories of exploitation seen as a direct effect of social conflict and class struggle under industrial capitalism. In the twentieth century feminism as a concept has come to pervade a much wider sphere of debate, mainly due to the growth of serious, scholarly investigation into the situation of women in relation to such issues as education, marriage and the family, employment and access to political power.

From the point of view of contemporary utopianism, feminism is of vital importance for the simple reason that any analysis of the need for fundamental qualitative change in society must at some stage tackle the many specific problems faced by women. Often these are problems which are rather distinctive, and which cannot simply be subsumed under the more general discussion of themes such as justice, liberty and equality (the inadequacy of the call for 'fraternity' speaks for itself in this respect). In its most radical form this perspective would lead us to the question of whether existing society is or is not patriarchal (male-dominated), and whether, therefore, women can ever hope to achieve true liberation without eliminating patriarchy altogether and replacing it with a system of true sexual equality (or possibly even matriarchy?).

Several utopian thinkers, from Charles Fourier in the early nineteenth century to Herbert Marcuse in the twentieth, have expressed the view that the liberation of women is in some sense a 'key' to the liberation of society in general, since women have a potential role to play in society which is crucial for the growth of relationships based on love, co-operation and true affection. There is the further argument, too, that exploitation in modern society is especially severe for women, for example in the way women are portrayed as 'sex objects' in literature and the mass media; in the lack of opportunity which women have, despite their large numbers, to exercise a correspondingly significant political role; in the complete closure of certain forms of education and employment to women; and so on.

As far as feminism is concerned, utopias can offer an extremely valuable perspective, since only a utopia can present us with an image of a society in which women's liberation has been accomplished. No actual, existing society can serve as such an image, since there is no working example (it would be argued by feminists) of the elimination of male domination. Probably the closest approximations are to be found in some of the communitarian experiments discussed in Chapter 8. The general view of these experiments as utopian is thus especially significant from the standpoint of women's liberation. It shows that we still have a long way to go before recognizing attempts to overcome the oppression of women as 'serious' and 'realistic'.

Utopian accounts of liberated woman vary in form from Fourier's bizarre speculations on *The New Amorous World* to Marcuse's *Eros and Civilisation* (an attempt to combine insights on modern capitalist society offered by Marx and Freud) and, within the last twenty years or so, a host of novels including Callenbach's *Ecotopia* (feminism linked to ecology) and (probably the most celebrated feminist novel) Marge Piercy's *Woman on the Edge of Time*.[39] Feminist movements which might reasonably be deemed utopian can also be traced back to the early socialism of the 1800–48 period, and since then there has been an unbroken tradition up to the New Left organizations and communitarianism of the 1960s. In recent years there has been a spectacular growth, in all Western countries, of exclusively female movements attempting to win the struggle for liberation. It may be that women can hope to achieve their goals with the assistance of men, but in some quarters it is believed that such co-operation between the sexes can only preserve the patriarchy which women's movements ought to be attacking.

Whether feminism stands much chance of emerging as a successful political movement also depends on several other factors. In the past women's movements have often drifted into a reaction *against* the 'threat' of radical change, partly because such movements have tended to be predominantly middle-class in terms of their social composition, and also because the winning of fundamental political rights (such as the right to vote) was frequently seen as a sufficient achievement which could be used by women to gradually improve their position through legislative measures. Deep-rooted cultural attitudes in Western societies, especially those linked to religious assumptions about women, marriage and the family, assumptions upheld in particular by the established Churches, have also served to hinder the mobilization of large measures of support for radical feminism. This is undoubtedly one reason why feminist movements have generally been most success-ful in the United States; in that country such traditional assumptions about the place of women in society have never been as strongly rooted as they have been in Europe.

Looking forward (with optimism)

The purpose of this chapter has been to show that utopianism still remains a key ingredient of political debate and political activity as we enter the 1980s. Those persons who regard themselves as 'modern', 'advanced', 'rational', 'scientific' and 'sensible', and hence as persons who must condemn utopianism for its naivety, are guilty of overlooking trends which point to the inescapable persistence of the utopian element in politics. Yet, at the same time, it must be recognized that in modern industrial societies man has become so accustomed to material comforts and satisfactions, the availability of welfare, and the instantaneous stimulation provided by the mass media that the question of moving forward to a *better* society in future has often been put off as irrelevant and unnecessary. History shows us that this question tends to emerge with force when dissatisfaction with the present social system becomes a powerful agent for change among specific groups. In the years since the end of World War II the initial enthusiasm for 'the affluent society' has gradually subsided as its inadequacies and what some people see as its inherent instability have become more apparent. Furthermore, self-satisfaction in the industrial societies cannot hide the fact that in the countries of the Third World the standard of living is so miserably low that, looking at global society *as a whole*, Western man must surely recognize the need to radically improve global conditions through the implementation of some kind of plan of utopian dimensions. In this book we have sought to show that utopian approaches to political problems, because they move beyond pragmatic responses to particular, narrow issues and seek to tackle the totality of the human condition, may under certain circumstances be absolutely essential as well as being the only solutions likely to lead to the clear, visionary thinking which is necessary at such times. The elements of present-day society in which people take pride, such as education, welfare, medicine, technology, communications and so on, would not have developed had not utopian visionaries in the past been willing to put their knowledge and insights to use despite being mocked by their contemporaries. The same may be said of most established religions and of most political doctrines and movements of any significant size which flourish today. How curious it is, then, that in a world where applications of science and technology are, in practice, changing our lives dramatically every few years, social and political observers still frequently condemn the utopian theorist and activist as dreamers of wild, fantastic and irrelevant dreams.

It is surely impossible to believe that mankind has now reached a stage of development from which no further avenues of social and political transformation open up. Yet that is the prospect offered to us by those commentators who wish to see the present situation as a kind of ultimate scenario against which mankind, for the rest of its history, will act out a drama in which there is no room at all for new, transcendent images of an alternative scenario. The scenario will either remain the same, we are told, or it will change very slowly and in a piecemeal fashion so that there is no point in being concerned with any more general, overall transformation. But, as we have already stated, in some fields of life – notably where applications of modern science and technology are made – the pace of change is actually quickening, and the extent of the impact of this change can be, and frequently is, so dramatic that societies do in fact undergo major transformations. The utopian merely asks that man should be sufficiently bold to formulate in advance an image of the kind of social future he considers desirable, so that he can then exert some definite control over his destiny. What needs to be realized, as William Morris pointed out so clearly a century ago, is that desire needs to be educated; and in this respect utopias perform a most valuable role by helping to reveal quite clearly what form of society is ethically, and perhaps aesthetically, most desirable as a goal worth striving for.[40] A purely analytical account of existing society, even if that account is highly critical, can never suffice as a framework for formulating a constructive, imaginative picture of a desirable alternative society.

The utopian approach to political theory and practice takes issue with the emphasis on politics as an activity concerned predominantly with individual and group 'interests' which characterizes so much of Western liberal-democratic thought and political activity. It seeks to direct attention to a broader conception of 'the Good Life' and a consequent need to view society as a joint enterprise in which the notion of a collective good can be expressed meaningfully, and can be seen to be expressed in progress towards greater happiness, fulfilment, wellbeing (both material and spiritual) and harmony. The quality of life thus becomes a central consideration for the utopian. At the same time the utopian does not disregard the importance of voluntarism and participation in shaping the progressive development of society. Although it is true, as we have seen in this book, that a certain type of application of utopianism can lead to political authoritarianism, there are also many traditions of utopianism which stand opposed to such authoritarianism, and which stress a route to utopia involving voluntary, collective effort based on the consent and agreement of participants rather than on an imposed solution backed up by the physical coercion of a governing elite.

Underlying all forms of utopianism is the conviction that optimistic, imaginative thought and action are capable of bringing about a change towards not only a new social existence, but a better one. The sources of such optimism are, in the last analysis, difficult to define, and it may be that the only logical justification for optimism is that optimism seems to be a characteristic of the individual's psychology and (arguably) biology.[41] What would life be like if optimism were eradicated from the individual's personality and his creative imagination? And what, furthermore, would be the consequences if optimism were eradicated from our attempts to comprehend and mould the society in which we live? In this book we have tried to show that a certain kind of optimism is a precondition for a worthwhile earthly existence. As long as man has the capacity to identify evil, then he is likely to feel the urge to transcend evil and seek goodness and beauty in his personal relationships, his artistic creations, his religious life and his social and political organization. Historically, beginning in the civilization of the ancient Greeks, the study of politics first emerged as a rigorous method of assisting man in this quest for the good life. Consciousness of the difference between existing reality and a non-existent, but potentially existent, future – a morally desirable future – was one of the most important ingredients of this quest. Unless we feel absolutely confident that we have now reached the limits of our capabilities and creativity, that we have advanced to perfection already, to dispense with utopianism would be to renounce a large part of what it is to be a political animal.

Suggested reading

One of the few attempts to give an account of utopianism which includes developments in the twentieth century is made by F. E. Manuel and F. P. Manuel in their *Utopian Thought in the Western World*. F. E. Manuel also included several essays dealing with twentieth-century aspects in his edited collection, *Utopias and Utopian Thought*. Socialist utopianism in the twentieth century is the theme of Z. Bauman, *Socialism: The Active Utopia*, and the issue of utopianism in relation to Marxism and the New Left could usefully be examined through two books by P. Anderson: *Arguments Within English Marxism* and *Considerations on Western Marxism*. R. Bahro's *The Alternative in Eastern Europe* is also essential reading. D. Bouchier, *Idealism and Revolution*, contains an interesting analysis of New Left thought, and includes a chapter on the Women's Liberation Movement. M. Kitchen, *Fascism*, and J. Meynaud, *Technocracy* offer good introductions to their respective subjects. On the theme of 'counter-utopias' the most fruitful approach would probably be to study the arguments of a representative thinker such as F. Hayek (*The Road to Serfdom*) and Dahrendorf's analysis of modern social science in 'Out of utopia', in *Essays in the Theory of Society*. R. Nozick's *Anarchy, State and Utopia* is also important. Material on recent communitarianism is included in R. M. Kanter's *Commitment and Community*; and the ecological perspective could usefully be studied through *A Blueprint for Survival* and articles in *The Ecologist*.

Notes and references

Chapter 1: Taking utopianism seriously

1 Succinctly expressed in *The Communist Manifesto* (1848), Part III:2.

2 J. Locke, *An Essay Concerning the True Original, Extent and End of Civil Government* (Everyman, 1924), p. 182.

3 J. Passmore, *The Perfectibility of Man* (Duckworth, 1970) shows the interconnections of such ideas. See also C. Vereker, *Eighteenth-century Optimism* (Liverpool University Press, 1951).

4 J. Servier, *Histoire de l'Utopie* (Gallimard, 1967), p. 354.

5 R. Mucchielli, *Le Mythe de la Cité Idéale* (Presses Universitaires de France, 1960), p. 238.

6 W. Godwin, *An Inquiry Concerning Political Justice* (London, 1793), Book VIII, 'Of private property'.

7 J. Rawls, *A Theory of Justice* (Harvard University Press, 1971).

8 See A. L. Morton, *The English Utopia* (Lawrence & Wishart, 1969) and V. Dupont, *L'Utopie et le Roman Utopique dans la Littérature Anglaise* (Didier, 1941). G. Duveau suggests that utopia flourished in England because the country 'retains a savour of childhood'! *Sociologie de l'Utopie* (Presses Universitaires de France, 1961), p. 13.

9 See, for example, the section on secondary literature in L. T. Sargent, *British and American Utopian Literature 1516–1975* (G. K. Hall, 1979).

10 R. Ruyer, *L'Utopie et les Utopies* (Presses Universitaires de France, 1951), pp. 4–5.

11 Servier, ch. xix.

12 See the article 'Liberty and equality' by E. Carritt for examples, in A. Quinton (ed.), *Political Philosophy* (Oxford University Press, 1967).

13 The phrase is used by Ruyer (p. 19) and also by H. Hudde, who calls utopia 'a projection of lateral possibilities in the name of mental exercise'. See his contribution to the Colloque de Cerisy: *Le Discours Utopique* (Union Générale d'Editions, 1978).

14 See H. Levin, *The Myth of the Golden Age in the Renaissance* (Indiana University Press, 1969).

15 The controversy is satirized by Swift in 'The battle of the books' (1697), *A Tale of a Tub* (Dent, 1909).

16 Rousseau's primitivism is disputed by A. Lovejoy, 'The supposed primitivism of Rousseau's discourse on inequality', in his *Essays in the History of Ideas* (Johns Hopkins Press, 1948). For a thorough account of noble savage myths see R. Meek, *Social Science and the Noble Savage* (Cambridge University Press, 1976).

17 S. Lukes, *Power: A Radical View* (Macmillan, 1974) discusses the importance of decision-blocking and similar devices. See pp. 24-6, 42-5 especially.

18 L. Marin, *Utopiques: Jeux d'Espaces* (Minuit, 1973), p. 120. Ch. 4 is devoted to analysing More's manipulation of proper names.

19 Mucchielli, ch. 1.

20 Z. Bauman, *Socialism: The Active Utopia* (Allen & Unwin, 1976), p. 13.

21 K. Mannheim, *Ideology and Utopia*, trans. L. Wirth and E. Shils (Routledge & Kegan Paul, 1936), p. 236.

22 T. More, *Utopia*, trans. P. Turner (Penguin, 1965), pp. 44ff.

23 J. Swift, *Gulliver's Travels* (Penguin, 1967), pp. 167-73.

24 See J. Bury, *The Idea of Progress* (Macmillan, 1932).

25 R. Dahrendorf, 'Out of Utopia' in *Essays in the Theory of Society* (Routledge & Kegan Paul, 1968), p. 110.

26 See B. Goodwin, *Social Science and Utopia* (Harvester, 1978), ch. 7.

27 Mucchielli, pp. 33-5.

28 R. Schérer in *Le Monde des Livres* (2 June 1972). His article is reminiscent of Marcuse's position in *Essay on Liberation* (Penguin, 1971). Similarly, an anonymous article in *Combat* (26 October 1971) entitled 'De Babeuf au mouvement de mai et aux communautés' argued that forgotten utopian authors can offer what Marxism cannot.

29 See R. Barthes, *The Pleasure of the Text*, trans. R. Miller (Cape, 1976) for an influential application of this approach to literary texts.

30 Mannheim, pp. 231-8.

31 J. Shklar, *After Utopia* (Princeton University Press, 1957).

32 H. Marcuse, *Eros and Civilisation* (Sphere, 1969); E. Fromm, *The Sane Society* (Routledge & Kegan Paul, 1956); F. Hayek, 'The principles of a liberal social order', in A. Crespigny and J. Cronin (eds.), *Ideologies of Politics* (Oxford University Press, 1975); R. Nozick, *Anarchy, State and Utopia* (Blackwell, 1974).

33 J. Freund emphasizes that insularity saves utopia from contamination by politics, adding that 'socialism in one country' was the only utopian element of Stalinism! *Utopie et Violence* (Rivière, 1978), p. 28.

34 F. Engels, 'Socialism: utopian and scientific', in *Marx and Engels: Selected Works* (Moscow, 1970), vol. 3, p. 121.

35 V. I. Lenin, *The State and Revolution*, in *Selected Works* (Lawrence & Wishart, 1953), vol. 2, pp. 249–51. 'We are not utopians, we do not indulge in "dreams" of dispensing at once with all administration, with all subordination.'

36 G. Lapouge, *Utopie et Civilisations* (Flammarion, 1978), *passim*.

37 K. Marx, 'The Jewish question', in *Early Texts*, trans. D. McLellan (Blackwell, 1971). 'The rights of the citizen are nothing but the rights of . . . eogistic man, man separated from other men and the community.' (p. 102).

Chapter 2: Taxonomy and anatomy

1 G. Negley and F. Patrick, *The Quest for Utopia* (H. Schuman, 1952); F. E. Manuel and F. P. Manuel, *Utopian Thought in the Western World* (Blackwell, 1979).

2 Extracts appear in F. E. Manuel and F. P. Manuel, *French Utopias* (Free Press, 1966).

3 The folk poem 'The Land of Cockayne' appears in A. L. Morton, *The English Utopia*, pp. 279–85.

4 *Utopia*, edn edited by H. Morley in *Ideal Commonwealths* (Routledge, 1890), p. 86.

5 The most cited utopian texts of Marx are *The Communist Manifesto* and his writings on the Paris Commune in *The Civil War in France*. See also B. Ollman's assertion of Marx's own utopianism, 'Marx's vision of communism: a reconstruction', in *Critique* (summer, 1977).

6 C. Péguy, *L'Esprit de Système* (Gallimard, 1953). J. Déjacque's *L'Humanisphère* is included in a reissue of his writings, ed. V. Pelosse, *A Bas les Chefs* (Champ Libre, 1971). For introductory information on the welfare socialism of the little-known Josef Popper-Lynkeus see Robert Plank's article, 'The Welfare State as utopia', in *Alternative Futures*, vol. 1, nos. 3–4 (Fall 1978).

7 Among Wells's utopian novels are *Men Like Gods* (London, 1905) and *A Modern Utopia* (Cassell, 1923).

8 *Eros and Civilisation*, pp. 152ff. The ideas in the following paragraphs all appear in this text.

9 Y. Friedman, *Utopies Réalisables* (Union Générale d'Editions, 1975), p. 23.

10 R. Nozick, *Anarchy, State and Utopia*, pp. 113–14.

11 ibid., p. 328.

12 ibid., p. 310.

13 ibid., p. 312.

14   ibid., pp. 322–3, 328–9.
15   ibid., ch. 7.
16   Friedman, p. 86.
17   ibid., pp. 89–90.
18   ibid., p. 269.
19   ibid., p. 226.
20   *Contingencies of Reinforcement* (Appleton–Century, 1969), ch. 2.
21   *Beyond Freedom and Dignity* (Cape, 1972), ch. 2.
22   ibid., ch. 9.
23   *Utopiques: Jeux d'Espaces*, p. 350.
24   *Socialism: The Active Utopia*, pp. 31–2.
25   H. J. N. Horsburgh, 'The relevance of the utopian', *Ethics*, vol. 67 (1957), pp. 127–38.
26   R. Ruyer, *L'Utopie et les Utopies*; G. Duveau, *Sociologie de l'Utopie*, Part II. Mucchielli offers an instructive comparison of More and Machiavelli in this light. See *Le Mythe de la Cité Idéale*, Part I, ch. 3.
27   Manuel and Manuel, *French Utopias*, p. 4.
28   ibid., pp. 45–7.
29   David Easton is famous for providing a systems analysis of politics on these lines. See especially *A Systems Analysis of Political Life* (Wiley, 1965).
30   C. B. Macpherson, *The Political Theory of Possessive Individualism* (Oxford University Press, 1966).
31   E. Fromm, *The Sane Society*, p. 196.
32   R. Owen, *Six Lectures Delivered in Manchester* (Manchester, 1837), p. 14.
33   This process is recorded in Michel Foucault's *Discipline and Punish*, trans. A. Sheridan (Allen Lane, 1977).
34   W. Godwin, *An Enquiry Concerning Political Justice*, 1st edn (Dublin, 1793), vol. 1, p. 109.
35   B. Baczko, *Lumières de l'Utopie* (Payot, 1978), p. 32. C. G. Dubois mentions the phenomenon of transparency in the service of control in *Problèmes de l'Utopie, Archives des Lettres Modernes*, no. 85 (1968), pp. 28, 52, and Mucchielli also discusses it. Lapouge says 'La cité idéale est vouée à la transparence' (*Utopie et Civilisations*, p. 37). This transparency, visibility and mutual surveillance make utopia similar to the ideal prison of the eighteenth century (e.g. Bentham's Panopticon) which had the same characteristics. See Foucault, Part IV.
36   F. Dostoevsky, *The Brothers Karamazov* (Penguin, 1958), vol. 1, pp. 292–305. The Inquisitor promises to relieve men 'of their great anxiety and of their present terrible torments of coming to a free decision themselves' (p. 304).

37　This classification of ascetic communist utopias, including those of
　　Mably and Morelly, was originally Durkheim's. See *Socialism and
　　Saint-Simon*, trans. C. Sattler (Antioch Press, 1958), ch. 3.
38　See J. Lacroix, *Le Désir et les Désirs* (Presses Universitaires de
　　France, 1975), which looks at Rousseau, Saint-Simon, Fourier and
　　Marx from this point of view.

Chapter 3: Ideology, science or symbol?

1　See B. Goodwin, *Social Science and Utopia*, especially ch. 7.
2　K. Marx and F. Engels, *Collected Works, 1844–5* (Lawrence &
　　Wishart, 1975), vol. 4, pp. 223–4.
3　'The main aim of an Owenite education was to produce a man able
　　to accept his role in the community'. M. Browning, 'Owen as an
　　educator', in J. Butt (ed.), *Robert Owen* (David & Charles, 1971),
　　p. 62. See also the other articles in this collection.
4　*The Condition of the Working Class in England*, in *Collected
　　Works*, vol. 4, p. 525.
5　*The Holy Family*, in *Collected Works*, vol. 4, p. 153.
6　ibid., p. 283.
7　K. Marx, *Capital*, trans. E. and C. Paul (Dent, 1972), pp. 796–7,
　　815.
8　M. Abensour, 'L'histoire de l'utopie et le destin de sa critique',
　　Textures, vols. 6–7 (1973), p. 17.
9　*Collected Works*, vol. 4, p. 84.
10　*The Communist Manifesto*, in *Marx and Engels: Selected Works*
　　(Moscow, 1970), vol. 1, p. 135.
11　*Selected Works*, vol. 1, p. 135, and vol. 3, p. 117.
12　For an account of Saint-Simon's influence on Marx, see R. Fakkâr,
　　Sociologie, Socialisme et Internationalisme Prémarxistes (Neu-
　　châtel, 1968).
13　Engels, *Socialism: Utopian and Scientific*, in *Selected Works*,
　　vol. 3, p. 122.
14　*Collected Works*, vol. 4, p. 526.
15　*Selected Works*, vol. 3, p. 117.
16　ibid., p. 116.
17　ibid., p. 126.
18　*Collected Works*, vol. 4, p. 615.
19　Abensour, p. 13.
20　Abensour, continuation of the same article in *Textures*, vols.
　　8–9 (1974), pp. 74–5. See also the contribution by G. Labica in
　　Le Discours Utopique for an account of Marxist criticism of
　　utopianism.
21　See J. Larrain, *The Concept of Ideology* (Hutchinson, 1979),

especially chs. 2–3, for a thorough exploration of the different interpretations given by different Marxists.

22 K. Mannheim, *Ideology and Utopia*, pp. 49–50.
23 ibid., p. 66.
24 ibid., p. 173.
25 ibid., p. 176.
26 ibid., p. 186–7. See also Y. Friedman, *Utopies Réalisables*, pp. 21ff.
27 Mannheim, p. 236.
28 Mucchielli, *Le Mythe de la Cité Idéale*, pp. 74–88.
29 A brief account of the New Left approach is offered in D. Howard's contribution to *Le Discours Utopique*.
30 C. M. Asperen, *Hope and History* (Utrecht University Press, 1973), p. 158.
31 ibid., p. 157.
32 Very few of Bloch's texts are available in English, although most are translated into French. For critical accounts of Bloch's work, see G. Raulet (ed.), *Utopie, Marxisme selon Ernst Bloch* (Payot, 1976), especially Raulet's introduction, and the articles on Bloch in the first part of *Le Discours Utopique*.
33 K. Popper, *The Logic of Scientific Discovery* (Hutchinson, 1968) is a classic statement of the Popperian thesis.
34 R. Dahrendorf, 'Out of utopia', in *Essays in the Theory of Society*.
35 Cited in Z. Bauman, *Socialism: The Active Utopia*, p. 36 (our italics).
36 M. Foucault, *Discipline and Punish*, pp. 226ff.
37 C.-H. de Saint Simon, 'Sur la querelle des abeilles et des frelons', in *Oeuvres de Claude-Henri de Saint-Simon* (Anthropos, 1966), vol. 2.
38 R. Ruyer, *L'Utopie et les Utopies*, p. 13.
39 Bauman, pp. 33–4.
40 For Adorno's view and similar hypotheses by Kolakowski and others, see Bauman, pp. 34–7.
41 Friedman, pp. 21ff.
42 Mucchielli, pp. 62–3.
43 G. Duveau, *Sociologie de l'Utopie*, Part 2, ch. 3 *passim*.
44 See R. Barthes, *The Pleasure of the Text*, and also *Leçon* (Seuil, 1978), pp. 23–5.
45 *Sade Fourier Loyola*, trans. R. Miller (Cape, 1977), pp. 4–6.
46 ibid., p. 3.
47 ibid., pp. 7–9 (our italics).
48 L. Marin, *Utopiques: Jeux d'Espaces*, pp. 10, 249.
49 ibid., pp. 181–2.
50 ibid., p. 22.
51 ibid., p. 346.
52 ibid., ch. 7.

Chapter 4: Utopia's enemies

1 Some of the arguments of this chapter appear in: B. Goodwin, 'Utopia defended against the liberals', *Political Studies*, vol. XXVIII/ 3 (September 1980).

2 *Magazine Littéraire* (July–August 1978, no. 139).

3 K. Popper, *The Open Society and its Enemies* (Routledge & Kegan Paul, 1945), vol. 1, p. 168.

4 The full statement of the six-point syndrome appears in C. J. Friedrich and Z. Brzezinski, *Totalitarian Dictatorship and Democracy*, 2nd edn (Praeger, 1965).

5 The result was *Plato Today* (Allen & Unwin, 1937). An extended account of the anti-totalitarian approach to utopianism can be found in G. Kateb, *Utopia and its Enemies* (Collier-Macmillan, 1963). For an examination of attacks on one particular 'totalitarian' see K. Taylor (ed.), *Henri Saint-Simon. Selected Writings* (Croom Helm, 1975), pp. 58-9.

6 Popper, vol. 1, pp. 157-68.

7 R. Levinson, *In Defence of Plato* (University of Massachusetts Press, 1953), ch. 9.

8 J. L. Talmon, *The Origins of Totalitarian Democracy* (Praeger, 1960), pp. 2-7, and *Political Messianism: The Romantic Phase* (Secker & Warburg, 1960), pp. 19-24.

9 F. A. Hayek, 'Liberalism: the principles of a liberal social order', in A. Crespigny and J. Cronin (eds.), *Ideologies of Politics*. The same ideas are expounded in his longer works such as *The Road to Serfdom* (Routledge & Kegan Paul, 1944).

10 M. Oakeshott, *Rationalism in Politics* (Methuen, 1962), p. 1.

11 ibid., p. 5.

12 E. M. Cioran, *Histoire et Utopie* (Gallimard, 1960), p. 181.

13 ibid., p. 145.

14 ibid., p. 155.

15 'Le lieu glissant de l'improbable', *Magazine Littéraire* (139), pp. 16-19.

16 *Utopie et Civilisations*, p. 199.

17 L. Schapiro, *Totalitarianism* (Macmillan, 1972), pp. 85-90.

18 M. Abensour, 'Le procès des maîtres rêveurs', *Libre*, no. 4 (1978), p. 213.

19 B. Barber, 'The conceptual foundations of totalitarianism', in C. J. Friedrich, M. Curtis and B. Barber, *Totalitarianism in Perspective* (Pall Mall, 1969), pp. 27ff.

20 For example, K. Arrow, *Social Choice and Individual Values* (Yale University Press, 1951) and subsequent references in his second edition, 1963.

21 A. Downs, *An Economic Theory of Democracy* (Harper & Row,

1957), ch. 3.

22 R. Owen, *A New View of Society* (Penguin, 1970), p. 198.

23 This logic was strongly criticized by G. E. Moore, but M. Warnock provides a defence of J. S. Mill in this respect in *Ethics Since 1900*, 2nd edn (Oxford University Press, 1966), pp. 19–27.

24 See the review in *Radical Philosophy*, no. 22 (Summer, 1979) by Hugh Tomlinson, of D. L. Phillips, *Wittgenstein and Science* (Macmillan, 1977). Referring to Popper's and Lakatos's demarcationist theory of science, he says 'the fear at the heart of demarcationism is that of a new set of rules being imposed on science and enforced through the use of power and force' (p. 39). The parallel with liberal political thought is clear.

25 T. Weldon, *The Vocabulary of Politics* (Penguin, 1953).

26 See, as a relatively early concession of the value-laden nature of theory, C. Taylor, 'Neutrality in political science', in P. Laslett and W. Runciman (eds.), *Philosophy, Politics and Society*, 3rd series (Blackwell, 1967).

27 J. Freund, *Utopie et Violence*, p. 249. On the utopia-and-violence question see also M. Lasky, *Utopia and Revolution* (University of Chicago Press, 1976) for a typically hostile view of utopianism.

28 J. S. Mill, *On Liberty* (Fontana, 1962), ch. 5 especially.

29 J. Déjacque, *L'Humanisphère*, reproduced in *A Bas les Chefs*, p. 91.

30 W. J. Stankiewicz, *Aspects of Political Theory* (Collier–Macmillan, 1976), p. 28.

31 R. Nozick, *Anarchy, State and Utopia*, p. 319n.

32 Such arguments are rehearsed by H. A. L. Hart in *The Concept of Law* (Clarendon Press, 1961), p. 38 especially.

33 N. Johnson gives a factual and theoretical account of these shortcomings in relation to British democracy in *In Search of the Constitution* (Pergamon, 1977). America's 'Watergate' episode is perhaps the most recent example of such failings.

34 Freund, p. 120.

35 P. Bachrach, *The Theory of Democratic Elitism* (London University Press, 1969) gives a useful account of such theories.

36 This is advocated by B. F. Skinner in *Beyond Freedom and Dignity*, ch. 8.

37 S. M. Lispet, *Political Man* (Mercury, 1963), p. 403.

38 Z. Bauman, *Socialism: The Active Utopia*. The book begins as a sympathetic account but becomes strongly critical of the utopian elements of socialism.

39 J. S. Mill, *On Representative Government* (1861). C. B. Macpherson makes a similar point (from a critical standpoint) about the development of liberalism in Chapter 1 of his *Democratic Theory* (Oxford University Press, 1973).

40 H. Marcuse, *One-Dimensional Man* (Sphere, 1965) and his essay in R. P. Wolff, B. Moore and H. Marcuse, *A Critique of Pure Tolerance* (Cape, 1969).

Chapter 5: The social origins of the utopian impulse

1 For further discussion of Cabet and Icarianism see K. Taylor, *The Political Ideas of the Utopian Socialists* (Cass, 1982), ch. 5.

2 The account which follows is based on sections of the introduction to Taylor.

3 Here we have the source of that distinction between governmental rule over men and the administrative control of things which reappears in the thought of a range of thinkers from Marx and Engels to Lenin, from Comte to the Fabian socialists.

4 L. A. Loubère, 'The intellectual origins of French Jacobin Socialism', *International Review of Social History*, vol. IV (1959), p. 422. See also B. H. Moss, 'Parisian producers' associations (1830–51): the socialism of skilled workers', in R. Price (ed.), *Revolution and Reaction. 1848 and the Second French Republic* (Croom Helm, 1975), pp. 73–86; and the same author's *The Origins of the French Labor Movement 1830–1914. The Socialism of Skilled Workers* (University of California Press, 1976), ch. 2.

5 A. L. Dunham, *The Industrial Revolution in France 1815–1848* (Exposition Press, 1955), p. 203.

6 See the writings by Moss referred to in note 4; also his 'Parisian workers and the origins of republican socialism, 1830–1833' in J. H. Merriman (ed.), *1830 in France* (New Viewpoints, 1975), pp. 203–21.

7 The *compagnonnages* originated under the guild system in the fifteenth century as associations of skilled journeymen (*compagnons*). Although their general significance was declining by the nineteenth century, they persisted in certain trades.

8 'The word "association" is being applied in our time only to narrow combinations that embrace but one type of interest' – so the leading Saint-Simonians complained in 1829. Instead they put forward the goal of 'universal association' – 'the association of all men on the entire surface of the globe in all spheres of their relationships'. G. G. Iggers (ed.), *The Doctrine of Saint-Simon: An Exposition. First Year, 1828–1829*, 2nd edn (Schocken, 1972), p. 58.

9 M. I. Thomis, *The Town Labourer and the Industrial Revolution* (Batsford, 1974), p. 194.

10 The *sociétés de secours mutuel* were essentially friendly societies providing their members with financial aid in cases of illness or death.

11   Both Fourier and Weitling welcomed an industrial society as a society based on productive labour, but they nevertheless detested the idea of traditional occupations being superseded by factory-based manufacturing. For Fourier agriculture (and, more specifically, horticulture) should remain the key occupation. Weitling, even though he recognized the need for greater mechanization, still considered it to be imperative to protect the position of handicraft.

12   R. M. Kanter, *Commitment and Community: Communes and Utopias in Sociological Perspective* (Harvard University Press, 1972), pp. 54–5.

13   This newspaper also issued fervent defences of the institution of private property in response to the Saint-Simonians, who, although they were not communists, wished to abolish the right of inheritance.

14   See, for example, A. Brisbane, *Association; or, A Concise Exposition of the Practical Part of Fourier's Social Science* (Tribune Office, 1843), p. 4. Fourier himself described Owen's notion of economic communism as 'so pitiful that it is not worthy of refutation': C. Gide (ed.), *Design for Utopia: Selected Writings of Charles Fourier* (Schocken, 1971), p. 128, quoting from *The New Industrial and Societary World.*

15   See R. C. Bowles, 'The reaction of Charles Fourier to the French Revolution', *French Historical Studies*, vol. 1 (1958–60), p. 355.

16   Some useful material on this point may be found in E. P. Thompson, *The Making of the English Working Class*, revised edn (Penguin, 1968), ch. 15, especially pp. 668–70.

17   For example: D. H. Pinkney, *The French Revolution of 1830* (Princeton University Press, 1972); R. Price, *The French Second Republic. A Social History* (Batsford, 1972); J. Godechot, *Les Révolutions de 1848* (Albin Michel, 1971); F. Rude, *L'Insurrection Lyonnaise de Novembre 1831. Le Mouvement Ouvrier à Lyon de 1827–1832* (Anthropos, 1970); R. J. Bezucha, *The Lyon Uprising of 1834: Social and Political Conflict in the Early July Monarchy* (Harvard University Press, 1974); M. Agulhon, *Une Ville Ouvrière au Temps du Socialisme Utopique: Toulon de 1815 à 1851* (Mouton/De Gruyter, 1970). The general hypothesis which emerges from these studies is that the chief participants in the upheavals of this period were artisans or newly proletarianized workers suffering the most severe consequences of socio-economic transition. The case of the silk-workers (*canuts*) of Lyons is the best documented.

18   Rude, pp. 697–711.

19   As we have seen, some modern critics of utopianism (e.g. Hayek,

Talmon and Popper) go even further and persistently equate utopianism and totalitarianism.

20 This was, in particular, one of the main points at issue in the continual disputes between Saint-Simonians and Fourierists.

21 R. A. Jones and R. M. Anservitz, 'Saint-Simon and Saint-Simonism: a Weberian view', *American Journal of Sociology*, vol. 80 (1975), pp. 1095-123.

22 See further the discussion in Chapter 8 below.

23 K. Mannheim, *Ideology and Utopia*, p. 173.

24 ibid., p. 175.

25 ibid., p. 174.

26 ibid., p. 174.

27 N. Cohn, *The Pursuit of the Millennium: Revolutionary Millenarians and Mystical Anarchists of the Middle Ages*, revised edn (Paladin, 1970), p. 29.

Chapter 6: Movements for utopia – 1

1 R. Levitas, 'Sociology and utopia', *Sociology*, vol. 13 (1979), p. 26.

2 From 'An appeal to all Englishmen' (1650), in G. H. Sabine (ed.), *The Works of Gerrard Winstanley* (Cornell University Press, 1941), p. 409.

3 N. Cohn, *The Pursuit of the Millennium*, p. 288.

4 K. Mannheim, *Ideology and Utopia*, p. 192.

5 ibid., p. 183.

6 ibid., p. 197.

7 See, for example, the extract from Saint-Simon's *Du Système Industriel* in K. Taylor (ed.), *Henri Saint-Simon: Selected Writings*, pp. 227-8.

8 Mannheim, p. 222.

9 See further the discussion on anarchism in Chapter 7.

10 See Mannheim, pp. 215-22; Z. Bauman, *Socialism: The Active Utopia*, pp. 36ff.

11 The account which follows is based on sections of the introduction to K. Taylor, *The Political Ideas of the Utopian Socialists*.

12 R. Heberle, *Social Movements: An Introduction to Political Sociology* (Appleton–Century–Crofts, 1951), p. 70.

13 C. H. Johnson, 'Etienne Cabet and the problem of class antagonism', *International Review of Social History*, vol. XI (1966), pp. 403-43; 'Communism and the working class before Marx: the Icarian system', *American Historical Review*, vol. 76 (1971), pp. 642-89; *Utopian Communism in France: Cabet and the Icarians, 1839-1851* (Cornell University Press, 1974).

14   Johnson, *Utopian Communism in France*, pp. 145–9. Unfortunately, Johnson himself is not entirely consistent in his overall
assessment of Icarianism as a social movement. On the one hand he
sees Icarianism as 'the first mass movement to accept the total
overthrow of the emerging capitalist society' (p. 299); but on other
occasions he tends to qualify this judgement. Thus Icarianism
'takes a place beside a wide variety of *transitional* social movements that arise in the earlier and more traumatic stages of indus-
trialisation but are inherently incapable of becoming viable mass
movements in the modern industrial context' (p. 16).

15   ibid., pp. 153–68. Johnson's analysis is here very useful, but it
occasionally leads to confusion owing to a lack of precision in the
terminology employed. In particular, the Icarian movement is said
to be neither proletarian nor petty-bourgeois. How, then, are we to
characterize it? Is the idea of an 'artisan movement' sufficiently
clear?

16   ibid., p. 160.

17   Heberle, p. 14.

18   G. G. Iggers (ed.), *The Doctrine of Saint-Simon*, p. xxiv.

19   ibid., p. xxiv.

20   The 'generational consciousness' at this time throughout Western
Europe, but especially in France, was truly remarkable. As Feuer
has written: 'Generational consciousness, in the sense of involving
an antagonism, first came into existence when the hopes of the
French Revolutionary era were unfulfilled, and those of the Restoration period were de-authorized in the eyes of the young. Thus
arose "the generation of 1830".' Lewis S. Feuer, *The Conflict of
Generations* (Heinemann, 1969), p. 35.

21   See Johnson, *Utopian Communism in France*, pp. 13 and 156n.

22   Quoted by Johnson, ibid., p. 207.

23   Furthermore, Fourierism never put forward any coherent religious
creed, nor did it ever form a deliberately organized sect. Religion
was encouraged, but no dogmatic beliefs were defined. As with
other aspects of the Fourierist doctrine, a considerable degree of
freedom was thought desirable.

24   An excellent account is provided by J. F. C. Harrison, *Robert
Owen and the Owenites in Britain and America: The Quest for the
New Moral World* (Routledge & Kegan Paul, 1969), pp. 195–232.

25   See E. P. Thompson, *The Making of the English Working Class*,
pp. 857–87; E. J. Hobsbawm, *The Age of Revolution* (Weidenfeld
& Nicolson, 1962), p. 210. Harrison (pp. 213–14) concludes that
Owenism constituted a mass movement only in 1833–4, the period
during which the Owenites succeeded in capturing the trade union
movement.

26 For example H. Katz, 'Social movements – an essay in definition', *Polish Sociological Bulletin*, no. 1 (1971), p. 65.

27 Thompson, p. 894.

28 ibid., pp. 869–70.

29 H. Pelling, *A History of British Trade Unionism* (Penguin, 1963), pp. 42–3.

30 Hobsbawm, p. 221.

31 A comprehensive analysis of this issue is provided by P. H. Noyes, *Organization and Revolution* (Princeton University Press, 1966). See also E. Shorter, 'Middle-class anxiety in the German Revolution of 1848', *Journal of Social History*, vol. 2 (1968–9), pp. 189–215.

32 There are brief comments in *The Communist Manifesto*, Part III, Section 1(c). Engels's *On the History of the Communist League* offers more detail.

33 M. A. Jones, *American Immigration* (University of Chicago Press, 1960), pp. 110–11.

34 See H. G. Gutman, *Work, Culture, and Society in Industrializing America* (Knopf, 1976), ch. 1.

35 K. J. R. Arndt, *George Rapp's Harmony Society 1785–1847*, revised edn (Fairleigh Dickinson, 1972), p. 6.

36 G. Lichtheim, *Marxism: An Historical and Critical Study*, 3rd impression (Routledge & Kegan Paul, 1967), p. 22.

Chapter 7: Movements for utopia – 2

1 Taken from F. Engels, *Principles of Communism*, trans. P. M. Sweezy (Pluto Press, n.d.).

2 K. Marx, *The Communist Manifesto*, in D. McLellan (ed.), *Karl Marx: Selected Writings* (Oxford University Press, 1977), pp. 231–7. Ten basic aims were listed (p. 237): 'Abolition of property in land and application of all rents of land to public purposes – A heavy progressive or graduated income tax – Abolition of all right of inheritance – Confiscation of the property of all emigrants and rebels – Centralisation of credit in the hands of the State, by means of a national bank with State capital and an exclusive monopoly – Centralisation of the means of communication and transport in the hands of the State – Extension of factories and instruments of production owned by the State; the bringing into cultivation of wastelands, and the improvement of the soil generally in accordance with a common plan – Equal liability of all to labour. Establishment of industrial armies, especially for agriculture – Combination of agriculture with manufacturing industries; gradual abolition of the distinction between town and country, by a more equable

distribution of the population over the country – Free education for all children in public schools. Abolition of children's factory labour in its present form. Combination of education with industrial production, etc., etc.'

3   ibid., pp. 237–8.
4   ibid., pp. 244–5.
5   See K. Mannheim, *Ideology and Utopia*, pp. 190–206, 218–19.
6   ibid., p. 195.
7   ibid., p. 125.
8   Quoted ibid., p. 196.
9   Quoted by M. Lasky, *Utopia and Revolution* (Macmillan, 1976), p. 74.
10 In E. Capouya and K. Tompkins (eds.), *The Essential Kropotkin* (Macmillan, 1975), pp. 74–5.
11 G. Lichtheim, *Marxism*, pp. 222–33.
12 In Capouya and Tompkins (eds.), p. 110.
13 See Mannheim, pp. 125, 202, 219, 223.
14 V. I. Lenin, *What is to be Done?*, trans. S. V. and P. Utechin (Panther, 1970), p. 164.
15 V. I. Lenin, *Letters on Tactics* (April 1917), in *Collected Works* (International Publishers, n.d.), vol. XX, Book I, p. 121.
16 See V. I. Lenin, *The State and Revolution*, in *The Essential Left: Four Classic Texts on the Principles of Socialism* (Unwin, 1960), especially chs. III and V.
17 D. Germino, *Modern Western Political Thought* (Rand McNally, 1972), p. 258.
18 See M. Oakeshott, 'On being conservative', in *Rationalism in Politics*.
19 See M. Oakeshott, *Social and Political Doctrines of Contemporary Europe* (Basic Books, 1940).
20 Mannheim, p. 207.
21 This characterization of Comte's positivism is suggested briefly in R. Aron, *Main Currents in Sociological Thought*, vol. 1 (Penguin, 1968), p. 74.
22 ibid., p. 77.
23 See R. Harrison, *Before the Socialists. Studies in Labour and Politics 1861–1881* (Routledge & Kegan Paul, 1965), ch. VI.
24 See R. L. Woodward (ed.), *Positivism in Latin America 1850–1900* (D. C. Heath, 1971).

Chapter 8: Utopia writ small: communitarianism and its legacy

1   A. O. Lewis, 'On utopian studies', *Alternative Futures*, vol. 1, no. 1 (Spring 1978), p. 89.

2 See R. S. Fogarty, *American Utopianism* (Peacock, 1972); 'Communal history in America', *Choice*, no. 10 (June 1973), pp. 578–90; 'American communes, 1865–1914', *Journal of American Studies*, vol. 9, no. 2 (1975), pp. 145–62; 'A radical nominalist looks at community', *Alternative Futures*, vol. 2, no. 2 (Spring 1979), pp. 55–71.

3 Fogarty, 'A radical nominalist looks at community', p. 61.

4 ibid., p. 70.

5 Quoted by Fogarty, ibid., p. 56.

6 Writing in 1973, Louis C. D. Joos pointed out that 'over the past 150 years, a European state has been born or has died on average every three years. . . . Under the system of nation-states, the average period of political stability has barely attained the average life of a car battery'. ('Are national frontiers natural frontiers?', in *European Community*, March 1973, pp. 20–21).

7 R. M. Kanter, *Commitment and Community*, pp. 246–7. The duration of the Shaker communities has been updated, since Kanter's analysis appeared in 1972. It should be noted, however, that the Shaker movement has recently dwindled further in size, so that it now faces the possibility of extinction.

8 ibid., p. 5.

9 ibid., p. 245.

10 ibid., p. 136.

11 ibid., pp. 136–7.

12 The analysis here follows Kanter, ibid., pp. 65–70.

13 ibid., p. 69.

14 ibid., pp. 70–74.

15 ibid., p. 72.

16 ibid., pp. 72–3.

17 ibid., p. 74.

18 ibid., ch. 4.

19 ibid., p. 113.

20 See the comprehensive list provided by H. Mariampolski in 'Communes and utopias, past and present: a bibliography of post-1945 studies', *Bulletin of Bibliography*, vol. 36, no. 3 (July 1979), pp. 119–27 and 143, especially the first section in 'Syntheses, analyses, and overviews'.

21 Kanter, ch. 6.

22 C. J. Erasmus, *In Search of the Common Good: Utopian Experiments Past and Future* (Free Press, 1977), p. 163.

23 ibid., p. 153.

24 ibid., p. 150.

25 ibid., p. 163.

26 ibid., p. 173.

27   Kanter, p. 245; Erasmus, pp. 113–14.
28   Erasmus, pp. 168–9.
29   H. Darin-Drabkin, *The Other Society* (Gollancz, 1962), p. 59.
30   See M. E. Spiro, *Kibbutz: Venture in Utopia*, new edn (Schocken, 1970), pp. 11–19.
31   Erasmus, p. 169.
32   ibid., p. 170.
33   ibid., p. 172.
34   ibid., p. 168.
35   Darin-Drabkin, pp. 76–7, 96–7.
36   Although, in this chapter, we have concentrated on two particular examples of communitarian utopianism – the American and the Israeli – it has to be realized that these cases really form the tip of a gigantic iceberg, and that communitarianism has had a practical impact in a large number of other countries, although this impact has usually been ignored in the study of politics. Our appreciation of this fact is just emerging, and there is need for much more work to be done before a full picture can be given. But already a sizeable literature exists, and the student interested in this area will find no shortage of material. (Reference may be made to Mariam-polski's bibliography cited in note 20.) The case of Britain is especially interesting, since until recently the orthodox view seemed to be that communitarianism has not played an important part in this country's political history. But beginning with W. H. G. Armytage's survey of utopian communities in the period 1560–1960 (*Heavens Below*, Routledge & Kegan Paul, 1961) there has gradually emerged a rather different view according to which a continuous tradition of communitarianism has been identified, just as some American scholars, including Fogarty, found such a tradition on an even grander scale in America. The spread of communes and the new youthful 'counter-culture' in the 1960s in Britain encouraged more research, much of it of a sociological nature, and books such as Andrew Rigby's *Alternative Realities* (Routledge & Kegan Paul, 1974) further reinforced the view that Armytage had put forward a decade earlier, that a continuous tradition of community-building could be identified. Even more recently, some very valuable material on nineteenth-century communities in England has been brought together by Dennis Hardy (*Alternative Communities in Nineteenth Century England*, Longman, 1979).
37   The following sources are especially useful: H. Rosenau, *The Ideal City in its Architectural Evolution* (Routledge & Kegan Paul, 1959); L. Benevolo, *The Origins of Modern Town Planning*, trans. J. Landry (Routledge & Kegan Paul, 1967); A. Blowers *et al.*

(eds.), *The Future of Cities* (Hutchinson/Open University Press, 1974), Part 1: 'The future city as seen in the past'.
38 C. B. Purdom, *The Letchworth Achievement* (Dent, 1963), p. 4.
39 In 1979 the British Town and Country Planning Association issued an outline prospectus: *A Third Garden City* (TCPA, 1979).

Chapter 9: Is utopia really necessary?

1 See B. Goodwin, *Social Science and Utopia*, pp. 161–71.
2 On the problems of average utility see J. Rawls, *A Theory of Justice*, pp. 27–8.
3 Satisficing is explained in S. Waldman, *The Foundations of Political Action* (Little, Brown, 1972), ch. 2. The idea was originally H. Simon's.
4 See C. B. Macpherson on the infinitely acquisitive man of liberal theory in *The Political Theory of Possessive Individualism*.
5 This would be Nozick's view as stated in *Anarchy, State and Utopia* and also that of many pluralist theorists.
6 M. Abensour, 'L'histoire de l'utopie et le destin de sa critique', *Textures* (1974), p. 57.
7 Fourier's scorn for morality and his conviction that it should only be observed if conducive to happiness is typical. See J. Beecher and R. Bienvenu (eds.), *The Utopian Vision of Charles Fourier* (Cape, 1972), pp. 157–60, 163–6.
8 R. Owen, *A New View of Society*, p. 103. The same point occurs throughout his writings.
9 H. J. N. Horsburgh, 'The relevance of the utopian', p. 136.
10 See again J. Lacroix, *Le Désir et les Désirs*.
11 J. Plamenatz, *Man and Society* (Longman, 1963), vol. 2, p. xvi.
12 Possible world analysis is now highly fashionable and specialized. For an explanation accessible to the layman see J. Elster, *Logic and Society* (Wiley, 1978), ch. 6. More advanced is N. Rescher, *A Theory of Possibility* (Blackwell, 1975), ch. 4.
13 Elster, pp. 190–1.
14 S. Kripke, 'Naming and necessity', in D. Davidson and G. Harman (eds.), *Semantics of Natural Language* (Reidel, 1972), p. 273 especially.
15 Rescher, p. 77.
16 Elster, p. 57.
17 Horsburgh, p. 133.
18 K. Arrow, *Social Choice and Individual Values*, 2nd edn (Yale University Press, 1963), pp. 59–60. Note Arrow's comment (p. 59): 'The word "unsatisfactory" in the above statement means that the social welfare function does not reflect individuals' desires

negatively' – a somewhat minimal requirement.

19   M. Olson, *The Logic of Collective Action* (Harvard University Press, 1971), p. 51.

20   W. Godwin, *Political Justice*, vol. I, p. 314.

21   L. Marin, *Utopiques: Jeux d'Espaces*, p. 351.

22   Y. Friedman, *Utopies Réalisables*, p. 16.

23   *Histoire de l'Utopie*, p. 364.

24   F. Engels, *Socialism: Utopian and Scientific*, in *Selected Works*, vol. 3, p. 117.

25   Horsburgh, pp. 128–31.

Chapter 10: The utopian impulse in twentieth-century politics

1   See the section on 'The living tradition' in Chapter 2.

2   K. Mannheim, *Ideology and Utopia*, pp. 222–36.

3   ibid., p. 225.

4   See F. Hayek, *The Counter-Revolution of Science* (Free Press, 1955), pp. 166–7.

5   See, for example, the articles collected in H. G. Skilling and F. Griffiths (eds.), *Interest Groups in Soviet Politics* (Princeton University Press, 1971).

6   Mannheim, p. 223.

7   ibid., p. 222.

8   ibid., p. 225.

9   ibid., p. 229.

10 ibid., p. 230.

11 ibid., p. 231.

12 ibid., p. 232–3.

13 ibid., p. 233–4.

14 See the lecture, 'Communism', in A. L. Morton (ed.), *Political Writings of William Morris* (Lawrence & Wishart, 1973), pp. 227–40.

15 ibid., p. 228.

16 See in particular C. A. R. Crosland, *The Future of Socialism* (Cape, 1961).

17 D. Bouchier, *Idealism and Revolution: New Ideologies of Liberation in Britain and the United States* (Edward Arnold, 1978), p. 160.

18 Z. Bauman, *Socialism: The Active Utopia*, p. 128.

19 In part the narrow social basis of the New Left conspired against the more general appeal which would have been required in order to ensure its success in established political circles. It was also an extremely fragmented movement, diluting its strength among a variety of independent organizations with little co-ordination.

Furthermore, the effectiveness of these organizations tended to fluctuate directly according to particular external factors, demonstrated most notably in the case of the American involvement in Vietnam, and as these factors declined in significance, so the new radicalism tended to lose strength.

20 Originally published in German as *Die Alternative* (Europäische Verlagsanstalt, 1977).

21 A remarkably large literature on nineteenth-century utopian socialism has appeared in recent years. See further the bibliographies included in B. Goodwin, *Social Science and Utopia*, and K. Taylor, *The Political Ideas of the Utopian Socialists*. The interesting case of the 'rediscovery' of William Morris is discussed in the Postscript to E. P. Thompson, *William Morris. Romantic to Revolutionary*, 2nd edn (Merlin Press, 1977).

22 R. Heberle, *Social Movements*, p. 37.

23 ibid., p. 277.

24 Mannheim, p. 130.

25 See, for example, the discussion in M. Kitchen, *Fascism* (Macmillan 1976), especially the concluding chapter, 'What is Fascism?'.

26 Mannheim, p. 125.

27 See W. W. Wagar, 'The steel-gray saviour: technocracy as utopia and ideology', *Alternative Futures*, vol. 2, no. 2 (Spring 1979), pp. 38–54.

28 The Synarchists were a conspiratorial group of technicians (many of them from the Ecole Polytechnique) who regarded themselves as 'outside politics' and sought to take over the running of French society. It is often alleged that many of these technicians actually gained power under the Vichy regime. See J. Meynaud, *Technocracy* (Faber, 1968), pp. 170–1. In 1930, in the Soviet Union, some 2000 engineers (forming a so-called 'Industrial Party') were accused of conspiring to take over the country's government. See K. E. Bailes, 'The politics of technology: Stalin and technocratic thinking among Soviet engineers', *American Historical Review*, vol. 79, no. 2 (April 1974), pp. 445–69.

29 See D. Bell, *The Coming of Post-Industrial Society* (Penguin, 1976), especially ch. 6, and *The End of Ideology*, 2nd edn (Collier–Macmillan, 1962). (Perhaps a more appropriate title for the latter book would be 'The end of utopia?'.)

30 R. Eccleshall, 'English conservatism as ideology', *Political Studies*, vol. XXV, no. 1 (March 1977), p. 65.

31 Mannheim, pp. 206–15.

32 ibid., p. 228.

33 R. Dahrendorf, 'Out of utopia', in *Essays in the Theory of Society*.

34 Eccleshall, p. 69.

35 R. M. Kanter, *Commitment and Community*, pp. 165–6.
36 ibid., p. 171.
37 ibid., pp. 194–5. See further pp. 201–12.
38 A. Bradshaw, 'Looking back to the future: utopian ecology', unpublished paper, Political Studies Association conference (1978), pp. 1–2.
39 M. Piercy, *Woman on the Edge of Time* (Women's Press, 1979).
40 For an illuminating analysis of this issue see E. P. Thompson, Part 4.
41 See L. Tiger, *Optimism: The Biology of Hope* (Simon & Schuster, 1979).

Urgent ☐

FOR _____

DATE _____ TIME _____

While You Were Out

M _____

OF _____

PHONE _____

CELL
FAX _____

Message

☐ TELEPHONED
☐ CAME TO SEE YOU
☐ RETURNED YOUR CALL
☐ PLEASE CALL
☐ WILL CALL AGAIN
☐ WANTS TO SEE YOU

Political Organizations

Ryan Andrews
K-college

248 931 2136

K-200
participate → Kettle korn

A-9711
T-3002   SIGNED

Bibliography

Abensour, M., 'L'histoire de l'utopie et le destin de sa critique', *Textures*, nos. 6–7, 8–9 (1973–4)

Abensour, M., 'Le procès des maîtres rêveurs', *Libre*, no. 4 (1978)

Agulhon, M., *Une Ville Ouvrière au Temps du Socialisme Utopique: Toulon de 1815 à 1851*, Mouton/De Gruyter, 1970

Anderson, P., *Considerations on Western Marxism*, New Left Books, 1976

Anderson, P., *Arguments Within English Marxism*, New Left Books, 1980

Aristotle, *The Politics*, trans. T. A. Sinclair, Penguin, 1962

Armytage, W. H. G., *Heavens Below: Utopian Experiments in England 1560–1960*, Routledge & Kegan Paul, 1961

Armytage, W. H. G., *Yesterday's Tomorrows: A Historical Survey of Future Societies*, Routledge & Kegan Paul, 1968

Arndt, K. J. R., *George Rapp's Harmony Society 1785–1847*, revised edn, Fairleigh Dickinson, 1972

Aron, R., *Main Currents in Sociological Thought*, vol. 1, Penguin, 1968

Arrow, K., *Social Choice and Individual Values*, 2nd edn, Yale University Press, 1963

Asperen, C. M. Van., *Hope and History*, Utrecht University Press, 1973

Augustine, Saint, *The City of God*, trans. H. Bettenson, Penguin, 1972

Bachrach, P., *The Theory of Democratic Elitism*, London University Press, 1969

Bacon, F., *New Atlantis*, in *Ideal Commonwealths*, revised edn, Collier, 1901

Baczko, B., *Lumières de l'Utopie*, Payot, 1978

Bahro, R., *The Alternative in Eastern Europe*, trans. D. Fernbach, New Left Books, 1978

Bailes, K. E., 'The politics of technology: Stalin and technocratic thinking among Soviet engineers', *American Historical Review*, vol. 79, no. 2 (April 1974)

Barber, B., 'The conceptual foundations of totalitarianism', in C. J. Friedrich, M. Curtis and B. Barber, *Totalitarianism in Perspective*, Pall Mall, 1969

Barthes, R., *The Pleasure of the Text*, trans. R. Miller, Cape, 1976
Barthes, R., *Sade, Fourier, Loyola*, trans. R. Miller, Cape, 1977
Barthes, R., *Leçon*, Seuil, 1978
Bauman, Z., *Socialism: The Active Utopia*, Allen & Unwin, 1976
Beccaria, C., *On Crimes and Punishment*, trans. H. Paolucci, Bobbs-Merrill, 1963
Beecher, J., and Bienvenu, R. (eds.), *The Utopian Vision of Charles Fourier*, Cape, 1972
Bell, D., *The End of Ideology*, 2nd edn, Collier–Macmillan, 1962
Bell, D., *The Coming of Post-Industrial Society*, Penguin, 1976
Bellamy, E., *Looking Backward 2000–1887*, Routledge, n.d.
Bellamy, E., *Equality*, Heinemann, 1920
Benevolo, L., *The Origins of Modern Town Planning*, trans. J. Landry, Routledge & Kegan Paul, 1967
Berneri, M. -L., *Journey through Utopia*, Schocken, 1972
Bestor, A. E., *Backwoods Utopias: The Sectarian and Owenite Phases of Communitarian Socialism in America: 1663–1829*, University of Pennsylvania Press, 1950
Bezucha, R. J., *The Lyons Uprising of 1834: Social and Political Conflict in the Early July Monarchy*, Harvard University Press, 1974
Bloch, E., *Geist der Utopie*, Berlin, 1923
Blowers, A. *et al.* (eds.), *The Future of Cities,* Hutchinson/Open University Press, 1974
Bouchier, D., *Idealism and Revolution: New Ideologies of Liberation in Britain and the United States*, Edward Arnold, 1978
Bowle, J., *Politics and Opinion in the Nineteenth Century: An Historical Introduction*, Cape, 1954
Bowles, R. C., 'The reaction of Charles Fourier to the French Revolution', *French Historical Studies*, vol. 1 (1958–60)
Bowman, S. E., *The Year 2000: A Critical Biography of Edward Bellamy*, Bookman Associates, 1958
Bradshaw, A., 'Looking back to the future: utopian ecology', unpublished paper, Political Studies Association conference (1978)
Brisbane, A., *Association: or, A Concise Exposition of the Practical Part of Fourier's Social Science*, Tribune Office, 1843
Brzezinski, Z., and Friedrich, C. J., *Totalitarian Dictatorship and Democracy*, 2nd edn, Praeger, 1965
Burnham, J., *The Managerial Revolution*, Putnam, 1942
Bury, J., *The Idea of Progress*, Macmillan, 1932
Butler, S., *Erewhon*, Dent, n.d.
Butler, S., *Erewhon Revisited*, Dent, n.d.
Butt, J. (ed.), *Robert Owen*, David & Charles, 1971
Cabet, E., *Voyage en Icarie*, 2nd edn, Paris, 1842
Callenbach, E., *Ecotopia*, Pluto Press, 1978

Campanella, T., *The City of the Sun*, in *Ideal Commonwealths*, Collier, 1901

Capouya, E., and Tompkins, K. (eds.), *The Essential Kropotkin*, Macmillan, 1975

Carritt, E., 'Liberty and equality', in A. Quinton (ed.), *Political Philosophy*, Oxford University Press, 1968

Cioran, E., *Histoire et Utopie*, Gallimard, 1960

Cohn, N., *The Pursuit of the Millennium: Revolutionary Millenarians and Mystical Anarchists of the Middle Ages*, revised edn, Paladin, 1970

Coleridge, S. T., *On the Constitution of Church and State*, Dent, 1972

Colloque de Cerisy, *Le Discours Utopique*, Union Générale d'Editions, 1978

Comte, A., *Cours de Philosophie Positive*, Culture Civilisation, 1969

Condorcet, M. J., *Sketch for a Historical Picture of the Progress of the Human Mind*, trans. J. Barraclough, Hyperion Press, 1979

Crosland, C. A. R., *The Future of Socialism*, Cape, 1951

Crossman, R., *Plato Today*, Allen & Unwin, 1937

Dahrendorf, R., 'Out of utopia', in *Essays in the Theory of Society*, Routledge & Kegan Paul, 1968

Daniels, N. (ed.), *Reading Rawls*, Blackwell, 1975

Darin-Drabkin, H., *The Other Society*, Gollancz, 1962

Davis, J. C., *Utopia and the Ideal Society*, Cambridge University Press, 1981

Déjacque, J., *L'Humanisphère*, in V. Pelosse (ed.), *A Bas les Chefs*, Champ Libre, 1971

Diderot, D., *Supplément au Voyage de Bougainville*, Garnier–Flammarion, 1972

Dostoevsky, F., *The Brothers Karamazov*, Penguin, 1958

Downs, A., *An Economic Theory of Democracy*, Harper & Row, 1957

Dubois, C. G., *Problèmes de l'Utopie*, Archives des Lettres Modernes no. 85, 1968

Dunham, A. L., *The Industrial Revolution in France 1815-1848*, Exposition Press, 1955

Dupont, V., *L'Utopie et le Roman Utopique dans la Littérature Anglaise*, Didier, 1941

Durkheim, E., *Socialism and Saint-Simon*, trans. C. Sattler, Antioch Press, 1958

Duveau, G., *Sociologie de l'Utopie*, Presses Universitaires de France, 1961

Easton, D., *A Systems Analysis of Political Life*, Wiley, 1965

Eccleshall, R., 'English conservatism as ideology', *Political Studies*, vol. XXV, no. 1 (March 1977)

Ecologist, The, *A Blueprint for Survival*, Penguin, 1972

Elster, J., *Logic and Society*, Wiley, 1978
Engels, F., *Principles of Communism*, trans. P. M. Sweezy, Pluto Press, n.d.
Erasmus, C. J., *In Search of the Common Good: Utopian Experiments Past and Future*, Free Press, 1977
Fâkkar, R., *Sociologie, Socialisme et Internationalisme Prémarxistes*, Neuchâtel, 1968
Fellman, M., *The Unbounded Frame: Freedom and Community in Nineteenth Century American Utopianism*, Greenwood Press, 1973
Fénelon, F. de, *Télémache*, Ormeraie, 1978
Feuer, L. S., *The Conflict of Generations*, Heinemann, 1969
Fishman, R., *Urban Utopias in the Twentieth Century: Ebenezer Howard, Frank Lloyd Wright and Le Corbusier*, Basic Books, 1977
Fogarty, R. S., *American Utopianism*, Peacock, 1972
Fogarty, R. S., 'Communal history in America', *Choice*, no. 10 (June 1973)
Fogarty, R. S., 'American communes, 1865–1914', *Journal of American Studies*, vol. 9, no. 2 (1975)
Fogarty, R. S., 'A radical nominalist looks at community', *Alternative Futures*, vol. 2, no. 2 (Spring 1979)
Foucault, M., *Discipline and Punish*, trans. A. Sheridan, Allen Lane, 1977
Freud, S., *Civilization and its Discontents*, trans. J. Rivière, Hogarth Press, 1963
Freund, J., *Utopie et Violence*, Rivière, 1978
Friedman, Y., *Utopies Réalisables*, Union Générale d'Editions, 1975
Friedrich, C. J., and Brzezinski, Z., *Totalitarian Dictatorship and Democracy*, 2nd edn, Praeger, 1965
Fromm, E., *The Sane Society*, Routledge & Kegan Paul, 1956
Fromm, E., *The Fear of Freedom*, Routledge, 1942
Galbraith, J. K., *The New Industrial State*, 2nd edn, Penguin, 1974
Germino, D., *Modern Western Political Thought*, Rand McNally, 1972
Gide, C. (ed.), *Design for Utopia: Selected Writings of Charles Fourier*, Schocken, 1971
Godechot, J., *Les Révolutions de 1848*, Albin Michel, 1971
Godwin, W., *An Enquiry Concerning Political Justice*, 3rd edn, London, 1798
Goodwin, B., *Social Science and Utopia*, Harvester, 1978
Goodwin, B., 'Utopia defended against the liberals', *Political Studies*, vol. XXVIII (1980)
Gutman, H. G., *Work, Culture, and Society in Industrializing America*, Knopf, 1976
Hardy, D., *Alternative Communities in Nineteenth Century England*, Longman, 1979

Harrington, J., *Oceana*, in *Ideal Commonwealths*, Collier, 1901

Harrison, J. F. C., *Robert Owen and the Owenites in Britain and America: The Quest for the New Moral World*, Routledge & Kegan Paul, 1969

Harrison, R., *Before the Socialists: Studies in Labour and Politics 1861–1881*, Routledge & Kegan Paul, 1965

Hart, H. A. L., *The Concept of Law*, Clarendon Press, 1961

Hayek, F., *The Road to Serfdom*, Routledge & Kegan Paul, 1944

Hayek, F., *The Counter-Revolution of Science*, Free Press, 1955

Hayek, F., 'The principles of a liberal social order', in A. Crespigny and J. Cronin (eds.), *Ideologies of Politics*, Oxford University Press, 1975

Heberle, R., *Social Movements: An Introduction to Political Sociology*, Appleton–Century–Crofts, 1951

Hine, R. V., *California's Utopian Colonies*, Huntington Library, 1953

Hitler, A., *Mein Kampf*, trans. R. Manheim, Hutchinson, 1972

Hobbes, T., *Leviathan*, ed. J. Plamenatz, Fontana, 1962

Hobsbawm, E. J., *Primitive Rebels*, Manchester University Press, 1959

Hobsbawm, E. J., *The Age of Revolution*, Weidenfeld & Nicolson, 1962

Holloway, M., *Heavens on Earth: Utopian Communities in America 1680–1880*, Turnstile Press, 1951

Horsburgh, H. J. N., 'The relevance of the utopian', *Ethics*, vol. 67 (1957)

Howard, E., *Garden Cities of To-Morrow*, ed. F. J. Osborn, Faber, 1945

Huxley, A., *Brave New World*, Penguin, 1955

Huxley, A., *Brave New World Revisited*, Chatto & Windus, 1960

Iggers, G. G. (ed.), *The Doctrine of Saint-Simon: An Exposition – First Year, 1828–1829*, 2nd edn, Schocken, 1972

Johnson, C. H., 'Etienne Cabet and the problem of class antagonism', *International Review of Social History*, vol. XI (1966)

Johnson, C. H., 'Communism and the working class before Marx: the Icarian system', *American Historical Review*, vol. 76 (1971)

Johnson, C. H., *Utopian Communism in France: Cabet and the Icarians, 1839–1851*, Cornell University Press, 1974

Johnson, N., *In Search of the Constitution*, Pergamon, 1977

Jones, M. A., *American Immigration*, University of Chicago Press, 1960

Jones, R. A., and Anservitz, R. M., 'Saint-Simon and Saint-Simonism: a Weberian view', *American Journal of Sociology*, vol. 80 (1975)

Joos, L. C. D., 'Are national frontiers natural frontiers?', *European Community* (March 1973)

Kamenka, E., *The Ethical Foundations of Marxism*, 2nd edn, Routledge & Kegan Paul, 1972

Kanter, R. M., *Commitment and Community: Communes and Utopias in Sociological Perspective*, Harvard University Press, 1972

Kateb, G., *Utopia and Its Enemies*, Collier–Macmillan, 1963

Katz, H., 'Social movements: an essay in definition', *Polish Sociological Bulletin*, no. 1 (1971)

Kitchen, M., *Fascism*, Macmillan, 1976

Knoedler, C. F., *The Harmony Society: A Nineteenth-Century American Utopia*, Vantage Press, 1954

Kripke, S., 'Naming and necessity', in D. Davidson and G. Harman (eds.), *Semantics of Natural Language*, D. Reidel, 1972

Kropotkin, P. A., *Mutual Aid: A Factor of Evolution*, Sargent, Porter, 1976

Krutch, J. W., *The Measure of Man*, Alvin Redman, 1956

Lacroix, J., *Le Désir et les Désirs*, Presses Universitaires de France, 1975

Lapouge, G., *Utopie et Civilisations*, Flammarion, 1978

Larrain, J., *The Concept of Ideology*, Hutchinson, 1979

Lasky, M., *Utopia and Revolution*, University of Chicago Press, 1976

Le Corbusier, *The City of Tomorrow and Its Planning*, trans. F. Etchells, 3rd edn, Architectural Press, 1971

Lenin, V. I., *The State and Revolution*, in *The Essential Left: Four Classic Texts on the Principles of Socialism*, Unwin, 1960

Lenin, V. I., *What Is to Be Done?*, trans. S. V. and P. Utechin, Panther, 1970

Lenin, V. I., *Letters on Tactics* (April 1917), in *Collected Works*, vol. XX, International Publishers, n.d.

Lenin, V. I., *Imperialism, the Highest Stage of Capitalism*, International Publishers, 1969

Levin, H., *The Myth of the Golden Age in the Renaissance*, Indiana University Press, 1969

Levinson, R., *In Defence of Plato*, University of Massachusetts Press, 1953

Levitas, R., 'Sociology and utopia', *Sociology*, vol. 13 (1979)

LeWarne, C. P., *Utopias on Puget Sound, 1885–1915*, University of Washington Press, 1975

Lewis, A. O., 'On utopian studies', *Alternative Futures*, vol. 1, no. 1, (Spring 1978)

Lichtheim, G., *Marxism: An Historical and Critical Study*, 3rd impression, Routledge & Kegan Paul, 1967

Lipset, S. M., *Political Man*, Mercury, 1963

Locke, J., *An Essay Concerning the True Original, Extent and End of Civil Government*, Everyman, 1924

Loubère, L. A., 'The intellectual origins of French Jacobin Socialism', *International Review of Social History*, vol. IV (1959)

Loubère, L. A., *Utopian Socialism: Its History since 1800*, Schenkman, 1974

Lovejoy, A., 'The supposed primitivism of Rousseau's Discourse on Inequality', in *Essays in the History of Ideas*, Johns Hopkins, 1948

Lukes, S., *Power: A Radical View*, Macmillan, 1974

Macpherson, C. B., *The Political Theory of Possessive Individualism*, Oxford University Press, 1966

Macpherson, C. B., *Democratic Theory*, Oxford University Press, 1973

Mandeville, B. de, *Fable of the Bees*, 4th edn, Tonson, 1725

Mannheim, K., *Ideology and Utopia*, trans. L. Wirth and E. Shils, Routledge & Kegan Paul, 1936

Manuel, F. E. (ed.), *Utopias and Utopian Thought*, Souvenir Press, 1973

Manuel, F. E., and Manuel, F. P., *French Utopias*, Free Press, 1966

Manuel, F. E., and Manuel, F. P. (eds.), *Utopian Thought in the Western World*, Blackwell, 1979

Marcuse, H., *One-Dimensional Man*, Sphere, 1965

Marcuse, H., *Eros and Civilisation*, Sphere, 1969

Marcuse, H., *Essay on Liberation*, Penguin, 1971

Mariampolski, H., 'Communes and utopias, past and present: a bibliography of post-1945 studies', *Bulletin of Bibliography*, vol. 36, no. 3 (July 1979)

Marin, L., *Utopiques: Jeux d'Espaces*, Minuit, 1973

Marx, K., *Early Texts*, ed. D. McLellan, Blackwell, 1972

Marx, K., *Capital*, trans. E. and C. Paul, Dent, 1972

Marx, K., *Selected Writings*, ed. D. McLellan, Oxford University Press, 1977

Marx, K., and Engels, F., *Selected Works*, vols. 1–3, Moscow, 1970

Marx, K., and Engels, F., *Collected Works*, vol. 4: 1844–5, Lawrence & Wishart, 1975

Meek, R., *Social Science and the Noble Savage*, Cambridge University Press, 1976

Meynaud, J., *Technocracy*, Faber, 1968

Mill, J. S., *On Liberty, On Representative Government, On the Subjection of Women*, Oxford University Press, 1975

Moment, G. B., and Kraushaar, O. F., *Utopias: The American Experience*, Scarecrow Press, 1980

More, T., *Utopia*, trans. P. Turner, Penguin, 1965

Morelly, *Code de la Nature*, Clavreuil, 1950

Morris, W., *News from Nowhere*, Routledge, 1970

Morton, A. L., *The English Utopia*, Lawrence & Wishart, 1969

Morton, A. L. (ed.), *Political Writings of William Morris*, Lawrence & Wishart, 1973

Moss, B. H., 'Parisian producers' associations (1830–51): The socialism of skilled workers', in R. Price (ed.), *Revolution and Reaction: 1848 and the Second French Republic*, Croom Helm, 1975

Moss, B. H., 'Parisian workers and the origins of republican socialism, 1830–1833', in J. H. Merriman (ed.), *1830 in France*, New Viewpoints , 1975

Moss, B. H., *The Origins of the French Labor Movement 1830–1914. The Socialism of Skilled Workers*, University of California Press, 1976

Mucchielli, R., *Le Mythe de la Cité Idéale*, Presses Universitaires de France, 1960

Mumford, L., *The Story of Utopias*, P. Smith, 1941

Negley, G., *Utopian Literature: A Bibliography*, Regents Press, 1978

Negley, G., and Patrick, J., *The Quest for Utopia*, H. Schuman, 1952

Noyes, P. H., *Organization and Revolution*, Princeton University Press, 1966

Nozick, R., *Anarchy, State and Utopia*, Blackwell, 1974

Oakeshott, M., *Social and Political Doctrines of Contemporary Europe*, Basic Books, 1940

Oakeshott, M., *Rationalism in Politics and Other Essays*, Methuen, 1962

Ollman, B., 'Marx's vision of communism: a reconstruction', *Critique*, no. 8 (Summer 1977)

Olson, M., *The Logic of Collective Action*, Harvard University Press, 1971

Orwell, G., *Nineteen Eighty-four*, Penguin, 1954

Owen, R., *Six Lectures Delivered in Manchester*, Manchester 1837

Owen, R., *A New View of Society*, Penguin, 1970

Parrington, V. L., *American Dreams: A Study of American Utopias*, Brown University Press, 1947

Passmore, J., *The Perfectibility of Man*, Duckworth, 1970

Péguy, C., *L'Esprit de Système*, Gallimard, 1953

Pelling, H., *A History of British Trade Unionism*, Penguin, 1963

Peters, V., *All Things Common: The Hutterian Way of Life*, University of Minnesota Press, 1965

Piercy, M., *Woman on the Edge of Time*, Women's Press, 1979

Pierson, S., *Marxism and the Origins of British Socialism*, Cornell University Press, 1972

Pierson, S., *British Socialists: The Journey from Fantasy to Politics*, Harvard University Press, 1979

Pinkney, D. H., *The French Revolution of 1830*, Princeton University Press, 1972

Plamenatz, J. P., *Man and Society*, vols. 1–2, Longman, 1963

Plank, R., 'The Welfare State as utopia', *Alternative Futures*, vol. 1, nos. 3–4 (Fall 1978)

Bibliography 283

Plath, D. W. (ed.), *Aware of Utopia*, University of Illinois Press, 1971

Plato, *Plato's Republic*, trans. H. D. P. Lee, Penguin, 1955

Plato, *Laws*, trans. T. Saunders, Penguin, 1970

Popper, K., *The Open Society and Its Enemies*, vols. 1–2, Routledge & Kegan Paul, 1945

Popper, K., *The Logic of Scientific Discovery*, revised edn, Hutchinson, 1968

Price, R., *The French Second Republic: A Social History*, Batsford, 1972

Purdom, C. B., *The Letchworth Achievement*, Dent, 1963

Rabelais, *Gargantua and Pantagruel*, trans. J. M. Cohen, Penguin, 1970

Raulet, G. (ed.), *Utopie – Marxisme selon Ernst Bloch*, Payot, 1976

Rawls, J., *A Theory of Justice*, Harvard University Press, 1971

Read, H., *The Green Child: A Romance*, Heinemann, 1935

Rescher, N., *A Theory of Possibility*, Blackwell, 1975

Rhodes, H. V., *Utopia in American Political Thought*, University of Arizona Press, 1967

Rigby, A., *Alternative Realities: A Study of Communes and Their Members*, Routledge & Kegan Paul, 1974

Rosenau, H., *The Ideal City in Its Architectural Evolution*, Routledge & Kegan Paul, 1959

Rousseau, J. -J., *The Social Contract and Discourses*, trans. G. D. H. Cole, revised edn, Dent, 1973

Rude, F., *L'Insurrection Lyonnaise de Novembre 1831: Le Mouvement Ouvrier à Lyon de 1827–1832*, Anthropos, 1970

Ruyer, R., *L'Utopie et les Utopies*, Presses Universitaires de France, 1951

Sabine, G. H. (ed.), *The Works of Gerrard Winstanley*, Cornell University Press, 1941

Saint-Simon, C. -H. de, *Oeuvres de Claude-Henri de Saint-Simon*, vols. 1–6, Anthropos, 1966

Sargent, L. T., *British and American Utopian Literature 1516–1975*, G. K. Hall, 1979

Schapiro, L., *Totalitarianism*, Macmillan, 1972

Schumacher, E. F., *Small is Beautiful*, Blond & Briggs, 1973

Servier, J., *Histoire de l'Utopie*, Gallimard, 1967

Shklar, J., *After Utopia*, Princeton University Press, 1957

Shorter, E., 'Middle-class anxiety in the German Revolution of 1848', *Journal of Social History*, vol. 2 (1968–9)

Simon, W. M., *European Positivism in the Nineteenth Century*, Harvard University Press, 1963

Skilling, H. G., and Griffiths, F. (eds.), *Interest Groups in Soviet Politics*, Princeton University Press, 1971

Skinner, B. F., *Walden Two*, Macmillan, 1962

Skinner, B. F., *Contingencies of Reinforcement*, Appleton–Century, 1969

Skinner, B. F., *Beyond Freedom and Dignity*, Cape, 1972

Spencer, H., *Principles of Ethics*, Liberty Fund, 1978

Spiro, M. E., *Kibbutz: Venture in Utopia*, new edn, Schocken, 1970

Stankiewicz, W. J., *Aspects of Political Theory*, Collier–Macmillan, 1976

Swift, J., *A Tale of a Tub*, Dent, 1909

Swift, J., *Gulliver's Travels*, Penguin, 1967

Talmon, J., *The Origins of Totalitarian Democracy*, Praeger, 1960

Talmon, J., *Political Messianism: The Romantic Phase*, Secker & Warburg, 1960

Taylor, C. 'Neutrality in political science', in P. Laslett and W. Runciman (eds.), *Philosophy, Politics and Society*, 3rd series, Blackwell, 1967

Taylor, K. (ed.), *Henri Saint-Simon. Selected Writings on Science, Industry and Social Organisation*, Croom Helm, 1975

Taylor, K., *The Political Ideas of the Utopian Socialists*, Cass, 1982

Thomis, M. I., *The Town Labourer and the Industrial Revolution*, Batsford, 1974

Thompson, E. P., *The Making of the English Working Class*, revised edn, Penguin, 1968

Thompson, E. P., *William Morris. Romantic to Revolutionary*, revised edn, Merlin Press, 1977

Tiger, L., *Optimism: The Biology of Hope*, Simon & Schuster, 1979

Tod, I., and Wheeler, M., *Utopia: An Illustrated History*, Harmony Books, 1978

Town and Country Planning Association, *A Third Garden City*, TCPA, 1979

Vairasse D'Allais, *Histoire des Sévérambes*, vols. 1–4, Clearwater, 1974

Vereker, C., *Eighteenth-Century Optimism*, Liverpool University Press, 1951

Wagar, W. W., 'The steel-gray saviour: technocracy as utopia and ideology', *Alternative Futures*, vol. 2, no. 2 (Spring 1979)

Waldman, S., *The Foundations of Political Action*, Little, Brown, 1972

Warnock, M., *Ethics since 1900*, 2nd edn, Oxford University Press, 1966

Weber, M., *Weber: Selections in Translation*, ed. W. G. Runciman, Cambridge University Press, 1978

Weitling, W., *Garantien der Harmonie und Freiheit*, Sozialistische Neudrucke, 1908

Weldon, T. W., *The Vocabulary of Politics*, Penguin, 1953

Wells, H. G., *Men Like Gods*, London, 1905

Wells, H. G., *A Modern Utopia*, Cassell, 1923
Wolff, R. P., *Understanding Rawls*, Princeton University Press, 1977
Wolff, R. P., Moore, B., and Marcuse, H., *A Critique of Pure Tolerance*, Cape, 1969
Wolin, S., *Politics and Vision*, Little, 1960
Woodcock, G., *Anarchism*, new edn, Penguin, 1975
Woodward, R. L. (ed.), *Positivism in Latin America 1850-1900*, D. C. Heath, 1971
Zamyatin, Y., *We*, Penguin, 1972

Index

Abensour, M., 73, 77, 97, 209
administration, 125
Adorno, T., 86
Amana Community, 186, 193, 195
America, 124, 130, 131, 132, 133,
    135, 142, 143, 145, 150, 151-2,
    154, 155, 159-60, 182-96, 197,
    199, 200, 237, 242, 245-6, 250
American Revolution, 187
Anabaptists, 168
anarchism, 46, 148, 167-72, 197, 237
Anservitz, R. M., 136
Aristotle, 41
Aron, R., 179
Arrow, K., 214-16
art, 124
association, 125-9, 133, 135, 147,
    148, 156, 157, 161, 166, 233
Augustine, Saint, 139
Aurora Community, 186, 193, 194
Austria, 170
authoritarianism, 127, 135-7, 153,
    155, 160, 184; see also
    totalitarianism
Axelrod, P., 173

Babeuf, G., 40, 44, 63, 103, 133
Bacon, F., 42, 140, 143, 237
Bahro, R., 235
Bakunin, M., 60, 169, 172
Barber, B., 98
Barbès, A., 133
Barthes, R., 88-90
Bauman, Z., 28, 58, 85, 113, 149
    234
Beccaria, C., 62
behaviourism, 122
Belgium, 170
Bell, D., 239
Bellamy, E., 47, 202, 237
Benjamin, W., 77
Bentham, J., 36, 58, 176, 177
Bergerac, C. de, 60

Berneri, M.-L., 93
Bethel Community, 186, 193, 194
Bimeler, J., 186, 193
Blanqui, A., 103, 127, 133, 158
Bloch, E., 77, 80-81, 90
Bolshevism, 172-6, 181
Bonald, L.G.A. vicomte de, 178
Borges, J. L., 64
bourgeoisie, 146, 147, 149, 153,
    160-61, 162, 163, 165, 166,
    173, 175, 236, 242
bourgeoisie, petit, 151, 154, 158
Bournville, 202
Bretonne, R. de la, 25, 28, 44, 61, 87
Brisbane, A., 131, 154
Britain, 125-6, 128, 132, 135, 143,
    144, 145, 155-7, 159, 161, 176
Bruderhof Community, 187, 193, 195
Buchez, P. J. B., 126
Bulwer-Lytton, E., 25
Burnham, J., 239
Butler, S., 25, 47, 62, 212, 218, 223

Cabet, E., 45, 65, 120-21, 124-37,
    144, 147, 150-52, 154, 158, 182,
    201, 202; see also Icarianism
Callenbach, E., 250
Campanella, T., 42, 59, 63, 140,
    143, 208
Camus, A., 33
capitalism, 49, 122-9, 130, 138,
    149, 150, 151, 158, 161, 163,
    165, 167, 169, 170, 173, 174,
    175, 176, 178, 202, 226, 234,
    242
Catholicism, 132, 139, 179
Chartism, 155, 157
chiliasm, 168-9, 170, 172, 237
Chomsky, N., 55
Christ, 132, 139, 140, 154
Christianity, 132, 133, 139, 140, 144,
    145, 151, 153, 154, 157, 158,
    179, 187, 245

75-7; and political theory, 15-37,
119-21; and science, 81-6, 90-91,
124, 125, 161, 163-8; and social
protest, 137-40; and social science,
32, 56, 82-4, 217; coercive nature
of, 102-5; constructive and critical
functions of, 28-31, 120-21,
223-5; definitions of, 15-17,
207-8; democracy in, 67; epistemology of, 98-100; practical imp
impact of, 120-22, 138, 149, 161,
229; psychological explanations of,
87-8, 219; realizability of, 167,
218-22; sociological context of,
121-2, 137-40, 160; symbolic
interpretations of, 86-90
utopian socialism, 16, 31, 66, 72-7,
122-37, 138, 147-62, 163, 164,
166, 171, 176, 181, 182, 197,
201, 248

Vairasse D'Allais, 43
Veblen, T., 237
violence, 103-5, 133, 154

Weitling; W., 45, 65, 103, 124-37,
147, 157, 158, 166, 167, 182
Weldon, T. W., 102
Wells, H. G., 47, 67, 220, 237
Winstanley, G., 144
working class, 123, 125, 126, 128,
129-37, 150, 151, 152, 153,
154, 155, 156-7, 158, 160-62,
163, 166, 167, 170, 171, 173,
174, 175
Wright, F. L., 201

Zamyatin, Y., 48, 109
Zasulich, V., 173
Zoar Community, 186, 193